First World War
and Army of Occupation
War Diary
France, Belgium and Germany

41 DIVISION
Divisional Troops
Royal Army Medical Corps
138 Field Ambulance
1 March 1918 - 31 May 1919

WO95/2628/2

The Naval & Military Press Ltd
www.nmarchive.com
Published in association with The National Archives

Published by

The Naval & Military Press Ltd

Unit 10 Ridgewood Industrial Park,
Uckfield, East Sussex,
TN22 5QE England
Tel: +44 (0) 1825 749494

www.naval-military-press.com
www.nmarchive.com

This diary has been reprinted in facsimile from the original. Any imperfections are inevitably reproduced and the quality may fall short of modern type and cartographic standards.

Contents

Document type	Place/Title	Date From	Date To
Miscellaneous	WO95/2628-2		
Heading	War Diary Of 138th Field Ambulance R.A.M.C. From March 1st 1918 To March 31st 1918 (Volume XV)		
War Diary	Allazia Italy	01/03/1918	07/03/1918
War Diary	Orville Map of Lens II. 1/100,000 5 E 95.60.	08/03/1918	11/03/1918
War Diary	Grille	12/03/1918	12/03/1918
War Diary	Humbercourt Map of Lens 11 1/100,000. 4 F. 50.55	13/03/1918	21/03/1918
War Diary	Savoy Camp. Bihucourt Lens 11.1/10000 5 J 6845	22/03/1918	22/03/1918
War Diary	Sht. Lens 11 1/100,000 5 J 83. Nr. Grevillers	23/03/1918	24/03/1918
War Diary	C.M.D.S. on Achut-Le-Petit-Bucqnay Rd Abmt 1/2 kilo Sum Bucqnoy (Lens 11 1/100,000 4 H 63 74)	25/03/1918	25/03/1918
War Diary	Hennes Camps Lens 11 1/100,000 4 H 8.0	26/03/1918	26/03/1918
War Diary	Fonquevillers and Bienvillers	27/03/1918	27/03/1918
War Diary	Bienvillers	28/03/1918	28/03/1918
War Diary	Fonquevillers 5 H. 66.70. Lens 11. 1/10000	29/03/1918	29/03/1918
War Diary	Essarts-Les-Bucquoy	30/03/1918	31/03/1918
Miscellaneous	A.D.M.S. 41st Division. Appendix "A"	31/03/1918	31/03/1918
Miscellaneous	Appendix "A"		
Miscellaneous	Distribution of Personnel. Appendix "B"		
Miscellaneous	Distributions of Wheeled Stretchers. Appendix "C"		
Miscellaneous	Appendix "B"		
Miscellaneous	Minimum Equipment For An Advanced Dressing Station. Limber No. 1. Appendix "C"		
Heading	War Diary of 138th Field Ambulance. From 1st April 1918. To. 30th April 1918 (Volume XVI)		
War Diary	Essarts-Les-Bucquoy.	01/04/1918	01/04/1918
War Diary	Brinnillers	02/04/1918	02/04/1918
War Diary	Grville	03/04/1918	03/04/1918
War Diary	Framecourt	04/04/1918	04/04/1918
War Diary	Schools Camp Sht. 27. T 3a.7.4.	05/04/1918	07/04/1918
War Diary	Moated Farm Sht. 28 Edition 3 1/40.000 H 2.d.8.2.	08/04/1918	28/04/1918
War Diary	Rousebrugge Sheet 19 W.17.c.0.4.	29/04/1918	29/04/1918
War Diary	Rousebrugge	30/04/1918	30/04/1918
Miscellaneous	List of appendices.		
Diagram etc	Diagram Showing Line of evacuation of Casualties. Appendix I		
Miscellaneous	Distribution of Personnel and Vehicles on Left Sector Appendix I a		
Map	Tracing Of Map 28 (1-20.000) Showing Posts Of Forward Line Of Evacuation 18-4-18 Appendix II		
Miscellaneous	Distribution of Personnel Vehicles etc on Right Sector. Appendix I		
Miscellaneous	Posts & Distribution of Personnel etc. Appendix I.		
Diagram etc	Diagram of Routes of evacuation Appendix 1d		
Heading	War Diary of 138th Field Ambulance From May 1-1918 To May 31st 1918 (Volume XVII.)		
War Diary	Rousebrugge Sheet 19 W.17c.04	01/05/1918	31/05/1918
Miscellaneous	Syllabus of Training Regimental Stretcher Bearers Class B. May 26 to June 2. 1918 Appendix II	26/05/1918	26/05/1918
Map	41st Division Appendix IV		

Map	41st Division (Sick) Appendix V		
Map	41st Division (Sick) 138th Fd. Ambce, Appendix VI		
Miscellaneous	Report on Action Taken concerning Points Raised at Conference held. Appendix VIII	19/05/1918	19/05/1918
Miscellaneous	41st. D.R.S., M.D.S. & Gas Centre. Report On Work Carried Out 1/5/18 to 31/5/18 Appendix X	01/05/1918	01/05/1918
Diagram etc	Development of Hopper Appendix IX		
Miscellaneous	List Of Articles Of Equipment Forwarded To Divisional Dump At St. Omer Appendix I	06/05/1918	06/05/1918
Miscellaneous	41st Division Table Shewing disposal of Officers and Other Ranks Who have Passed Through M.D.S., D.R.S. & Gas Centre. Appendix III		
Miscellaneous	Appendix VII Detached Field with Pears Under Main Dressing Locations		
Heading	War Diary of 138th Field Ambulance R.A.M.C. From June 1st 1918 To June 30th 1918 (Volume XVIII.)		
War Diary	Rousbrugge Sheet 19 W 17 C.O.4	01/06/1918	01/06/1918
War Diary	Rousbrugge	02/06/1918	04/06/1918
War Diary	Le Communal Sheet 27a. J 24 b. 8.0.	05/06/1918	05/06/1918
War Diary	Le Communal	05/06/1918	25/06/1918
War Diary	Rubrouck Map Ref (H.8.d.8.7.) Sheet 27	25/06/1918	25/06/1918
War Diary	Rubrouck	25/06/1918	26/06/1918
War Diary	Rietveld Map Ref. (Sht 27. I 4b.8.6)	26/06/1918	26/06/1918
War Diary	Rietveld.	27/06/1918	29/06/1918
War Diary	Ryveld J 27 b.3.2. (Sheet 27)	30/06/1918	30/06/1918
War Diary	Ryveld.	30/06/1918	30/06/1918
Map	Chart Showing Cases of Influenza Admitted Evacuated To CCS And Returned To Duty. During June 1918 Appendix-2		
Miscellaneous	138th Field Ambulance Syllabus of Training Appendix-1		
Miscellaneous	List of Appendices accompanying War Diary for month of June, 1918.	01/07/1918	01/07/1918
Heading	War Diary of 138th Field Ambulance From July 1st To July 31st 1918. (Volume XIX)		
War Diary	Rweld (Sh 27 J 27b 2.2.)	01/07/1918	02/07/1918
War Diary	Rweld	03/07/1918	31/07/1918
Map	Chart Showing. 41st Division (Sick).		
Map	41st D.R.S. (July 1918)		
Map	To 2nd Army Rest Camp Appendix IV		
Miscellaneous	Orders for Patients Proceeding to Baths App 1		
Miscellaneous	Admissions App 2		
Miscellaneous	To A.D.M.S. 41st Div.	01/08/1918	01/08/1918
Heading	War Diary of 138th Field Ambulance From August 1st To August 31st 1918. (Volume-XX)		
War Diary	Rweld (41 Divs R.S.) Sh. 27 J. 27b. 3.2.	01/08/1918	02/08/1918
War Diary	Div R.E.	03/08/1918	08/08/1918
War Diary	Div R.E.	05/08/1918	15/08/1918
War Diary	Rweld (DRS)	16/08/1918	28/08/1918
War Diary	Hallines Sheet 36D F1.d 8.8.	29/08/1918	29/08/1918
War Diary	La Wattine Sheet 27A. P 32.d 5.0.	30/09/1918	30/09/1918
War Diary	Hallines Sheet 36 D F2.d.4.6.	31/08/1918	31/08/1918
Diagram etc	Disposal Admitted App 3		
Map			
Heading	War Diary of 138th Field Ambulance From 1/9/18 To 30/9/18 (Volume XXI)		

War Diary	Hallines.	01/09/1918	01/09/1918
War Diary	Remy Siding (Sheet 27. L 23.a.4.7.)	02/09/1918	03/09/1918
War Diary	Remy (HQ)	03/09/1918	17/09/1918
War Diary	Hooggraaf Sheet 28. (G26.c.4.4)	18/09/1918	18/09/1918
War Diary	Hooggraaf HQ.	19/09/1918	26/09/1918
War Diary	Hooggraaf	27/09/1918	28/09/1918
War Diary	Swan Chateau. 28/I 19 C.5.7.	29/09/1918	29/09/1918
War Diary	Verbranden Molen 28/I.28.d. 6.6.	30/09/1918	30/09/1918
Miscellaneous	Advanced Army Dysentery Centre App 1	00/09/1918	00/09/1918
Map	Casualties app 2		
Heading	War Diary of 138th Field Ambulance October 1st To 31st 1918. (Volume XXII)		
War Diary	Kortewilde 28/P.14.a.3.9	01/10/1918	01/10/1918
War Diary	A.D.S. ? Cox at 28/P 34 6.5.6	02/10/1918	02/10/1918
War Diary	A.D.S. J.36.c.7.3.	03/10/1918	03/10/1918
War Diary	J 36 c.7.3.	04/10/1918	04/10/1918
War Diary	Gheluvelt 28/J 21.b.1.5. A.D.5. (Forward HQ)	05/10/1918	05/10/1918
War Diary	Gheluvelt A.D.S.	06/10/1918	16/10/1918
War Diary	Moorseele 28/L 23 b. 5.7. ADS. HQ.	17/10/1918	17/10/1918
War Diary	Moorseele ADS. HQ.	18/10/1918	20/10/1918
War Diary	ADS & H.Q. Courtrai H.31.d. 2.7. Sheet 29	21/10/1918	21/10/1918
War Diary	Sweveghem ADS & H.Q. 29/O.I.C.8.3.	22/10/1918	22/10/1918
War Diary	Sweveghem. ADS & HQ.	23/10/1918	27/10/1918
War Diary	Belleghem 29/N. 29.c.1.8.	28/10/1918	28/10/1918
War Diary	Belleghem.	29/10/1918	31/10/1918
Miscellaneous	From 8 am. to noon 23/10/18 App 2	23/10/1918	23/10/1918
Miscellaneous	8 Pm to 8 am. 23-24 Oct 1918	23/10/1918	23/10/1918
Miscellaneous	8 a.m. to 6 pm	24/10/1918	24/10/1918
Miscellaneous	Oct 24-25th 1918 8. pm to 8. am.	24/10/1918	24/10/1918
Miscellaneous	25/10/18 08.00 hours to 16.00 hours.	25/10/1918	25/10/1918
Miscellaneous	From 20.00 hours 25/10/18 to 08.00 hours 26/10/18	25/10/1918	25/10/1918
Miscellaneous	08.00 To 1800 hours	26/10/1918	26/10/1918
Miscellaneous	20.00 hours 26-10-18 to 0800-27-10-18	26/10/1918	26/10/1918
Miscellaneous	Medical Scheme Of Evacuation 138 Field Amb App 1	12/10/1918	12/10/1918
Miscellaneous	20.00 hours	22/10/1918	22/10/1918
Miscellaneous	1200 hours	23/10/1918	23/10/1918
Miscellaneous	ADMS. 35 Div.	24/10/1918	24/10/1918
Miscellaneous	ADMS 41/Div Location herewith	24/10/1918	24/10/1918
Miscellaneous	ADMS 35/Div Left Bde	25/10/1918	25/10/1918
Miscellaneous	Situation Report.	25/10/1918	25/10/1918
Miscellaneous	Locations 122 Brigades	26/10/1918	26/10/1918
Miscellaneous	O.C. 106th Field Ambulance Hd. Qrs 106th Infantry Bde. Appendix 3	24/10/1918	24/10/1918
Heading	War Diary of 138th Field Ambulance November 1st To 30th-1918. (Volume XXIII)		
Miscellaneous	Cover for Documents. Nature of Enclosures.		
War Diary	Belleghem Map References Sheet 29	01/11/1918	01/11/1918
War Diary	Belleghem	02/11/1918	02/11/1918
War Diary	Sheet 29.		
War Diary	Sheet 29 HQ Near Ooteghem O.6.a.5.2	03/11/1918	03/11/1918
War Diary	HQ/O.6.a.5.2.	04/11/1918	04/11/1918
War Diary	Sheet 29 HQ.0.6.a.5.2.	05/11/1918	05/11/1918
War Diary	HQ J.32.c.9.8. Vicinity Ingoyghem.	06/11/1918	06/11/1918
War Diary	Sheet 29 HQ. J.32.c.9.8.	07/11/1918	09/11/1918
War Diary	Sheet 29 HQ. & Ads Grijkourt Near Berchem Q.21.b.8.7	10/11/1918	10/11/1918

War Diary	HQ. & Ads. Nukerke R.21.b.38.	11/11/1918	11/11/1918
War Diary	Nukerke.	11/11/1918	11/11/1918
War Diary	Sheet 30 HQ. & Ads Nederbrakel N 17. Central.	12/11/1918	12/11/1918
War Diary	HQ. & Ads Nederbrakel	13/11/1918	13/11/1918
War Diary	Sheet 30 HQ. & Ads Nederbrakel	14/11/1918	14/11/1918
War Diary	HQ. & Drs. Nederbrakel	15/11/1918	16/11/1918
War Diary	Sheet 30		
War Diary	HQ. & Drs Nederbrakel.	17/11/1918	18/11/1918
War Diary	Sheet 38 HQ. Chateau Deux Acren C.6.a.4.2.	19/11/1918	19/11/1918
War Diary	HQ. Deux Acren	20/11/1918	20/11/1918
War Diary	HQ. Sarlardinge 30/U.10.a.6.4.	21/11/1918	21/11/1918
War Diary	HQ. Sarlardinge.	22/11/1918	30/11/1918
Miscellaneous	A.D.M.S 41 Div	01/11/1918	01/11/1918
Miscellaneous	The positions of the various lines to be taken up by 41 Div during advance are as under:-		
Miscellaneous	Medical Arrangements	17/11/1918	17/11/1918
Miscellaneous	Locations A.D.S. C.P.S. R.A.Ps. Etc.		
Miscellaneous	Locations.		
Miscellaneous	Locations		
Heading	War Diary Of 138th Field Ambulance Dec 1st To 31st 1918 (Vol XXIV Pages I to X)		
War Diary	HQ. Drs.Sarlardinge Sheet 30/U.10.a.6.4.	01/12/1918	01/12/1918
War Diary	HQ. & Drs Sarlardinge	02/12/1918	03/12/1918
War Diary	HQ. & Drs. Sarlardinge.	04/12/1918	11/12/1918
War Diary	'A' Day Of March Program	11/12/1918	11/12/1918
War Diary	Sarlardinge.	12/12/1918	12/12/1918
War Diary	Brussels 6 Map	12/12/1918	12/12/1918
War Diary	Terlinden	13/12/1918	13/12/1918
War Diary	Bierghes	14/12/1918	14/12/1918
War Diary	Brussels 6 Map.		
War Diary	Nauthier Braine.	15/12/1918	16/12/1918
War Diary	Plancenoit	17/12/1918	17/12/1918
War Diary	Moha.	28/12/1918	31/12/1918
War Diary	Brussels 6 Map.		
War Diary	Tilly	18/12/1918	18/12/1918
War Diary	Sombreffe.	19/12/1918	19/12/1918
War Diary	Namur 8 Map St Servais.	20/12/1918	20/12/1918
War Diary	Liege No 7 Map Moha.	21/12/1918	21/12/1918
War Diary	Moha.	22/12/1918	27/12/1918
Heading	41th Div Box 2444 War Diary. Jan 19 To 19 138 Field Amb. May 1919.		
Heading	War Diary Of 138th Field Ambulance R.A.M.C. Went to Germany 8/1/19 From 1-1-1919 To 31-1-1919 Volume XXX		
War Diary	Map 7 Liege Moha.	01/01/1919	04/01/1919
War Diary	Moha.	05/01/1919	07/01/1919
War Diary	Huy	08/01/1919	08/01/1919
War Diary	No 9 Train.	09/01/1919	09/01/1919
War Diary	Urbach 7 Miles S.E Of Cologne.	10/01/1919	10/01/1919
War Diary	Urbach.	11/01/1919	31/01/1919
Heading	War Diary 138 Field Amb. March 1919 Vol XXVII Appendices. March 1919. I. Defence Scheme. IA. First Amendment to Medical Defence Scheme II. Div Admin. Instruction No 7. III. March Tables. IV. Brigade Operation Order No 263.		
Miscellaneous	Defence Scheme Left Division. Appendix I		

Miscellaneous	Brigade Sector.		
Miscellaneous	Defensive System. Lap.		
Miscellaneous			
War Diary	Vickers Machine Guns.	28/02/1919	28/02/1919
Miscellaneous	Appendix "A". Table Of Permanent Guards And Picquets Found.		
Miscellaneous	41st Division Administrative Instruction No 7 Appendix II.	07/03/1919	07/03/1919
Miscellaneous	1st Amendment To 41st Divisional Medical Defence Scheme dated 24-2-19 Appendix 1a.	24/02/1919	24/02/1919
Miscellaneous	B.M.538. Appendix III.	10/03/1919	10/03/1919
Miscellaneous	March Table "A", "Move To Position Of Readiness.		
Miscellaneous	March Table "B" Move To Battle Positions.		
Miscellaneous	March Table "C", "Occupy Much-Drabenderhche Line".		
Operation(al) Order(s)	122nd. Infantry Brigade Operation Order No. 263. Appendix IV.	20/03/1919	20/03/1919
Operation(al) Order(s)	122nd Infantry Brigade Operation Order No. 264. Appendix 1.	06/04/1919	06/04/1919
War Diary	Urbach. 7 Miles S.E Of Cologne.	01/04/1919	03/04/1919
War Diary	Urbach.	04/04/1919	31/05/1919
Miscellaneous	Syllabus Of Training for Regimental Stretcher Bearers Appendix 1.		
Miscellaneous	ADMS. London Div.	01/06/1919	01/06/1919

Mar. 1918

ITALY

Vol 23

14 0/2983

CONFIDENTIAL.

WAR DIARY

OF

138th FIELD AMBULANCE R.A.M.C.

FROM MARCH 1st 1918. TO MARCH 31st 1918.

(VOLUME XV.).

Instructions regarding War Diaries and Intelligence Summaries are contained in F. S. Regs., Part II. and the Staff Manual respectively. Title pages will be prepared in manuscript.

WAR DIARY
or
INTELLIGENCE SUMMARY.
(Erase heading not required.)

Volume XV Page I

Army Form C. 2118.

Place	Date	Hour	Summary of Events and Information	Remarks and references to Appendices
Abbazia Italy	1.3.18		Weather :- Dull rain during night.	
			Lieut. Vercoe proceeded to Fontaniva Railway Station at 7.30 a.m. for the purpose of acting as Entraining Medical Officer to the 122nd Inf. Bde Group. He was accompanied by one RAMC N.C.O and two privates. Lieut. Leslie, V.S. M.O.R.C., with similar personnel, proceeded to the same station at the same hour in order to catch the first Bde. Train, and depart for the detraining station in France (i.e. Doullens), there to act as Detraining Medical Officer to the 122nd Bde. Group. Necessary medical equipment was sent with both the above officers.	
			Strength :- Officers 8, O.R. — RAMC 8 / 182; A.S.C. H.T. – / 25; A.S.C. M.T. – / 13; P.B. men – / 7; Total 8 / 227	
			Four motor ambulances were sent to Fontaniva for entrainment of Battalion trains. One M.A.C. car was also sent to Fontaniva for use of Entraining Medical Officer.	

Strength :-	Officers	O.R.
R.A.M.C.	8	182
A.S.C. H.T.	–	25
A.S.C. M.T.	–	13
P.B. men	–	7
Total	8	227

Instructions regarding War Diaries and Intelligence Summaries are contained in F. S. Regs., Part II. and the Staff Manual respectively. Title pages will be prepared in manuscript.

WAR DIARY
or
INTELLIGENCE SUMMARY.
(Erase heading not required.)

Army Form C. 2118.

Volume XV Page 2.

Place	Date	Hour	Summary of Events and Information	Remarks and references to Appendices
—	2.3.18		Weather :- Dull	
			Unit marched out of billets at Abbazia at 1.15 p.m. and entrained at Fontaniva. Train left Fontaniva at 8.15 p.m. Entraining medical Officer (St. Vincent Ramb) and his party were left behind at entraining Station to proceed to France by last Brigade Train.	WRG
—	3.3.18		Weather :- Dull.	
			One patient, who had been left at the Station, Turin by a previous train, was evacuated to a British Hospital in Turin by this unit.	WRG
—	4.3.18.		Weather :- Dull and cold with deep snow. — Altitude about 4000 feet.	
			Arrived at Bardonecchia at 2.30 a.m. Held up for about 24 hours owing to railway accident outside the further end of Mont Cenis Tunnel.	WRG
			No casualties passed through this unit.	
			Night was intensely cold.	

D. D. & L., London, E.C.
(A7883) Wt. W809/M1672 350,000 4/17 Sch. 52a Forms/C/2118/14

Instructions regarding War Diaries and Intelligence Summaries are contained in F. S. Regs., Part II. and the Staff Manual respectively. Title pages will be prepared in manuscript.

WAR DIARY
or
INTELLIGENCE SUMMARY. Volume XV Page 3
(*Erase heading not required.*)

Army Form C. 2118.

Place	Date	Hour	Summary of Events and Information	Remarks and references to Appendices
—	5.3.18		Weather :- Bright & sunny but cold. Left Bardonecchia at 3 a.m., & continued journey towards Modane.	WRG
—	6.3.18.		Weather :- Bright, but cold. Nothing of importance to report	WRG
—	7.3.18		Weather :- Dull and mild Detrained at Doullens at 9 a.m. Proceeded by march-route to billets at Orville, arriving there at 2.30 p.m. Map ref. of Orville :- Lens 11. 1/100,000. 5E 95.60	WRG
ORVILLE Map ref. - Lens 11. 1/100,000. 5E 95.60.	8.3.18		Weather :- Bright, sunny and mild. Lt Leslie U.S.M.O.R.C. and party returned to this unit upon the detrainment of the Division being completed Lt Vercoe and party also returned Hospital established in a wooden hut — patient-accommodation - 50 O Rs	WRG

D. D. & L., London, E.C.
(A7883) Wt. W803/M1672 350,000 4/17 Sch. 52a Forms/C/2118/14

Instructions regarding War Diaries and Intelligence Summaries are contained in F. S. Regs., Part II. and the Staff Manual respectively. Title pages will be prepared in manuscript.

WAR DIARY
or
INTELLIGENCE SUMMARY.
(Erase heading not required.)

Army Form C. 2118.

Volume XV Page 4

Place	Date	Hour	Summary of Events and Information	Remarks and references to Appendices
ditto.	9.3.18		Weather :- Bright, sunny, and warm.	
			A.D.M.S. S33 received. Lieut. Leslie U.S.M.O.R.C. posted for temporary duty as	
			Medical Officer % 11th R.W. Kents in relief of Captain Cruickshank, who proceeded	WRG
			on leave to the United Kingdom. Camp visited by D.A.D.M.S. & D.A.D.V.S. 41st Div.	
ditto	10.3.18		Weather :- Bright, but cold.	
			122nd Inf Bde. W.O. 24 Copy 11 received at 12.17	
			Capt J. La T. Lander D.S.O. M.C. RAMC and 4 O.Rs. proceeded on leave to U.K. (on 14 days	WRG
			leave)	
ditto.	11.3.18.		Weather :- Warm & Bright.	
			Received wire from A.D.M.S. 41st Division at 8 pm. instructing this unit to march out of Orville	
			before 12 noon on 12.3.18, and to proceed to Thumbercourt.	WRG
			Major L. V. Thurston D.S.O. R.A.M.C. has been posted provisionally to this unit from	
			to-days date for duty.	

D. D. & L., London, E.C.
(A7883) Wt. W809/M1672 350,000 4/17 Sch. 52a Forms/C/2118/14

Army Form C. 2118.

Instructions regarding War Diaries and Intelligence Summaries are contained in F. S. Regs., Part II, and the Staff Manual respectively. Title pages will be prepared in manuscript.

WAR DIARY
or
INTELLIGENCE SUMMARY.
(Erase heading not required.)

Volume XV Page 5

Place	Date	Hour	Summary of Events and Information	Remarks and references to Appendices
Grville	12.3.18		This unit marched out of Grville at 9.30 a.m., and proceeded to billets at Humbercourt, arriving there at 12.45 p.m. New location of unit notified to A.D.M.S. 41st Div., 122nd Inf. Bde. Hd. Qrs. and 41st DS Column. Map ref. Lens 11 1/100,000 4F 50.55. Great difficulty was experienced in finding sufficient billet-accommodation in Humbercourt. Hospital, with accommodation for 50 patients, was established in wooden huts, which had formerly been used as Military Baths.	MRG
Humbercourt Map ref.- Lens 11 1/100,000 4F 50.55.	13.3.18.		Weather :- Fine & Bright. Cold in morning. This camp was visited by D.D.M.S. IV corps. Amendment to 41st Div. A.I. No.14 received. All the Field Ambulance equipment was carefully checked, and repacked in wagons again. P.H. helmets, Iron rations, Box-Respirators, Identity discs, Brassards, and Steel-helmets of all personnel were ~~[illegible]~~ inspected at 2 p.m. Personnel received instruction in use of Box-respirator, and practised Box-respirator drill from 2.30 p.m. to 3.30 p.m.	MRG

D. D. & L., London, E.C.
(A7883) Wt. W809/M1672 350,000 4/17 Sch. 52a Forms/C/2118/14

Instructions regarding War Diaries and Intelligence Summaries are contained in F. S. Regs., Part II, and the Staff Manual respectively. Title pages will be prepared in manuscript.

WAR DIARY
or
INTELLIGENCE SUMMARY.
(Erase heading not required.)

Army Form C. 2118.

Volume XV Page 6.

Place	Date	Hour	Summary of Events and Information	Remarks and references to Appendices
ditto	14.3.18		Weather :- Fine, Sunny, but cold in early morning	
			Several wagons were sent No 2 Coy 41st Div Train for repairs.	WRG
			All ranks practised box-respirator drill for one hour	
ditto	15.3.18		Weather :- Bright, but cold.	
			Health-inspection of unit carried out; men found to be in good condition.	
			Stretcher-drill was practised for one and a half hours with all men wearing box-respirators.	WRG
			Wagons, which had been sent to No. 2 Coy 41st Div Train for repairs, returned, the necessary repairs having effected	
ditto	16.3.18		Weather :- Bright, but cold.	
			Four O.Rs proceeded to U.K on 14 days leave; 21 O.Rs returned from leave to U.K.	WRG
			Capt. E.W.H. Cruickshank, R.A.M.C. M.O. i/c 11th R.W. Kents, who is at present on leave in U.K, is taken on the strength of this unit from to-days date, as that battalion has now been disbanded. Lieut Leslie U.S.M.O.R.C., who was doing duty as temporary medical	

(continued overleaf)

D. D. & L., London, E.C.
(A7883) Wt. W809/M1672 350,000 4/17 Sch. 52a Forms/C/2118/14

Instructions regarding War Diaries and Intelligence Summaries are contained in F. S. Regs., Part II, and the Staff Manual respectively. Title pages will be prepared in manuscript.

WAR DIARY
or
INTELLIGENCE SUMMARY.
(Erase heading not required.)

Army Form C. 2118.

Volume XV Page 7

Place	Date	Hour	Summary of Events and Information	Remarks and references to Appendices
ditto	16.3.18 (continued)		officer to 11th R.W. Kents during the absence of Captain Cruickshank R.A.M.C., has to-day returned to this unit. The medical and surgical equipment, etc, and British Red Cross Stores of the 11th R.W. Kents have been collected, and brought to this unit for disposal. M. Noren, French Interpreter, who was attached to 11th R.W. Kents, has now been attached to this unit for rations, accommodation, etc.	WRG
			Lieut.-Col. W. Ross Gardner, D.S.O., R.A.M.C. made a reconnaissance of the 51st and 25th Divisional forward-areas.	
ditto	17.3.18		Weather:- Fine, but cold.	
			Commanding officer attended conference at A.D.M.S. office at 11 a.m.	
			Non-conformist Service held at hospital of this unit at 11 a.m.	
			Respirators were fitted on horses and mules to-day, and worn for ½ hour.	WRG
			All ranks received one hour's box-respirator drill.	
			Lieut. J. F. Leslie, U.S.M.O.R.C. proceeded to 41st Divisional Machine Gun Battalion for temporary duty as Medical Officer in charge. The Regtal Medical and Surgical equipment, taken over from 11th R.W. Kents, was handed over to 41st Divl M.G. Battn.	

D. D. & L., London, E.C.
(A7883) Wt. W809/M1672 350,000 4/17 Sch. 52a Forms/C/2118/14

Instructions regarding War Diaries and Intelligence Summaries are contained in F. S. Regs., Part II. and the Staff Manual respectively. Title pages will be prepared in manuscript.

WAR DIARY
or
INTELLIGENCE SUMMARY.
(Erase heading not required.)

Army Form C. 2118.

Volume XV Page 8

Place	Date	Hour	Summary of Events and Information	Remarks and references to Appendices
ditto	18.3.18		Weather:- Fine, warm, & sunny.	
			41st Div A.I. No. 15 received: this cancels A.I. No. 14	
			One N.C.O. was sent to 4th Corps Anti-Gas School in order to go through a course	
			of instruction in anti-gas measures; course will last until 24.3.18	WRG
			All ranks received one hour's box-respirator drill. Two more isolation-tents were	
			pitched in hospital-grounds, making a total of 3 isolation-tents (bell).	
ditto	19.3.18		Weather:- Rainy.	
			All ranks were paraded at 8.50 a.m. for inspection by G.O.C. 41st Division at 9.15 a.m.;	
			all transport, with animals hooked in, was paraded at same hour for G.O.C.'s	
			inspection. At 9 a.m. wire was received from 41st Div. "Q" cancelling	
			G.O.C's inspection.	WRG
			Three O.Rs proceeded to U.K. on 14 days' leave.	
			Received W.O. B.M.177 of 18.3.18 warning this unit that 41st Div will move from the	
			Mondicourt-Pas Area to Baizieux on 21.3.18.	
			A.D.M.S. S53 of 18.3.18 received (Arrangements for collecting sick of 19th Middlesex	
			Regt & 228 Fd. Coy R.E. on march to Arras)	

D. D. & L., London, E.C. (A7883) Wt. W809/M1672 350,000 4/17 Sch. 52a Forms/C/2118/14

Instructions regarding War Diaries and Intelligence Summaries are contained in F. S. Regs., Part II. and the Staff Manual respectively. Title pages will be prepared in manuscript.

WAR DIARY
or
INTELLIGENCE SUMMARY.
(Erase heading not required.)

Army Form C. 2118.

Volume XV Page 9.

Place	Date	Hour	Summary of Events and Information	Remarks and references to Appendices
ditto	19.3.18 (continued).		One Ramb N.C.O. and one Ramb private left the Hd-Qrs. of this unit at 7 a.m. with two horse-ambulances in order to follow these two units on the line of march, and to collect their sick. At 11.30 a.m. Lieut. R.H. Vercoe, Ramb proceeded to Arras with one motor-ambulance for the purpose of carrying back to this unit the sick collected by the horse-ambulances. The horse-ambces will return to this Hd-Qrs to-morrow, leaving Arras at 7.30 a.m. Weather improved somewhat at 12 noon. Heavy rain from 2 p.m. to 3 p.m. A.D.M.S. S 57 of 19.3.18 received at 7.30 p.m. — instructions regarding move to another area.	WRG
ditto.	20.3.18		Weather :- Dull in morning with rain. Bright at noon. A.D.M.S. S 56 of 20.3.18 received at 6.20 a.m. — instructions regarding move. 122 I. Bde O.O. 173 received at 7 a.m. All the horse-transport, with the exception of 1 Limbered-wagon, 1 Water-cart, & 2 horse-ambulances, proceeded from this Hd-Qrs under the Transport officer (Capt S.S.C. Roche, M.C. Ramb) at 9.45 a.m. to report to O.C. No 2 Coy. 41st Div. Train at Pommera.	WRG

D. D. & L., London, E.C. (A7883) Wt. W809/M1672 350,000 4/17 Sch. 52a Forms/C/2118/14

Instructions regarding War Diaries and Intelligence Summaries are contained in F. S. Regs., Part II. and the Staff Manual respectively. Title pages will be prepared in manuscript.

WAR DIARY
or
INTELLIGENCE SUMMARY.
(Erase heading not required.)

Army Form C. 2118.

Volume XV Page 10.

Place	Date	Hour	Summary of Events and Information	Remarks and references to Appendices
ditto	20.3.18 (continued).		and there join up with remainder of 122 Inf Bde Transport.	
			122 Inf. Bde. SCB.811 of 20.3.18 received at 10.20 a.m. —— Captain J. J. H. Ferguson RAMC, accompanied by the French Interpreter, M. Noren, proceeded from this Hd-Qrs at 11.30 a.m as billetting officer for this unit, and reported to the 122 Inf. Bde. Billetting officer at the Church Halloy at 12 noon.	[illegible]
			At 2 p.m. the box-respirators, steel-helmets, iron-rations, identity discs, and first-Field-Dressings of all personnel of this unit were inspected.	
			Amendment to O.O. 173 received at 10.30 a.m.	
			O.C. proceeded with A.D.M.S to the Baizieux Area, that is, the area to which the division is about to proceed.	
ditto.	21.3.18		Weather:- Dull, thick mist.	
			Transport arrived at HEILLY at 2.15 p.m.	
			Personnel of Field Ambulance entrained at Mondicourt at 5 p.m, and horse-transport, which remained behind with personnel at Humbercourt entrained at 8 p.m. at Saulty	[illegible]
			Motor-ambulances proceeded to Heilly by road.	

D. D. & L., London, E.C. (A7883) Wt. W803/M1672 350,000 4/17 Sch. 52a Forms/C/2118/14

Instructions regarding War Diaries and Intelligence Summaries are contained in F. S. Regs., Part II. and the Staff Manual respectively. Title pages will be prepared in manuscript.

WAR DIARY
or
INTELLIGENCE SUMMARY.
(Erase heading not required.)

Army Form C. 2118.

Volume XV page 11

Place	Date	Hour	Summary of Events and Information	Remarks and references to Appendices
Savoy Camp Behucourt. Sheet 11 1/40000 5 J 68 45	22.3.18		Weather:- Misty and cold in early morning; during day bright sunshine. Personnel and horse-transport, which entrained at Saulty, arrived at Achiet-le-Grand at about 2 a.m., and detrained at that station. Then marched to Savoy Camp at Behucourt (Map ref. Sht Sens 11. 5 J 68 45) Transport which spent the previous night at Heilly, left Heilly at 6 a.m., and proceeded by route-march to Behucourt arriving there at 5 pm. Motor-ambulances arrived at Behucourt about 12 noon. The entire Field Ambulance proceeded by route-march at 10 pm to Grévillers, and on arrival there took over the site vacated by No3 C.C.S, and established a C.M.D.S for Walking Wounded (Map ref. 5 J 8 3) R.A.M.C. O.O. 44 received together with S75 - modification of O.O. 44. Evacuation of wounded was carried out by 16 M.A.C. and 3rd Army Aux. Bus Coy	WRG
Sht. Sens 11 1/10000 5 J 8 3 nr Grévillers.	23.3.18.		Weather:- Bright & sunny. Secret Preliminary Order Copy No 5 received. Camp was heavily shelled during the afternoon and evening; also throughout the night. — two of R.A.M.C. personnel	WRG

D. D. & L., London, E.C. (A7883) Wt. W809/M1672 350,000 4/17 **Sch. 52a** Forms/C/2118/14

Instructions regarding War Diaries and Intelligence Summaries are contained in F. S. Regs., Part II, and the Staff Manual respectively. Title pages will be prepared in manuscript.

WAR DIARY
or
INTELLIGENCE SUMMARY.
(Erase heading not required.)

Army Form C. 2118.

Volume XV Page 12

Place	Date	Hour	Summary of Events and Information	Remarks and references to Appendices
ditto	23.3.18 (continued).		was wounded. Gas alert was ordered at 7 p.m. Total number of casualties evacuated = 1,300 (approx). A few gas-shells landed in the vicinity during the night.	WPS
ditto.	24.3.18		Weather: Bright & sunny. Casualties amongst Fd. Amb. personnel = 3 O.Rs. A.D.M.S. 980, d. 24.3.18 received. An advance party proceeded at 2 p.m. to establish a new site for the C.M.D.S on the Achiet-le-Grand — Miraumont Road at 5I 95.44; enemy commenced shelling, and new site was abandoned. Another site was selected in Buchanan Camp situated near Achiet-le-petit, but this was also abandoned on account of the retirement of the line. Finally a site was chosen on the Achiet-le-petit — Bucquoy Road about ½ kilometre from Bucquoy. About 8 p.m., all casualties having been evacuated from the C.M.D.S. at Grevillers, this Dressing Station was closed, and the personnel proceeded to the new site, and re-established the C.M.D.S	WPS

D. D. & L., London, E.C.
(A7883) Wt. W809/M1672 350,000 4/17 Sch. 52a Forms/C/2118/14

Instructions regarding War Diaries and Intelligence Summaries are contained in F. S. Regs., Part II. and the Staff Manual respectively. Title pages will be prepared in manuscript.

WAR DIARY
or
INTELLIGENCE SUMMARY.
(Erase heading not required.)

Volume XV Page 13

Army Form C. 2118.

Place	Date	Hour	Summary of Events and Information	Remarks and references to Appendices
C.M.D.S on Achiet-le-Petit–Bucquoy Rd about ½ kilo from Bucquoy (Lens 11 1/100000 4 H 63 74)	25.3.18.		Weather: Bright, but cold.	
			About 500 cases evacuated.	
			Owing to continued retirement the Field Ambulance withdrew to Hannescamps at 3 p.m., and opened the C.M.D.S at 4 H 8 0. at 5 p.m., when about 320 casualties were dealt with.	WRG
			Lt J F Leslie, U.S.M.O.R.C., temporarily attached to 41st Div. M.G. Batt. was wounded and evacuated to C.C.S.	
Hannescamps (Lens 11 1/100000 4 H 8.0.)	26.3.18		Weather: Cold, but bright	
			The M.D.S. at Hannescamps was closed down at 9.30 a.m. The Division came out of the line at Bucquoy and went into support in the Gommecourt area. This unit proceeded by route march across country to Bienvillers, and was instructed, on arrival at that village, to take charge of the forward-evacuation from the division. Two officers and 50 O.Rs. proceeded forward to the Foncquevillers–Gommecourt area, and established touch with the R.M.Os of the Division. A Collecting Post was formed in Foncquevillers.	WRG

D. D. & L., London, E.C. (A7883) Wt. W809/M1672 350,000 4/17 Sch. 52a Forms/C/2118/14

Instructions regarding War Diaries and Intelligence Summaries are contained in F. S. Regs., Part II. and the Staff Manual respectively. Title pages will be prepared in manuscript.

WAR DIARY
or
INTELLIGENCE SUMMARY.
(Erase heading not required.)

Army Form C. 2118.

Volume XV Page 14.

Place	Date	Hour	Summary of Events and Information	Remarks and references to Appendices
Foncquevillers and Bienvillers	27.3.18		Weather - Dull & cold.	
			At 1 a.m. the Division returned from the Gommecourt area, and proceeded into reserve at Bienvillers. All the personnel of this unit in the Gommecourt - Foncquevillers area were withdrawn, and billetted in Bienvillers.	WRG
			All R.M.Os were supplied with stretchers, shell-dressings, etc according to their requirements	
Bienvillers	28.3.18.		Weather - Wet and stormy.	
			One bearer subdivision reported to this unit from 139th and 140th Field Ambulances. Division proceeded into support in the Gommecourt area. This Fd. Amb. (with the exception of a few details left at Bienvillers) proceeded with the 3 Inf. Brigades to the forward-area. A C.P. was formed at Foncquevillers at 2.30 p.m.; the O.C. Forward-Bearers established his Hd-Qrs at Gommecourt in the vicinity of the Hd-Qrs. of the 3 Inf Bdes. Touch was maintained with all R.M.Os. Casualties, which were few in number, were evacuated by hand-carriage and wheeled-stretcher from R.A.P's to Hd Qrs of O.C. Forward-bearers, thence to A.D.S. (139 Fd. Amb.) at Bienvillers (via C.P. at Foncquevillers).	WRG

D. D. & L., London, E.C.
(A7883) Wt. W809/M1672 350,000 4/17 Sch. 52a Forms/C/2118/14

Instructions regarding War Diaries and Intelligence Summaries are contained in F. S. Regs., Part II, and the Staff Manual respectively. Title pages will be prepared in manuscript.

WAR DIARY
or
INTELLIGENCE SUMMARY.
(Erase heading not required.)

Army Form C. 2118.

Volume XV Page 15.

Place	Date	Hour	Summary of Events and Information	Remarks and references to Appendices
Foncquevillers	29.3.18		Weather:- High wind, rain during morning, sunshine in afternoon.	
57D. 66.70			R.A.M.C. O.O. No 46 copy 3 dated 29/3/18 received. A shell struck a billet occupied by	
Lens 11 1/100000			personnel, and severely wounded one man.	
			Lieut Pearce RAMC was posted to 10th Queens (R.W.S) as M.O. temporarily in charge.	WRG
			Transport, which was attached to 41st Div Train since commencement of enemy-	
			offensive, was reported to be at Authie.	
			Division relieved the 42nd Div. in the Bucquoy line during the night. This unit	
			proceeded to Bucquoy Sector. Head-Qrs details remained at Bienvillers. Commanding	
			Officer established his Hd-Qrs at Essarts-les-Bucquoy in a sap along with 124	
			Inf Bde. Hd-Qrs. For location of other posts, methods and routes of evacuation,	
			distribution of personnel, etc. please see attached report (Appendix "A")	
Essarts-les-Bucquoy	30.3.18		Weather:- Heavy rain - high wind.	
			Ford-car, to replace the one abandoned near Bucquoy, arrived from Workshops.	
			Capt Davies RAMC arrived for temporary duty from 10th Queens (R.W.S).	WRG
			Capt J J H. Ferguson was posted to 10th R.W.Kents & 11th Queens as M.O. temporarily in charge.	
			Throughout the day forward-area was heavily shelled.	

D. D. & L., London, E.C. (A7883) Wt. W803/M1672 350,000 4/17 Sch. 52a Forms/C/2118/14

Army Form C. 2118.

Instructions regarding War Diaries and Intelligence Summaries are contained in F. S. Regs., Part II. and the Staff Manual respectively. Title pages will be prepared in manuscript.

WAR DIARY
or
INTELLIGENCE SUMMARY.
(Erase heading not required.)

Volume XV Page 16.

Place	Date	Hour	Summary of Events and Information	Remarks and references to Appendices
Essarts-lès-Bucquoy.	31.3.18.		Weather:- Bright, & stormy.	
			W.O. 41st Div G 378 d 31.3.18 received — Division being relieved by 42nd Div on night of 1/2 April	
			Strength:- Off. / O.Rs.	
			R.A.M.C. 7 / 174	
			A.S.C. H.T. / 24	WRG
			" M.T. / 13	
			R.B. / 7	
			Total 7 / 218	
			Throughout the day shell-fire in Forward Area was of moderate intensity. Casualties evacuated about 300	

D. D. & L., London, E.C.
(A7883) Wt. W809/M1672 350,000 4/17 Sch. 52a Forms/C/2118/14

Instructions regarding War Diaries and Intelligence Summaries are contained in F. S. Regs., Part II. and the Staff Manual respectively. Title pages will be prepared in manuscript.

WAR DIARY
or
INTELLIGENCE SUMMARY.
(*Erase heading not required.*)

Army Form C. 2118.

Volume XV Page 17.

Place	Date	Hour	Summary of Events and Information	Remarks and references to Appendices
Month of March, 1918.			General Remarks:- Since the commencement of the enemy-offensive the horse-transport of this Field Ambulance (with the exception of one "A.D.S." limbered wagon, and one water-cart) has been attached to the 41st Div. Train, and has moved from place to place with that unit.	
			When this unit is responsible for the evacuation from the Forward-Area, the following procedure is adopted in order to maintain close contact with the Inf. Bde Hd-Qrs. and also with the R.M.Os:-	
			(1) A runner is posted to each Inf. Bde Hd-Qrs; the duty of this runner is to convey messages from the Inf. Bde Hd-Qrs. to the nearest Fd. Amb. officer.	WRS
			(2) A runner and one squad of 4 bearers are posted to all Regtl M.Os. The runner is for the purpose of keeping the O.C. Forward-Bearers informed of the position of the R.A.P. of the R/M.O. to whom he is attached, and also for the purpose of conveying messages from the R.M.O. concerned to O.C. Forward-Bearers.	—
			During the enemy-offensive this method of "maintaining touch" was again made use of, and was found to be of even greater value than hitherto, when practised during the British offensives, as during an advance touch is	

D. D. & L., London, E.C.
(A7883) Wt. W809/M1672 350,000 4/17 Sch. 52a Forms/C/2118/14

Instructions regarding War Diaries and Intelligence Summaries are contained in F. S. Regs., Part II. and the Staff Manual respectively. Title pages will be prepared in manuscript.

WAR DIARY
or
INTELLIGENCE SUMMARY.
(Erase heading not required.)

Volume XV Page 18

Army Form C. 2118.

Place	Date	Hour	Summary of Events and Information	Remarks and references to Appendices
			General remarks (continued):-	
			more easily maintained, and, if lost, not so difficult to re-establish.	
			A copy of the instructions issued to runners, attached to R.M.Os, is attached (see appendix "B").	
			For contents of "A.D.S." Limber, see appendix "C".	

M Ross Gardner
Lieut Colonel RAMC
Commanding 138th Field Ambulance

D. D. & L., London, E.C.
(A7883) Wt. W809/M1672 350,000 4/17 Sch. 52a Forms/C/2118/14

A.D.M.S.
41st Division.

Appendix "A"

Reference Map, Sheet 57D 1/40,000, I have to report on the evacuation of wounded from the Forward Area as under:–

R.A.P's of all the Battalions of the Division have been visited, and the evacuation of wounded from all these R.A.P's is entirely satisfactory.

Map references of the R.A.P's are shewn in Appendix "A" attached.

All evacuation from the Forward Area to the C.P. at ESSARTS is carried out by wheeled stretcher or hand carriage, and owing to the very muddy condition of the roads resulting from the recent heavy rains the use of the wheeled stretcher carriage has become more or less limited to the two semi-metalled roads in the area, namely: the ESSARTS–BUCQUOY Road and the road leading from ESSARTS to the MONCHY–BUCQUOY Road.

The casualties from the 3 Left R.A.P's, i.e. 26th R.F's, 10th R.W. Kents (11th Queens) and 19th Middlesex are evacuated to the Relay Post at DIERVILLE FARM; thence to the C.P. at ESSARTS via the Relay Post near the Cross Roads at F20. B1.9.

casualties from the 3 Right R.A.P's, i.e. 20th D.L.I., 10th Queens and 12th E. Surreys are evacuated to the C.P. at ESSARTS by wheeled stretcher along the main BUCQUOY – ESSARTS Road. Evacuation from the R.A.P. of the 18th K.R.R.C. takes place along the branch road in which the R.A.P. is situated to the Relay Post at the Cross Roads; thence to ESSARTS.

REMARKS

At night Ford Cars could be taken to the R.A.P's of the 10th Queens and 20th D.L.I. along the main ESSARTS – BUCQUOY Road, and also, in the event of an improvement in the weather conditions, to the Relay Post at the Cross Roads at F.20. B.1.9.

DISTRIBUTION OF R.A.M.C. PERSONNEL.

See appendix "B" attached.

DISTRIBUTION OF WHEELED STRETCHERS.

See appendix "C" attached.

Three R.A.P's have not been supplied with wheeled stretchers, as they could not be used for evacuation from these R.A.P's

The R.A.P. of the 23rd Middlesex has the use of wheeled stretchers at the Relay Post (at the Cross Roads), which is adjacent to that R.A.P.

GENERAL REMARKS.

Throughout the day BUCQUOY has been much more heavily shelled than during the previous 24 hours. Heavy shelling occurred during the night of the 31st. The Cross Roads at F.20 B.1.9. was continuously shelled for several hours.

W Ross Gardner
Lt. Col. RAMC
31/3/18 O.C. 138th Field Ambce.

APPENDIX "A".

R.A.P.	MAP REF.	M.O.	REMARKS	PERSONNEL
20 D.L.I.	L.2.B.2.9.	Lieut. Milner	Deep Sap	5
10 Queens	F.26.D.4.2.	" Vercoe	Damaged cellar	5
26 Roy. Fus.	F.27.B.5.0.	Capt. Wilson	Deep Sap	5
10 R.W. Kents } 11 Queens }	F.22.d.6.4.	" Ferguson	Deep Sap	5
19 Middlesex	F.22.d.5.7	" Crosse		9
23 Middlesex	F.14.d.2.2.	" Powell	Small Dug-out	5
18 K.R.R.C.	F.20.d.8.3.	" Godfrey	" "	5
15 Hants	F.20.a.3.2.	" Reynolds	" "	5
12 E. Surrey	F.26.a.9.0.	" Christie	Deep Sap.	5
				49

Appendix "B"
Distribution of Personnel.

POST		OFFICERS	O.R.'s
Bde. Hqrs.	RUNNERS	—	3
ESSARTS		* 2 * includes O.C. F.A.	10
RELAY POST at Cross Roads F. 20 B 1.9.		1 O.C. Forward Bearers.	30
RELAY POST at DIERVILLE FARM		1	19
Each R.A.P. (Except 19th Middlesex, which has 1 runner & 2 squads.)		0	5 {1 Runner, 4 Bearers. 49
	Total.	4	111.

Appendix "C".

Distribution of Wheeled Stretchers.

POST	NUMBER.	
Relay Post at Cross Roads F.20 B.1.9	5	Road from Relay Post to C.P. at ESSARTS is suitable for wheeled stretchers.
DIERVILLE FARM.	3	– Road to Cross Roads is now unsuitable for W.S. owing to muddy condition.
R.A.P. 19 Middlesex	1	
" 20 D.L.I.	1	
" 12 E. Surreys	1	
" 18 K.R.R.C.	1	
" 15 Hants	1	
Total	13.	

Appendix "B"

To No 777 PTE Jones, J. R.A.M.C.

You are posted as runner to M.O. i/c 10th Blankshire Regt,

Your duties will be as follows:-

(1) To convey messages from the Regtal M.O. to the nearest Field Ambce Officer.

(2) Whenever the Regtal M.O. moves from his R.A.P. to a new R.A.P., you will, on arrival at new R.A.P., at once proceed to the nearest Fld Ambce Officer, and inform him of the site of the new R.A.P; if possible the Map Reference of the new R.A.P should be obtained from the R.M.O., and conveyed to the Fld Ambce Officer.

(3) You will not act as a stretcher-bearer.

(4) You will remain attached to above R.M.O until relieved by another runner from this unit, or until instructed to rejoin this unit by an <u>Officer of this Fld Ambce</u>

(5) You will show these instructions to the above R.M.O.

DATE:-

R.A.M.C.

O.C. Fld Ambce

APPENDIX "C"

MINIMUM EQUIPMENT FOR AN ADVANCED DRESSING STATION.

LIMBER NO: 1.

Pannier "F"	Complete, ONE.
Pannier "H"	" ONE.
Field Medical Pannier.	No. 1.
Field Surgical Pannier.	No. 1.
Medical Comfort Pannier.	1.
Surgical Haversacks.	3.
Medical Companion.	1.
Butchers Set.	1.
Entrenching Tool Bag. (Complete).	1.
Poles for pendant flags.	4.
Tow Surgeons.	10 lbs.
Lamps, hurricne. (In addition to 2 in "F" Pannier.)	2.
Stove, Oil, Primus.	1.
Bed Pan.	1.
Parraffin.	5 Gallons.
Cresol.	1. "
Reserve Dressing Box.	1.
Buckets, Canvas.	2.
Operating Table.	1.
" " (Cushion for)	1.
Bottles, Water.	3.
Box Containing Stationery.	1.
Office Table.	1.
Oxygen Cylinder.	1.
Feeder. (In "F" Pannier)	2.
Funnel Tin. " ") ½ Pint.	1.
Kettle, Enamelled (In "F" Pannier).	1.
Basins, 11" ("F" Pannier)	2.
" 14" ("H" Pannier).	2.
Brushes Scrubbing. ~~xxx~~ ("F" Pannier)	3.
Pannikins, Pint. ("H" Pannier).	12.
Methylated Spirit. "F" Pannier)	1 tin.
Lamps, Operating.	1.
Towels, " ("H" Pannier)	3.
Anti-tetanic serum. "F" Pannier)	1 box.
" " " Syringe.	1.
Tressles.	2.

No. 2 LIMBER.

Shell Dressings.	~~4~~ 6 Haversacks.
~~Stretchers.~~	~~12~~.
Blankets.	50.
Ground Sheets.	50.
Soyers Stove.	1.
Oxo, Boxes.	1.
Tea Boxes.	1.
Sugar boxes.	1.
Stretchers.	6.

-oOoOoOo-

1

Vol 24

apr. 1918

CONFIDENTIAL

140/3076

WAR DIARY

OF

138TH FIELD AMBULANCE.

FROM. 1ST APRIL 1918. TO. 30TH APRIL 1918.

(VOLUME XVI)

Instructions regarding War Diaries and Intelligence Summaries are contained in F. S. Regs., Part II. and the Staff Manual respectively. Title pages will be prepared in manuscript.

WAR DIARY
or
~~INTELLIGENCE~~ SUMMARY.
(Erase heading not required.)

Army Form C. 2118.

Volume XVI Page. I.

Place	Date	Hour	Summary of Events and Information	Remarks and references to Appendices
Essarts-les-Bucquoy	1/4/18		Weather: Bright & dry.	
			Ramb. O.O 47 received 8 a.m. Bienvillers, and Essarts-les-Bucquoy were heavily shelled throughout the day. The bearer-subdivision and wheeled-stretchers, which were attached to this unit from the 140th Fd Amb, were returned at 3.30 p.m. to their unit at La Cauchie. Bearer-subd. and wheeled-stretchers, attached from 139th Fd Amb, were also returned to their unit at Bienvillers. One Ford-car, which was damaged in Forward-Area, was sent to Workshops. A new Triumph motor-cycle was received from workshops.	
			A.D.M.S. Secret letter 93 received. 122 Inf. Bde. O.O. 174 received.	
			138th Field Amb was relieved in the line by 1/1st East Lancs. Fd. Amb. 42nd Division. Relief was completed at midnight.	
			Strength:- R.A.M.C. 7 offs 174 O.Rs; A.S.C. H.T. 24; " M.T. 13; R.E. 7; Total 7 – 218.	
			All personnel assembled at Bienvillers.	
Bienvillers	2/4/18		Weather:- Dull, but dry.	
			Personnel proceeded from Bienvillers by motor-ambulance to Authie, joining transport of this unit there. At 6.30 a.m. personnel and transport proceeded from Authie by march-route to billets at Orville, arriving there at 9.30 a.m.	

D. D. & L., London, E.C. (A7883) Wt. W803/M1672 350,000 4/17 Sch. 52a Forms/C/2118/14

Instructions regarding War Diaries and Intelligence Summaries are contained in F. S. Regs., Part II. and the Staff Manual respectively. Title pages will be prepared in manuscript.

WAR DIARY
or
INTELLIGENCE SUMMARY.
(Erase heading not required.)

Army Form C. 2118.

Volume XVI Page 2.

Place	Date	Hour	Summary of Events and Information	Remarks and references to Appendices
	2/4/18 (continued)		122 I. Bde. W.O. No B.M.559 received, also 41st Div A.I. No 21 received. Lieuts J. Cullen, and C.R. Wilkins RAMC were posted to this unit, & taken on strength accordingly.	
Grville	3.4.18.		Weather:- Dull & cold.	
			Personnel left billets at Grville at 7.30 a.m., and proceeded by march-route to embussing-point at Mondicourt. Embussed at Mondicourt at 11 a.m., and were conveyed to Framecourt, debussing at the latter place at 12.30 p.m. Transport (horse) joined No 2 Coy 41st Div Train at the southern end of Grville at 7 a.m., and proceeded with that company to Framecourt by road, arriving there about 3 p.m. Motor-ambulances accompanied the buses, which conveyed the personnel.	WRS
			At 7 a.m. a medical officer, with 5 O.Rs, the necessary medical equipment, and a motor-ambulance, was sent by road to both detraining stations (i.e. Pezelhoek and Hopoutre) to act as Detraining Medical Officer. At the same time a billetting-party, consisting of the Interpreter and one N.C.O., was sent to the Detraining Area to arrange for billets for this unit.	WRS
			The Field Ambulance spent the night in billets at Framecourt.	

D. D. & L., London, E.C.
(A7883) Wt. W809/M1672 350,000 4/17 Sch. 52a Forms/C/2118/14

Instructions regarding War Diaries and Intelligence Summaries are contained in F. S. Regs., Part II. and the Staff Manual respectively. Title pages will be prepared in manuscript.

WAR DIARY
or
INTELLIGENCE ~~SUMMARY~~.
(Erase heading not required.)

Volume XVI Page 3

Army Form C. 2118.

Place	Date	Hour	Summary of Events and Information	Remarks and references to Appendices
Framecourt	4.4.18		Weather: Rain in early morning. Dull during day	
			Transport (horse) left Framecourt at 4.45 a.m., and proceeded to Entraining Station (Petit Houvin) arriving there at 5.15 a.m. Personnel proceeded to Entraining Station (Petit Houvin) at 9.15 a.m., arriving at station at 9.45 a.m. Owing to delay in the departure of previous trains, entrainment of this unit was not completed until 11 a.m.	
			Motor-ambulances proceeded by road to Detraining Area, leaving Framecourt at 11 a.m.	
			Train conveying this unit left Petit Houvin at 11.45 a.m., and arrived at Detraining Station at 5.10 p.m. (Detraining Stat. = Peselhoek). Detrainment of unit was completed at 5.45 p.m. Personnel were conveyed by lorries to billets at School's Camp (Sht 27 L 3 a 7.4); transport proceeded by march-route to Schools Camp. Motor-ambs also arrived at same camp.	WRG
Schools Camp Sht 27 L 3 a 7 4.	5.4.18		Weather: Very wet & cold.	
			Detraining Medical officers (together with personnel, equipment, & motor-ambulances used at Detraining Stations) reported back to this unit at Schools camp	WRG
			Informed that Army Commander (Gen. Sir H. Plumer) will inspect the Division	

D. D. & L., London, E.C.
(A7883) Wt. W809/M1672 350,000 4/17 Sch. 52a Forms/C/2118/14

Instructions regarding War Diaries and Intelligence Summaries are contained in F. S. Regs., Part II. and the Staff Manual respectively. Title pages will be prepared in manuscript.

WAR DIARY
or
INTELLIGENCE SUMMARY.
(Erase heading not required.)

Army Form C. 2118.

Volume XVI Page 4.

Place	Date	Hour	Summary of Events and Information	Remarks and references to Appendices
	5/4/18 (continued)		at 9.30 a.m. on 6 inst.	
			Capts T.R. Thomas & R.H. Clements reported to this unit for duty, and were taken on the strength. One O.R. reported as a reinforcement. Lieut. R.H. Vercoe RAMC returned to this unit from 10th Queens (R.W.S.), where he had been doing temporary duty. Location of unit was notified to A.D.M.S. 41st Div, 122 Inf. Bde Hd-Qrs, 41st D.S.Col, and 139th & 140th Field Ambulances	WRG
ditto	6/4/18		Weather:- Fine and Bright.	
			This unit paraded with 122 Inf. Bde. in Schools Camp at 9 a.m., and was inspected by the Corps Commander (General Hunter Weston) at 9.30 a.m. Owing to unforeseen circumstances, the Army Commander was unable to ~~attend~~ inspect the Division.	WRG
			O.C. (Colonel W. Ross Gardner D.S.O.) made a reconnaissance of the forward area (i.e. St Jean - Wieltje - Potijze - Frost House Sectors) along with the A.D.M.S. 41st Division prior to this unit taking over from the 87th & 88th Field Ambulances 29th Division.	
			R.A.M.C. O.O. No 48. & A.D.M.S. S80 received. Also 122 Inf. Bde. O.O. 175 received.	

D. D. & L., London, E.C. (A7883) Wt. W809/M1672 350,000 4/17 Sch. 52a Forms/C/2118/14

Instructions regarding War Diaries and Intelligence Summaries are contained in F. S. Regs., Part II. and the Staff Manual respectively. Title pages will be prepared in manuscript.

WAR DIARY
or
~~INTELLIGENCE SUMMARY.~~
(Erase heading not required.)

Army Form C. 2118.

Volume XVI Page 5.

Place	Date	Hour	Summary of Events and Information	Remarks and references to Appendices
	6/4/18 (continued).		One runner and one squad of 4 bearers were attached to each battalion of the 122 Inf. Bde. One runner was attached to 122 Inf. Bde. H.Q. Anti-trench foot powder and soap supplied to all units of the 122 Inf. Bde. group. Medical stores supplied to R.M.Os. of affiliated Bde. group.	WRG
Do.	7/4/18.		Weather: Bright, much warmer. Personnel proceeded by motor-lorries to Moated Farm, Vlamertinghe; transport proceeded by road to the same camp, arriving there at 1 p.m. Moated Farm (H2d.5.2 Sht.28 1/40,000), which was being used as a D.R.S. by the 87th Fd. Amb., was taken over as the Hd. Qrs. of this unit. The 122 Inf. Bde. went into the line just south of Passchendaele, and the following R.A.M.C. posts, situated behind the Brigade Front, were taken over from the 88th Fd. Ambulance, 29th Division by this unit:-	WRG
			Ref. map:- Sht. 28 Edition 3 1/40.000.	
			(a) Tyne Cott - D17 a 4.4 - Taken over as R.A.Ps by R.M.Os of 12 E. Surreys, 15 Hants, & 18 K.R.R.	See Appendix I
			(b) Ingot Relay Post - D16 b 8.8	
			(c) Daring Crossing R.P. - D16 d 6.3	

D. D. & L., London, E.C.
(A7883) Wt. W809/M1672 350,000 4/17 Sch. 52a Forms/C/2118/14

Instructions regarding War Diaries and Intelligence Summaries are contained in F. S. Regs., Part II. and the Staff Manual respectively. Title pages will be prepared in manuscript.

WAR DIARY
or
~~INTELLIGENCE SUMMARY.~~
(Erase heading not required.)

Army Form C. 2118.

Volume XVI Page 6.

Place	Date	Hour	Summary of Events and Information	Remarks and references to Appendices
"	7/4/18 (continued)		(d) Jersey Relay Post = D 16 d. 13	
			(e) Joy Loading Post - D 27 a 4 4 } Still held by 2/3 North Midland Fd Amb.	
			(f) Frost House A.D.S - D 25 a 6.2 } 59th Division, but were reinforced by	See Appendix I.
			(g) Potyze A.D.S. - I 4 a 2 0 } personnel of this unit so that 122 Inf Bde casualties could be evacuated via these posts.	WRG
			Relief was completed in above Sector about 12 midnight.	
			Received the following :- RAMB O.O No 49, 41st Divn A.I Nr 25 under A.D.M.S. S95, and 124 I.Bde. O.O. 173.	
Moated Farm Sht. 28. Edition 3 1/40.000 H 2 d 8 2	8/4/18		Weather :- Bright & dry	
			One bearer-subdivision and one Sunbeam motor-amb. reported to this unit for duty from 139th Fd. Ambulance. One O.R posted to Divisional Baths at Vlamertinghe. One N.C.O. and 2 men posted to Trench foot Preparation Centre near St. Jean.	WRG
			The 88th Fd. Amb, 29th Division was relieved in the Left Sector VIII Corps Front by this unit, and the following posts were taken over (see appendix I) :- Ref Map. Sht 28 1/40.000	
			(1) Bill-boxes 13 & 10 (as R.A.Ps Left Bde) = D 4 b 5.1 & D 4 a 8 4 respectively	

D. D. & L., London, E.C. (A7883) Wt. W803/M1672 350,000 4/17 Sch. 52a Forms/C/2118/14

Instructions regarding War Diaries and Intelligence Summaries are contained in F. S. Regs., Part II. and the Staff Manual respectively. Title pages will be prepared in manuscript.

WAR DIARY
or
~~INTELLIGENCE~~ SUMMARY.
(Erase heading not required.)

Volume XVI Page 7.

Army Form C. 2118.

Place	Date	Hour	Summary of Events and Information	Remarks and references to Appendices
	8/4/18 (continued)		(2) Bellevue Saps (as R.A.Ps Rt Bde) — D 4 d 5.5.	
			(3) Waterloo R.P. — D 10 c 5.9.	
			(4) Gravenstafel Relay Post — D 9 c 7.2.	
			(5) Somme A.D.S. — D 13 d 6.6.	
			(6) Bridge House Dressing Station — C 24 a 3.6.	
			(7) Wieltje A.D.S. — C 28 b 5.5.	
			(8) St Jean A.D.S. — I 3 a 5.5.	WEG
			For methods of evacuation, see appendix I.	
			Relief was completed at 6 p.m.	
			During the night the 124 Inf Bde. took over the Right Brigade Sector. A runner was posted to the 124 Inf Bde. Hd-Qrs, and a runner and a squad of 4 bearers were posted to all the R.M.Os of the battalions of the Bde. These R.M.Os were situated in Bellevue saps, as previously indicated.	
			Casualties - slight. Forward area - very quiet.	

D. D. & L., London, E.C.
(A7883) Wt. W803/M1672 350,000 4/17 Sch. 52a Forms/C/2118/14

Instructions regarding War Diaries and Intelligence Summaries are contained in F. S. Regs., Part II, and the Staff Manual respectively. Title pages will be prepared in manuscript.

WAR DIARY
or
~~INTELLIGENCE SUMMARY.~~
(Erase heading not required.)

Army Form C. 2118.

Volume XVI Page 8

Place	Date	Hour	Summary of Events and Information	Remarks and references to Appendices
ditto	9 4/18		Weather: dull	
			Forward-area was quiet throughout the day. Casualties very few	
			During the night the 123rd Inf Bde took over the Left Brigade Sector. A runner was posted to 123rd Inf Bde Hd-Qrs. runners and bearer squads were posted to R.A.Ps (Pill-Boxes 10913) of the R.M.Os of that Brigade.	MRG
			The methods of evacuation from the three Inf Bdes, at present in the line, are shown the attached diagrams (appendix I).	
ditto	10 4/18		Weather: Dull	
			A.D.M.S. 41st Div visited Hd-Qrs of this unit at Moated Farm.	
			Increased shell-fire in forward-area. Casualties slight.	
			It was reported at 11 p.m that an enemy-attack was expected in the morning on our right (along Menin Road). Instructions were issued from this office at 12 midnight to all officers in the forward-area informing them of the probable attack, and of the action to be taken in the event of a withdrawal from the present line.	MRG

D. D. & L., London, E.C. (A7853) Wt. W809/M1673 350,000 4/17 Sch. 52a Forms/C/2118/14

Instructions regarding War Diaries and Intelligence Summaries are contained in F. S. Regs., Part II. and the Staff Manual respectively. Title pages will be prepared in manuscript.

WAR DIARY
or
~~INTELLIGENCE SUMMARY.~~
(*Erase heading not required.*)

Army Form C. 2118.

Volume XVI. Page 9.

Place	Date	Hour	Summary of Events and Information	Remarks and references to Appendices
Ditto	11/4/18		Weather: Dull and mild.	
			Contrary to expectations, enemy did not attack in the night along the Menin Rd.	
			O.O. 176 122 Inf. Bde & 1st Amendment received. O.O. 42 A.D.M.S. 59 Div received.	
			Steel-helmets, iron-rations, box-respirators, haversacks, and identity-discs of all personnel were inspected, and found to be in a satisfactory condition.	
			122 Infantry Bde. was relieved in the Left Brigade Sector, Right Division VIII Corps Front by the 176 Infantry Brigade, 59th Division during the night.	
			The posts — Ingot, Dawning Crossing, and Jersey — were handed over to the 2/3 North Midland Field Ambulance 59th Division. The personnel and motor transport attached to the posts — Joy, First House, and Potijze, were withdrawn, and returned to Hd-Qrs of this unit at Moated Farm.	WEG
			Relief was completed at 8 pm.	
			The 122 Inf. Bde on relief, proceeded into camps in the Wieltje area. Contact with the RMOs of this Bde, was established by the officer in charge of the Wieltje A.D.S.	

D. D. & L., London, E.C. (A7883) Wt. W819/M672 350,000 4/17 Sch. 52a Forms/C2118/14

Instructions regarding War Diaries and Intelligence Summaries are contained in F. S. Regs., Part II, and the Staff Manual respectively. Title pages will be prepared in manuscript.

WAR DIARY
or
~~INTELLIGENCE SUMMARY.~~

(Erase heading not required.)

Army Form C. 2118.

Volume XVI Page 10

Place	Date	Hour	Summary of Events and Information	Remarks and references to Appendices
ditto	12 4/18		Weather: Bright & sunny	
			Received - R.A.M.C. O.O. 50 dated 12 4/18 (A.D.M.S. 41st Div), 122 Inf Bde O.O. 177, & Med. Arrangements 29th Div under A.D.M.S. 41 Div S119.	
			One Sgt and 28 men reported for duty from 140 Fd. Amb.	
			During the night 59th Division was completely withdrawn from the line, and the front-line held by this Division, and that given up by 59th Division were held as an outpost-line by 4 battalions of this Division.	
			The R.A.M.C. posts, which were held by the 2/3 North Midland Fd Amb., 59th Division, were taken over by this unit. Please see appendix , which gives these posts, and also the distribution of personnel, vehicles, etc.	WCG
			For distribution of personnel, posts, etc on left (St Jean - Wieltje - Somme Sector) half of Forward-area, please see appendix . It will be noticed from the appendices that all posts forward of the Army Battle Zone line were held with a minimum personnel.	
			The Prison (or Arsenal) Ypres, which was formerly the C.M.D.S., was taken over by this unit as an A.D.S. Hd-Qrs of this unit remained at Moated Farm	

D. D. & L., London, E.C. (A7883) Wt. W809/M1672 350,000 4/17 Sch. 52a Forms/C/2118/14

Instructions regarding War Diaries and Intelligence Summaries are contained in F. S. Regs., Part II, and the Staff Manual respectively. Title pages will be prepared in manuscript.

WAR DIARY
or
~~INTELLIGENCE SUMMARY.~~
(Erase heading not required.)

Army Form C. 2118.

Volume XVI Page 11.

Place	Date	Hour	Summary of Events and Information	Remarks and references to Appendices
ditto	13/4/18.		Weather :- Dull & cold.	
			Forward-area was moderately quiet throughout the day. Casualties few.	
			Personnel in Trench Foot Preparation Centre near St Jean were withdrawn, and all	
			stores in F. Preparation Centre were removed to Moated Farm. A holding-party	
			was put in a Trench Foot Preparation Centre near Potijze, which was handed	WRG
			over by the 2/3 North Midland Fd Ambulance 59th Division, later in the	
			day all stores in this T. Foot Preparation Centre were removed to Moated	
			Farm, and holding-party was withdrawn.	
ditto	14/4/18.		Weather :- Dull, cold, & wintry.	
			122 Inf. Bde. O.O. 178 received.	
			C.O. (Lt. Col. W. Ross Gardner D.S.O. RAMC) visited A.D.M.S. office about 4 p.m., and was shown	WRG
			copy of R.A.M.C. O.O. 51 d. 14/4/18, which was about to be issued.	
			During the night 14th and 15th the troops of the 41st Division, which were in the Army	
			Battle Zone line, were withdrawn to a line (approximately) running from Wieltje to	
			the White Chateau on the Ypres-Menin Road.	

D. D. & L., London, E.C.
(A7883) Wt. W809/M1672 350,000 4/17 Sch. 52a Forms/C/2118/14

Instructions regarding War Diaries and Intelligence Summaries are contained in F. S. Regs., Part II, and the Staff Manual respectively. Title pages will be prepared in manuscript.

WAR DIARY or ~~INTELLIGENCE SUMMARY.~~

(Erase heading not required.)

Army Form C. 2118.

Volume XVI Page 12.

Place	Date	Hour	Summary of Events and Information	Remarks and references to Appendices
	14/4/18 (continued)		The Vlamertinghe Mill (H.8.a.9.8) was taken over from the 139th Fd Ambulance and was organised as an Adv Dressing Station. Hd-Qrs of this unit remained at Moated Farm. The Prison Ypres became Hd-Qrs of O.C. Forward-Bearers of all the forward-area (i.e. both right & left sectors). In view of the proposed withdrawal of the outposts from Passchendaele line to the Army Battle Zone line on the following night, the personnel in all the forward-posts were reduced to a minimum. One officer still remained at Wieltje in charge of forward-bearers of left sector; similarly one officer remained at Potyze in charge of Forward-bearers of right sector. The A.D.S. at the Vlamertinghe Mill was ready to receive casualties at 8.30 p.m.	WRG
ditto	15/4/18.		Weather: Dull and cold. R.A.M.C. O.O. 51 Copy 3 d 14/4/18 received at 6 a.m. All stores in the Posts in the Forward-Area, with the exception of a few stretchers blankets and dressings, were removed, and conveyed back to the Moated Farm and to the C.M.D.S. at Brandhoek. Altogether about 10 G.S. wagon-loads and 9 Sunbeam motor-amb-loads were removed. The surplus stores	WRG

D. D. & L., London, E.C. (A7883) Wt. W809/M1672 350,000 4/17 Sch. 52a Forms/C/2118/14

Instructions regarding War Diaries and Intelligence Summaries are contained in F. S. Regs., Part II. and the Staff Manual respectively. Title pages will be prepared in manuscript.

WAR DIARY
or
~~INTELLIGENCE SUMMARY.~~
(Erase heading not required.)

Army Form C. 2118.

Volume XVI Page 13

Place	Date	Hour	Summary of Events and Information	Remarks and references to Appendices
	15/4/18 (continued)		at the Prison Ypres, which was now being used as a Collecting Post and as H.Q. of O.C. Forward-Area, were also removed, and dumped at Moated Farm.	
			Throughout the day the forward-area was quiet; casualties slight	
ditto	16/4/18		Weather:- Dull, but dry	
			The Vlamertinghe Mill was handed over to the 16th Fd. Ambulance 6th Division, and the Adv. Dressing Station of this unit was transferred to Moated Farm.	
			The withdrawal of the Passchendaele outpost-line commenced about 4 a.m. The withdrawal of the R.A.M.C. forward-posts commenced at the same hour. Touch was maintained with the infantry, and ~~the~~ each forward RAMC post withdrew as the infantry in front retired upon it. RAMC withdrawal was completed at 6.30 a.m.	WRG
			On completion of withdrawal the posts held by this unit, and the distribution of the personnel were as shown on attached appendix	
			During the withdrawal no casualties occurred, with the exception of 2 or 3 men of the demolition-party, who were accidentally injured when blowing up a "pill-box dug-out"	
			During the night (16th/17th) the Prison C. Post Ypres was very heavily shelled from a	

D. D. & L., London, E.C. (A7883) Wt. W809/M1672 350,000 4/17 Sch. 52a Forms/C/2118/14

Instructions regarding War Diaries and Intelligence Summaries are contained in F. S. Regs., Part II, and the Staff Manual respectively. Title pages will be prepared in manuscript.

WAR DIARY
or
~~INTELLIGENCE SUMMARY.~~
(Erase heading not required.)

Army Form C. 2118.

Volume XVI Page 14

Place	Date	Hour	Summary of Events and Information	Remarks and references to Appendices
	16 4/18 (continued)		south-eastern direction. The Town Major Ypres, who was billeted over the Prison C.P., was buried amongst a mass of bricks in his room, as a result of a shell having struck the building immediately above. Capt J.J.H. Ferguson, RAMC (O.C. Prison C.P.), on hearing the Town Major cry for help, boldly rushed from the C.P. and, after a careful search, succeeded in discovering the whereabouts of the imprisoned and buried officer. Capt Ferguson, assisted by a small party of R.A.M.C., worked for 4 hours under the heaviest shell fire, and finally rescued the Town-Major from his perilous situation. During the night 2 R.A.M.C. privates were slightly wounded.	WRG
Do	17 4/18		Weather: Dull Enemy still continued to shell the Prison, Ypres. Entrances to the Prison C.P., which were blocked as a result of the shelling, were reopened. A supply of reserve rations and a number of picks and shovels were stored in the Prison C.P. in the event of the occupants being imprisoned by the entrances and exits being blown in again. All surplus stores at Moated Farm — ordnance, red-cross, medical, etc — were removed by lorry from Moated Farm, and conveyed to 140th Fd Ambulance at Nine Elms.	WRG

D. D. & L., London, E.C. (A7883) Wt. W809/M1672 350,000 4/17 Sch. 52a Forms/C/2118/14

Instructions regarding War Diaries and Intelligence Summaries are contained in F. S. Regs., Part II. and the Staff Manual respectively. Title pages will be prepared in manuscript.

WAR DIARY
or
~~INTELLIGENCE~~ SUMMARY.
(Erase heading not required.)

Volume XVI Page 15

Army Form C. 2118.

Place	Date	Hour	Summary of Events and Information	Remarks and references to Appendices
	17/4/18 (continued)		Horse transport of this unit, not required at Moated Farm, was sent back to 139th Fd Amb at Red Farm (G 5 d 8 3 Sht 28 1/40000), and parked there.	
			Notification was received that Capt J. Le F. Lander D.S.O., M.C., RAMC was to be struck off the strength of this unit from 25/3/18, having been passed unfit for General Service by a Medical Board in the U. Kingdom.	WRG
			Casualties evacuated from Forward Area during past 24 hours = about 40	
ditto	18/4/18		Weather: Dull & cold.	
			A D M S 41st Division visited this Hd. Qrs.	
			Enemy shelled Vlamertinghe; no damage was done to Moated Farm.	WRG
			Shell-fire in Ypres was less intense to-day. Forward area was moderately quiet.	
ditto	19/4/18		Weather:- Stormy with hail and snow showers.	
			Captain F. P. Joscelyne M.C., RAMC was posted to this unit for duty, and was taken on the strength accordingly.	WRG
			Captain P. A. Clements RAMC was struck off the strength of this unit upon being	

Army Form C. 2118.

Instructions regarding War Diaries and Intelligence Summaries are contained in F. S. Regs., Part II. and the Staff Manual respectively. Title pages will be prepared in manuscript.

WAR DIARY
or
~~INTELLIGENCE SUMMARY.~~
(Erase heading not required.)

Volume XV Page 16

Place	Date	Hour	Summary of Events and Information	Remarks and references to Appendices
	19/4/18		posted to the 18th K.R.R. Corps as Medical officer in charge	
	(continued)		Eleven O.Rs arrived as reinforcements	
			The Vlamertinghe Chateau and Cottage were thoroughly cleaned up by a party of men from this unit.	
			Forward-area was quiet throughout the day, with exception of an enemy-attack, which was launched against our outpost-line about noon. About 12 casualties were evacuated. Ypres remained quiet during the day. There was marked aerial activity (enemy) during the night.	WRG
ditto	20/4/18		Weather:- Bright & sunny	
			D.D.M.S and D.A.D.M.S II nd Corps visited this Ad. Qrs this morning, afterwards proceeding to the Prison Collecting Post	
			The Commanding Officer and the D.A.D.M.S. 41st Division visited the forward-area in the afternoon.	WRG
			Soup-kitchens were established by this unit at Dead End Canal (I 2 c 3 7), and at the Ramparts Ypres (I 8 d 1.7). —— 3 Soyer's stoves at the former	

D. D. & L., London, E.C. (A7883) Wt. W809/M1672 350,000 4/17 Sch. 52a Forms/C/2118/14

Instructions regarding War Diaries and Intelligence Summaries are contained in F. S. Regs., Part II. and the Staff Manual respectively. Title pages will be prepared in manuscript.

WAR DIARY
or
~~INTELLIGENCE~~ SUMMARY.
(Erase heading not required.)

Army Form C. 2118.

Volume XVI Page 17.

Place	Date	Hour	Summary of Events and Information	Remarks and references to Appendices
	20/8 (continued)		place, and also those at the latter. Soup, tea, cocoa, etc supplied free. Hours:- From 6 a.m to 11 a.m., and from 7 p.m to 11 p.m.	
			More "Walking Wounded" Signs were put up in Forward Area.	
			The W.W.P at the Ramparts was heavily shelled by the enemy with Gas-shells. Ten RAMC O.Rs were gassed, of these 7 were evacuated to the M.D.S at Red Farm and 3 were detained at the A.D.S. Menin Farm. All R.A.M.C posts were warned in writing by O.C. Prison C.P. that the N.C.O i/c must place a gas-sentry on duty, and that he must keep a record of the tour of duty of the gas-sentry, giving the times and the name of sentry. Also that each gas-sentry must be instructed to moisten all gas-blankets with water at the commencement of his tour of duty. These records will be inspected periodically by O.C Prison C.P. N.C.Os were instructed to hand over these records, when relieved, to relieving N.C.Os.	WRG
			Wheeled-stretchers were supplied to several Regtl M.Os.	
			About 22 casualties were evacuated by this unit during the past 24 hrs, of these 18 were gassed-cases; 25 sick were also evacuated.	

D. D. & L., London, E.C. (A7883) Wt. W809/M1672 350,000 4/17 Sch. 52a Forms/C/2118/14

Instructions regarding War Diaries and Intelligence Summaries are contained in F. S. Regs., Part II. and the Staff Manual respectively. Title pages will be prepared in manuscript.

WAR DIARY
or
INTELLIGENCE ~~SUMMARY.~~
(Erase heading not required.)

Army Form C. 2118.

Volume XVI Page. 18.

Place	Date	Hour	Summary of Events and Information	Remarks and references to Appendices
ditto	21/4/18		Weather:- Bright & sunny. Received:- 123 I. Bde. Defence Scheme; A.D.M.S. Med. Def. Scheme (S145) & Med. Arrangements (S145)	
			O.C. (Lt-Col. W. Ross Gardner D.S.O. RAMC) attended conference of O.Cs Fd. Ambulances at A.D.M.S. office at 10.30 a.m.; the following questions were discussed:-	
			(1) Runners attached to Inf. Bde. Hd-Qrs and Regtal M.Os. from Field Ambulances.	
			O.C. this unit was instructed by A.D.M.S. to forward to O.Cs 139th and 140th Fd. Ambs. for their information copies of the instructions, which are issued by this unit to RAMC runners attached to Inf. Bde. H.Qs and to Regtal M.Os	WRG.
			(2) R.A.M.C. working-party for Dead End Canal Relay Post and W. W. Post — to construct and repair dug-outs under the direction of the Royal Engineers, 41st Div.	
			Soup-kitchens, established at Ramparts Relay Post and Dead End Canal Relay Post, are working satisfactorily. The gas-protection of all R.A.M.C. posts in forward-area was improved to-day; new gas-blankets were fitted on many doors and windows. Five suits of hospital-clothing were forwarded to the Prison C.P. to be held in readiness there in the event of the clothing of gassed patients having to be removed. A steaming-chamber was fitted up at the Prison C.P. for the purpose of dealing with gassed-clothing.	

D. D. & L., London, E.C.
(A7883) Wt. W803/M1672 350,000 4/17 Sch. 52a Forms/C/2118/14

Instructions regarding War Diaries and Intelligence Summaries are contained in F. S. Regs., Part II. and the Staff Manual respectively. Title pages will be prepared in manuscript.

WAR DIARY
or
~~INTELLIGENCE SUMMARY.~~
(Erase heading not required.)

Army Form C. 2118.

Volume XVI Page 19.

Place	Date	Hour	Summary of Events and Information	Remarks and references to Appendices
ditto	21/4/18 (continued)		One N.C.O and 15 men, who reported from 139th Fd Amb to-day, and 1 N.C.O and 15 men from this Hd Qrs proceeded to Dead End Canal at 5 p.m. as a working-party for the construction and repair of dug-outs. One G.S. wagon-load of R.E material (picks, shovels, sand-bags, timber, etc) was obtained from the Hop Factory R.E Dump Vlamertinghe, and forwarded to Dead End Canal.	
			Three RAMC O.Rs were evacuated from the Ramparts suffering from the effects of shell-gas (mustard).	WRG
			A.D.M.S. S 147 & S 148 received.	
ditto	22/4/18		Weather:- Fine and bright	
			1st Lieut. E.P. Norwood, U.S.M.O.R.C arrived at 10 a.m. for temporary duty with this unit from 139th Field Ambulance. This officer proceeded with 1 runner, 4 bearers, and the necessary medical & surgical equipment to Wieltje dug-outs to report to O.C. Outpost Line as temporary M.O. in charge of Outpost Line.	WRG
			The 19th Middlesex Regt moved back from Forward Area; R.A.P of that battalion is now at H 11 b 0.1 (Sht 28 1/40000). The working-party commenced work on the	

D. D. & L., London, E.C.
(A7883) Wt. W809/M1672 350,000 4/17 Sch. 52a Forms/C/2118/14

Instructions regarding War Diaries and Intelligence Summaries are contained in F. S. Regs., Part II. and the Staff Manual respectively. Title pages will be prepared in manuscript.

WAR DIARY
or
~~INTELLIGENCE SUMMARY.~~
(Erase heading not required.)

Army Form C. 2118.

Volume XVI Page 20

Place	Date	Hour	Summary of Events and Information	Remarks and references to Appendices
	22 4/18 (continued)		dug-outs at Dead End Canal Relay Post at 5.30 a.m to-day. A considerable amount of "sand-bagging" was done. Party works in two shifts —— 1st Shift from 5.30 a.m to 12 noon, 2nd shift from 12 noon to 6.30 p.m.	
			Capt Joscelyne, M.C. RAMC proceeded from this Hd-Qrs to take over charge of the Prison C.P from Capt. Roche M.C RAMC. Capt. Roche has been instructed to return to this H.Q to-morrow when the "handing over" of C.P. has been completed.	WRG
			The attached diagram (appendix) shows the present positions of all forward-posts (including R.A.Ps), also routes of evacuation and sites of "Walking Wounded" signs. Present disposition of personnel, cars, bicycles, and wheeled-stretchers is shown on attached appendix.	
ditto	23 4/18		Weather:- Fine and bright.	
			123 I.B. O.O. No 183 received.	
			As Ypres has been heavily shelled with gas-shells for the past few nights, A.D.M.S. 41st Div. to-day instructed this unit to remove the Collecting Post from the Prison to Dead End Canal. This afternoon the required "moves" were carried out. Only	WRG

D. D. & L., London, E.C. (A7883) Wt. W803/M1672 350,000 4/17 Sch. 52a Forms/C/2118/14

Instructions regarding War Diaries and Intelligence Summaries are contained in F. S. Regs., Part II. and the Staff Manual respectively. Title pages will be prepared in manuscript.

WAR DIARY
or
~~INTELLIGENCE~~ SUMMARY.
(Erase heading not required.)

Army Form C. 2118.

Volume XVI Page 21.

Place	Date	Hour	Summary of Events and Information	Remarks and references to Appendices
"	23 4/18 (continued)		one N.C.O and 4 men, together with a few stretchers, blankets and dressings, and a wheeled-stretcher, were left at the Prison Ypres as a holding party, and also for the purpose of dealing with local casualties. All surplus personnel and equipment at the Prison were removed to Dead End Canal, and the Collecting Post was re-established at that site. The soup-kitchen at the Ramparts was removed, and re-established along with the other soup-kitchen at Dead End Canal. Only 1 N.C.O and 4 men, with a wheeled-stretcher and a few dressings, blankets and stretchers, were left at the Ramparts; these personnel serve the same purpose as those left at the Prison. The surplus personnel and equipment from the ramparts were returned to Hd-Qrs at Moated Farm. The R.M.Os of 26th Royal Fusiliers, 20th D.L.I., and 10th Queens were informed of the above "moves", and were instructed to inform the RAMC runners and squads attached to them, that all cases from their R.A.Ps would now be evacuated direct to Dead End Canal Collecting Post, and not to the Ramparts Relay Post as hitherto, also that Hd Qrs. of O.C. Forward-bearers would now be at Dead End Canal C.P. Runners from the above R.M.Os were sent to Dead End Canal C.P. so that they might	WRG

D. D. & L., London, E.C. (A7883) Wt. W809/M1672 350,000 4/17 Sch. 52a Forms/C/2118/14

Instructions regarding War Diaries and Intelligence Summaries are contained in F. S. Regs., Part II, and the Staff Manual respectively. Title pages will be prepared in manuscript.

WAR DIARY
or
~~INTELLIGENCE~~ SUMMARY.
(*Erase heading not required.*)

Army Form C. 2118.

Volume XVI Page 22

Place	Date	Hour	Summary of Events and Information	Remarks and references to Appendices
"	23/4/18 (continued)		familiarise themselves with the new route. Rainbrunners attached to 123rd and 124th Inf. Bde Hd-Qrs were also sent to Dead End canal for the same purpose, and the Bde. Hd-Qrs were informed of the transference of the Collecting Post and Hd-Qrs. of O.C. Forward Bearers from the Prison to Dead End Canal.	
			The necessary alterations were made in the "Walking Wounded" signs, established along the First House - Potyze Road, so that the new routes of evacuation might be indicated. These new routes of evacuation are as follows:-	WRG
			(1) From R.A.P. 26th Roy. Fus to Dead E. canal — via continuation of Menin-Zhluvelt Rd. around N.E. side of Ypres	
			(2) " " 20th D.L.I " " " " } — via Saville Road, then to the left on	
			(3) " " 10th Queens " " " " } St Jean - Dead End Road.	
			Forward area was quiet throughout the day.	
			Two anti-gas chambers were fitted up in the Prison Ypres. Men, whose clothes have been contaminated with gas, before entering the Prison pass into the first chamber there they undress, then pass into the second chamber, and re-dress in fresh	

D. D. & L., London, E.C. (A7883) Wt. W809/M1672 350,000 4/17 Sch. 52a Forms/C/2118/14

Instructions regarding War Diaries and Intelligence Summaries are contained in F. S. Regs., Part II. and the Staff Manual respectively. Title pages will be prepared in manuscript.

WAR DIARY
or
~~INTELLIGENCE SUMMARY.~~
(Erase heading not required.)

Army Form C. 2118.

Volume XV Page. 23

Place	Date	Hour	Summary of Events and Information	Remarks and references to Appendices
"	23 4/18 (continued).		clothes. By this method contamination of the atmosphere of the Prison with gas is prevented.	
			Ypres was heavily shelled from 9.30 p.m. till 11.30 p.m. with gas-shells. It is not yet known if many casualties have resulted.	WRG
			Major J.S.C. Roche M.C. RAMC reported to this Hd-Qrs. from Dead End Canal about 6 p.m., the "handing-over" of the Forward-area to Capt Joscelyne M.C. having been completed. 124 Inf. Bde. O.O 176 received.	
ditto	24 4/18.		Weather:- Dull, but dry. A.D.M.S. 41st Div. visited this H.Q. at 10 a.m.	
			One wheeled-stretcher was forwarded to M.O. i/c 20 D.L.I. for use by his Regtl. stretcher bearers. Five hundred sandbags were sent to the Prison Ypres for the purpose of strengthening certain portions of the cellar.	WRG
			Lieut. Wilkins reported for duty to O.C. Dead End Canal C.P. in relief of Lieut. Bullen, who returned to this Hd-Qrs. One private was forwarded to Dead End Canal C.P. to report to officer in charge as carpenter for that Post. One Sunbeam ambulance was brought back from Dead E.C. C.P. to this H.Qrs, leaving only one car for duty	

D. D. & L., London, E.C.
(A7883) Wt. W809/M1672 350,000 4/17 Sch. 52a Forms/C/2118/14

Instructions regarding War Diaries and Intelligence Summaries are contained in F. S. Regs., Part II. and the Staff Manual respectively. Title pages will be prepared in manuscript.

WAR DIARY
or
~~INTELLIGENCE SUMMARY.~~
(Erase heading not required.)

Army Form C. 2118.

Volume XVI Page 24.

Place	Date	Hour	Summary of Events and Information	Remarks and references to Appendices
"	24 4/18 (continued)		at Dead End. Ten sets of S.D. uniform were forwarded to Dead E.C.C.P. for use of gassed-cases. Telephone was fitted up in Officers' mess at Dead E.C.C.P., and constructive work, which is being carried out at that post, has progressed rapidly. At the Prison Ypres all gas shell-holes in dangerous proximity to the entrances and exits were covered with fresh earth. Soup-kitchen is working satisfactorily; seven Soyer stoves of soup were prepared and distributed during the night. An inspection of the Box-respirators, steel-helmets, iron-rations, brassards, and identity-discs of all R.A.M.C. & ASC personnel was held at 2 p.m. to-day. Everything was found to be in a satisfactory condition. Enemy was quiet throughout the day. Casualties and sick very light. 123 I.Bde OO 186 and 187 received.	WRG
ditto.	25 4/18		Weather:- Dull, but dry. Rain during the night. Forward-area was shelled during the day. Dead End Canal was heavily shelled until noon, and again after 6 p.m. Four R.A.M.C. O.Rs were wounded, of these 3 were evacuated to the M.D.S. and one was returned to duty.	WRG

D. D. & L., London, E.C. (A7883) Wt. W809/M1672 350,000 4/17 Sch. 52a Forms/C/2118/14

Instructions regarding War Diaries and Intelligence Summaries are contained in F. S. Regs., Part II. and the Staff Manual respectively. Title pages will be prepared in manuscript.

WAR DIARY
or
~~INTELLIGENCE SUMMARY.~~

(Erase heading not required.)

Army Form C. 2118.

Volume XVI Page 25

Place	Date	Hour	Summary of Events and Information	Remarks and references to Appendices
"	25/4/18 (Continued)		During early hours of the morning a raid was carried out by our troops on an enemy-position opposite right flank of 41st Div. Outpost-line. M.O. 26 Royal Fusiliers selected a temporary R.A.P. at Barvana House [at C 30 c 6.4 (Sht 28 1/40000)] so as to be in close proximity to the Outpost line in the event of heavy casualties. Twelve stretcher bearers were held in readiness at Dead End Canal for the purpose of proceeding if necessary, to Barvana House to assist squad, attached to M.O. 26 Royal Fus. to evacuate from Barvana House to Potyze chateau. A Ford-car was forwarded from this Hd-Qrs to Potyze Chateau with instructions to evacuate from Potyze to Dead End Canal C.P. The additional bearers were, however, not required as only 4 or 5 casualties resulted from the raid.	WRG
			Four O.Rs were attached to O.C. 40 Sanitary Section to undergo a course of instruction in Sanitation.	
			Lt. R H VERCOE RAMC (T.C) evacuated to CCS and struck off the strength of the Division accordingly. Capt H M GODFREY RAMC (T.C.) reported his arrival for duty and was taken on the strength of this unit (Auth ADMS. 41st Div.)	WRG.

D. D. & L., London, E.C. (A7883) Wt. W809/M1672 350,000 4/17 Sch. 52a Forms/C/2118/14

Instructions regarding War Diaries and Intelligence Summaries are contained in F. S. Regs., Part II. and the Staff Manual respectively. Title pages will be prepared in manuscript.

WAR DIARY
or
~~INTELLIGENCE~~ SUMMARY.
(Erase heading not required.)

Army Form C. 2118.

Place	Date	Hour	Summary of Events and Information	Remarks and references to Appendices
	26/4/18		Weather dull showery. RAMC Preliminary OO received and the Collecting Post at Dead End Canal was brought back to MOATED FARM. The ADS at MOATED FARM was moved back to RED FARM (Sheet 28 G 5 d. 7 3)	
			123 I B OO 188 received 123 I Bde OO 189 received.	WRG
			Capt J. La F LAUDER DSO MC reported his arrival for duty & taken on the strength accordingly. One OR RAMC (Pte SULLIVAN RAMC) Killed.	
	27/4/18		Weather - dull. Soup Kitchen at Dead End closed down at 2.30 am. A/Major W. CHESNEY MC RAMC and Capt J La F LAUDER DSO MC RAMC evacuated to CCS wounded & struck off the strength. Vicinity of Red Farm shelled with high velocity guns & dump in vicinity exploded wrecking the house & camp. Six officers & 30 OR wounded - but 2 officers & 6 OR evacuated to CCS -	
			1 mule & 2 Riders also killed by the explosion. A temporary new site for an ADS selected at BRANDHOEK (Sheet 28 G 12 b. 8 8.)	WRG
			Amendment to Med Defence scheme received from ADMS. New location notified to ADMS & all Brigades.	

D. D. & L., London, E.C.
(A7883) Wt. W809/M1672 350,000 4/17 Sch. 52a Forms/C/2118/14

Instructions regarding War Diaries and Intelligence Summaries are contained in F. S. Regs., Part II, and the Staff Manual respectively. Title pages will be prepared in manuscript.

WAR DIARY

or

~~INTELLIGENCE SUMMARY.~~

(Erase heading not required.)

Army Form C. 2118.

Place	Date	Hour	Summary of Events and Information	Remarks and references to Appendices
	28/4/18		Weather dull & showery. 75 OR reported for salvage work under instructions from ADMS. Material salved to be collected into one heap for removal by train to PROVEN – time of arrival of train to be notified later by ADMS. – RAMC OO No 52 from ADMS received.	MRG
ROUSEBRUGGE Sheet 19 W.17c.0.4	29/4/18		Weather dull. Loading party of 1 NCO & 27 OR commenced loading the train at 9am. All trucks fully loaded & small unloading party sent off with the train to PROVEN. All material salved was taken to the 2nd Corps Dump PROVEN on arrival & stacked there. ADS BRANDHOEK ~~followed~~ to DIRTY BUCKET CAMP Sheet 28 A 30 Central & BRANDHOEK retained as a walking wounded post. Responsibility for evacuation of the forward area passed to O.C. 140th FA at 5pm. This unit proceeded to the site previously occupied by 36 CCS at Sheet 19 W 17 c 0.4. & established the Main Dressing Station & Divisional Rest Station there. Lt. J. CULLEN RAMC (TC) took over charge of the Aid Post at the TOWN Hall POPERINGHE at 11-30 am relieving Capt MONTGOMERY & personnel of 140th FA.	MRG

D. D. & L., London, E.C. (A7883) Wt. W809/M1672 350,000 4/17 Sch. 52a Forms/C/2118/14

Army Form C. 2118.

Instructions regarding War Diaries and Intelligence Summaries are contained in F. S. Regs., Part II. and the Staff Manual respectively. Title pages will be prepared in manuscript.

WAR DIARY
or
~~INTELLIGENCE~~ SUMMARY.
(Erase heading not required.)

Place	Date	Hour	Summary of Events and Information	Remarks and references to Appendices
ROUSEBRUGGE	30/9/18		Weather dull. Remainder of personnel from forward area reported to new site on relief. Responsibility for evacuation of all posts in the forward area passed to O.C. 140th F.A. at 5.30 pm & all personnel belonging to this unit withdrawn at that hour. Notification sent to ADMS. Evacuation of wounded from ADS (Sheet 28 A 30 central) to MDS Sheet 19 W 17 c 0 4 by Light Railway. Off loading point is on the main PROVEN – ROUSEBRUGGE road. Unloading party of One NCO & 5 OR posted at this point in accordance with Instructions received from ADMS. Hot food provided at this unloading point night & day.	WRG

General Remarks

Strength of unit: Officers 8; 148 RAMC OR, 22 ASC HT OR, 7 PB

During the month 3 officers 36 RAMC OR have been evacuated from all causes 3 ASC HT and 1 ASC MT and 2 Permanent Base men making a total of 3 officers and 42 OR

W Ross Gardner
Lieut Colonel RAMC
Commanding 138th Field Ambulance

D. D. & L., London, E.C.
(A7883) Wt. W803/M1672 350,000 4/17 Sch. 52a Forms/C/2118/14

List of Appendices.

No	
1	Diagram shewing line of Evacuation of Casualties.
1 a.	Distribution of personnel & vehicles on left Sector.
1 b.	Distribution of personnel & vehicles on right Sector.
1 c.	Posts & Distribution of personnel, &c.
1 d.	Diagram of Routes of Evacuation.
2.	Map shewing Posts of Forward Line of Evacuation.

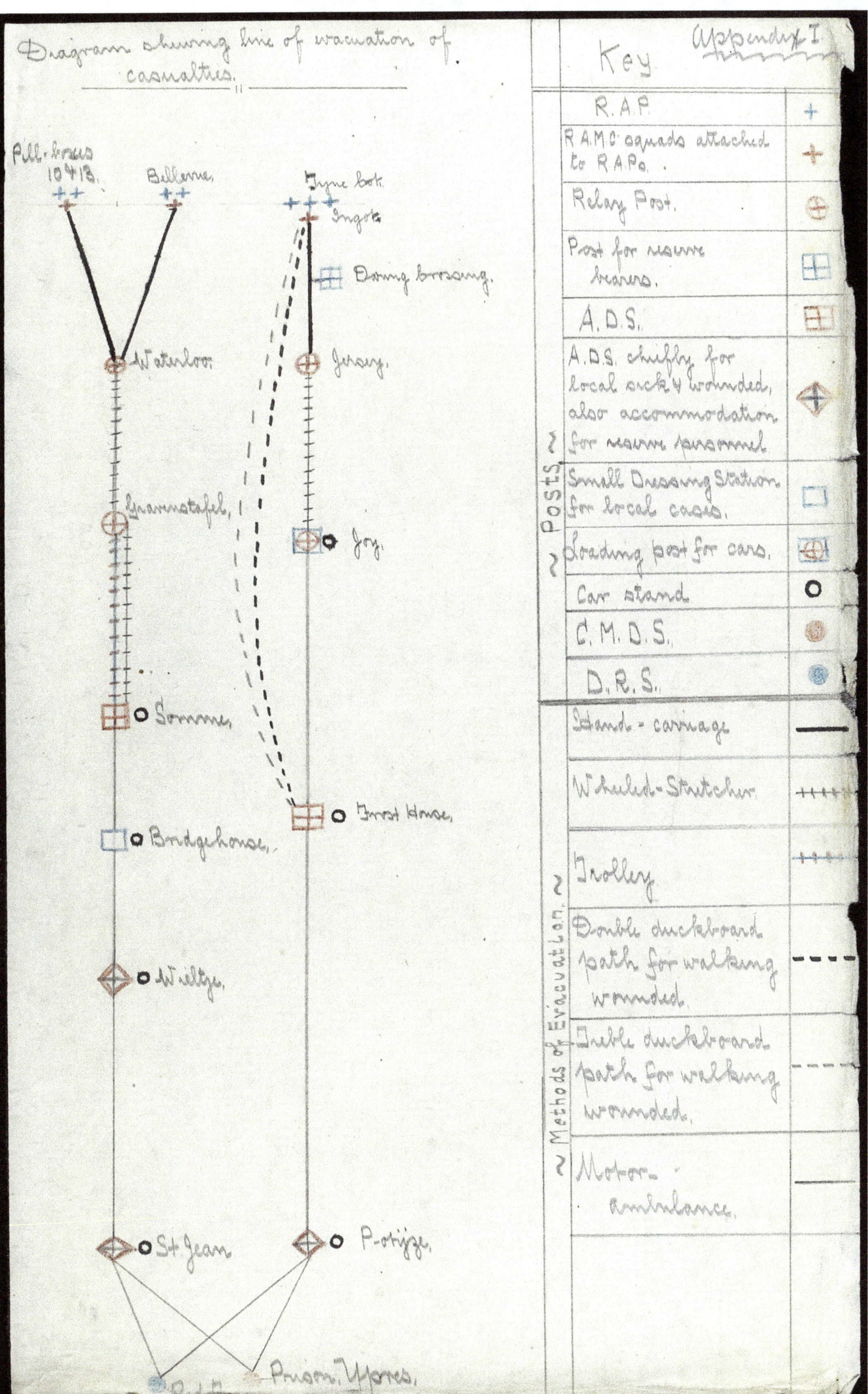
Diagram shewing line of evacuation of casualties.
Appendix I
Pill-boxes 10 & 13.
Bellevue.
Tyne Cot.
Ingot.
Dochy Crossing.
Waterloo.
Jersey.
Gravenstafel.
Joy.
Somme.
Frost House.
Bridgehouse.
Wieltje.
St Jean
Potijze.
Prison, Ypres.
Key
R.A.P.
R.A.M.C. squads attached to R.A.Ps.
Relay Post.
Post for reserve bearers.
A.D.S.
A.D.S. chiefly for local sick & wounded, also accommodation for reserve personnel
Small Dressing Station for local cases.
Loading post for cars.
Car stand
C.M.D.S.
D.R.S.
Posts
Hand-carriage
Wheeled-Stretcher
Trolley
Double duckboard path for walking wounded.
Treble duckboard path for walking wounded.
Motor-ambulance.
Methods of Evacuation.

Appendix Ia

Distribution of personnel and vehicles on left Sector

Posts.		Officers	R.A.M.C. O.Rs.	Sunbeam motor-ambs	Bicycles	Wheeled-Stretchers
Pill-box 13 (R.A.P)			1 runner 4 bearers.			
Bellevue R.A.P			ditto.			
Waterloo Relay P.			1 N.C.O 4 men			1
Gravenstafel R.P.			ditto			1
Somme R.P.			1 N.C.O 7 men		1	2
Bridgehouse Relay Post			1 N.C.O 4 men		1	1
Wieltje - H.Q. of O.C. Forward - Bearers.		2.	3 N.C.O. 32 men	1		1
St. Jean Car-Post			1 N.C.O 5 men	1		
123 & 124 Inf. Bde. H.Q			1 runner each			

Map refs. of above posts are given on pages 6 & 7 of War Diary.

Appendix:- II

Vlamerlinghe

← To. RED FARM.

DEAD END

Salvation Corner

PRISON

YPRES

RAMPARTS

St. Jean

REFERENCE

⊕ R.A.Ps.

1 11th QUEENS
2 23rd MIDDLESEX
3. 10th QUEENS
4 20th D.L.I.
5. 26th R.F.
6 19th MIDDLESEX.
7. 10th R.W.K. DUGOUT. I.24.
8. M.G. BATN

RELAY POSTS & W.W.P

COLLECTING POST

A.D.S. & H.Q. 138 Fd. Amb.

← Route of Evacuation

← Alternative routes in event of shell-fire in Ypres or on Salvation Corner Road.

TRACING OF MAP 28 (1 : 20,000) SHOWING POSTS OF FORWARD LINE OF EVACUATION 18-4-18.

Appendix I b

Distribution of personnel, vehicles, etc on Right Sector

Posts	Officers	R.A.M.C. O.Rs.	Sunbeam Motor Ambs.	Wheeled Stretchers	Bicycles
Tyne Cott. R.A.P.		{1 runner {4 bearers			
Jury R.A.P. (D 21 d 6.3)		ditto.			
Jersey Relay Post.		4 bearers		1	
Joy Relay Post.		{1 N.C.O {2 bearers		1	1
First House Car-Post.		{1 N.C.O {6 men	1	1	
Potyze C.P. = H.Q of O.C. Forward-Bearers of Rt Sector.	2	{2 N.C.Os {17 men	1		1
122 Inf. Bde. H.Q		1 runner.			

Map refs of all above posts (except Jury) given on pages 5 & 6 of War Diary

<u>A.D.S.</u> for all Forward-Area (both Rt & Lt Sectors).

Location	Officers	R.A.M.C O.Rs.	Sunbeam Motor-ambs	Wheeled Stretchers	Bicycles
Prison & Arsenal Ypres	2.	{3 N.C.Os {22 men.	2.	2	1

Appendix Ic

Posts & Distribution of personnel, etc.

Posts	Officers	R.A.M.C. O.Rs.	Motor Ambulances	Wheeled Stretchers	Bicycles
St Jean Relay Post		1 N.C.O. 5 bearers		2	1
Dead End Canal Relay Post & Walking Wounded Post		1 N.C.O. 7 men	1 Sunbeam	2	1
Ramparts (Ypres) Relay Post & Walking Wounded Post		1 N.C.O. 12 men.		2	1
Prison (Ypres) Collecting Post & Hd-Qrs of O.C. Forward Bearers	2	3 N.C.O. 20 men	1 Sunbeam	3	1
Moated Farm A.D.S. & Hd-Qrs. of Fd. Amb.	7	Remainder of Personnel	Remainder at Moated Farm		
122, 123, & 124 Inf. Bde Hd-Qrs		1 runner each			
R.A. Po.		1 runner & 4 bearers } Each			

Appendix 1d

Diagram of Routes of evacuation.

10th R.W. Kts
Div. M.G. Batt.
11th Queens
23rd Middlesex
19th Middlesex
10th Queens
20th D.L.I.
26th R. Fus

St. Jean
Ramparts (Ypres)
Dead End Canal
Rd. around N.E. side of Ypres
via Cloth Hall
Prison (Ypres) C.P.
Schoolhouse Corner & Switch Rd.
Vlamertinghe - Ypres Rd.

18th K.R.R.C.
12th E Surreys
15th Hants
Reserve Bde

A.D.S. & H.Q. Moated Farm Vlamertinghe

M.D.S. Red Farm

~ Key ~

~ Posts ~	R.A.P.	+
	Relay Post	⊕
	Walking Wounded Post.	o
	Collecting Post	⊞
	Adv. Dress Station	⊞ (circled)
Methods of evacuation	Hand-carriage	- - - -
	Wheeled-stretcher	——
	Motor-ambulance	——
	Alternative routes in event of shell-fire in Ypres or Dead E.C.	→
~ Map refs ~ Sheet 28 1/40 000	10 R.W. Kents	I 1 b 7.4.
	41st Div M.G. Battalion	I 1 b 9.8
	11 Queens	C 27 c 7.2
	23 Middlesex	I 3 b 2.8
	19 Middlesex	I 8 b 0.5
	10 Queens	I 3 c 2.4
	20 D.L.I.	I 9 a 2.9
	26 Roy. Fus	I 9 d 1.5
	Ramparts R.P. & W.W.P.	I 8 d 1.7
	St Jean R.P.	I 3 a 8.9
	Dead End Canal R.P. & W.W.P.	I 2 c 3.7
	Prison (Ypres) C.P.	I 7 b 1.1
	Moated Farm A.D.S. & H.Q.	H 2 d 8.9.
	18 K.R.R.C.	H 6 a 7.4.
	12 E Surreys	H 11 b 5.2.
	15 Hants.	H 5 d 8.5.

11

CONFIDENTIAL

May 1918

Vol 25
140/3076.

WAR DIARY

OF

138TH FIELD AMBULANCE

FROM MAY 1-1918 TO MAY 31ST 1918

(VOLUME. XVII.).

Army Form C. 2118.

Instructions regarding War Diaries and Intelligence Summaries are contained in F. S. Regs., Part II. and the Staff Manual respectively. Title pages will be prepared in manuscript.

WAR DIARY
or
~~INTELLIGENCE SUMMARY.~~
(*Erase heading not required.*)

Vol XVII Page I

Place	Date	Hour	Summary of Events and Information	Remarks and references to Appendices
ROUSEBRUGGE	1.5.18		Weather fair.	
Sheet 19			ADMS visited the M.D.S., DRS & GAS CENTRE.	
W17c04			The following received: Medical Defence Scheme No 3, with first amendment	
			S159 Location of Units	
			Medical arrangements No 14	WRG
			Strength: Officers — O.R.	
			RAMC 8 148	
			ASC H.T. - 20	
			A.S.C MT. - 13	
			P.B men - 7	
			Total 8 168	
			Animals: Riders: 8 — HD: 12 — Mules 16 —	
	2.5.18		Weather fine & sunny.	
			42825 C/Sgt Strachan W. awarded Military Medal	WRG
			18 Fd Ambce open a Dressing Station on the same site as this Fd Ambce	

D. D. & L., London, E.C.
(A7883) Wt. W809/M1672 350,000 4/17 Sch. 52a Forms/C/2118/14

Instructions regarding War Diaries and Intelligence Summaries are contained in F. S. Regs., Part II. and the Staff Manual respectively. Title pages will be prepared in manuscript.

WAR DIARY
or
INTELLIGENCE SUMMARY.
(Erase heading not required.)

Army Form C. 2118.

Vol XVII Page 2.

Place	Date	Hour	Summary of Events and Information	Remarks and references to Appendices
Continued				
	2.5.18		The following received: Medical Arrangements II Corps	
			Medical Arrangements 41 Div –	WRG
			Location of Units 41 Div –	
	3.5.18		Weather fine –	WRG
			Telephone applied for.	
	4.5.18		Weather fair –	
			G.O.C. 41 Div & ADMS visited the DRS & MDS.	
			Later DDMS II Corps visited DRS & MDS.	WRG
			Lieut. H. Farncombe RAMC reported for duty.	
	5.5.18		Weather fair at first, stormy in the evening –	
			Capt. C.G.H. Moore RAMC reported for duty.	WRG
			Major. L.S.C. Roche reported back II Corps Gas-Course.	

D. D. & L., London, E.C.
(A7883) Wt. W803/M1672 350,000 4/17 Sch. 52a Forms/C/2118/14

Army Form C. 2118.

Instructions regarding War Diaries and Intelligence Summaries are contained in F. S. Regs., Part II, and the Staff Manual respectively. Title pages will be prepared in manuscript.

WAR DIARY
or
INTELLIGENCE SUMMARY.
(Erase heading not required.)

Place	Date	Hour	Summary of Events and Information	Remarks and references to Appendices
	6.5.18		Weather fine.	
			Lieut J Cullen RAMC struck off the strength of this unit. He reported for duty as MO i/c to 77 Bde RGA.	
			A quantity of surplus medical equipment sent to ST OMER by lorry to be stored until required (Authority: ADMS 41 M5/23 dated 6.5.18 List of stores attached	WRG Appendix I
			The following received: ADMS S 164 (Ref Well water & contamination by yellow + gas) ADMS Location of Transport lines of Division	
	7.5.18		Weather Rainy	
			Lieut Wilkins & RAMC party (5 OR) holding the Aid Post in Town Hall cellars cellars POPERINGHE relieved by 139 Fd Ambce (Auth: ADMS M877 dated 6.5.18)	
			Sunbeam Ambulance Car broke down & was towed to Workshops	
			Packstore & Recreation Rooms completed.	
			The following received: 41 Div Medical Arrangements (Ref Infectious Cases & Locations of Sanitary Sections)	WRG

D. D. & L., London, E.C.
(A7883) Wt. W809/M1672 350,000 4/17 Sch. 52a Forms/C/2118/14

Instructions regarding War Diaries and Intelligence Summaries are contained in F. S. Regs., Part II, and the Staff Manual respectively. Title pages will be prepared in manuscript.

WAR DIARY
or
INTELLIGENCE SUMMARY.
(Erase heading not required.)

Army Form C. 2118.

VOL. XVII Page 4.

Place	Date	Hour	Summary of Events and Information	Remarks and references to Appendices
Continued.				
ROUSBRUGGE	8.5.18		Weather: fine.	
		11.45am	Inspection of DRS & MDS by Major-General S. Guise-Moore CB.	
			CMG. AMS DMS II Army.	WRG
		6.00pm	Cinema performance by No 4 M.A.C to DRS patients	
			ADMS, S 165 location of units 41 Div. received.	
	9.5.18		Weather: fine	
			Capt C.G.H. Moore RAMC assumes the duties of Transport Officer to the	
			unit in relief of Major L.S.C. Roche RAMC.	WRG
		5pm	Div! Concert Party gave a performance to D.R.S Patients.	
			Gassed Cases: admission for last 36 hrs (ending 4 pm): 1 Officer, 88 O.R.	
			evacuated to CCS 21	
			Skin Cases - To be sent from now onwards to II Corps Skin depot TUBBY CAMP	
			Sh. 19 - W17d19	
	10.5.18		Weather Dull.	
			The following awards for gallantry in the field announced:	WRG
			Military Medal 51480 S/Sgt Jones ~~RAMC~~ — 36214 Pte Beal A.C.	

D. D. & L., London, E.C.
(A7883) Wt. W809/M1672 350,000 4/17 Sch. 52a Forms/C/2118/14

Army Form C. 2118.

Instructions regarding War Diaries and Intelligence Summaries are contained in F. S. Regs., Part II. and the Staff Manual respectively. Title pages will be prepared in manuscript.

WAR DIARY
or
INTELLIGENCE SUMMARY.
(Erase heading not required.)

VOL XVII Page 5

Place	Date	Hour	Summary of Events and Information	Remarks and references to Appendices
	10.5.18 Contd		60479 Pte Kennedy J M. Rame — M2/053834 Pte Chalmers J. ASC (MT)	
			A court of Enquiry to investigate & report on the circumstances leading to the death of Mlle Madeleine Merrian a Belgian civilian, knocked over by an ambulance car 5/5/18 belonging to this unit and driven by 052134 Pte Groom ASC (MT), was held.	WRG
	11.5.18		Weather bright.	
			Major-General Sir S. T. B Lawford KCB G.O.C 41 Div visited Camp.	
			The following award announced: MILITARY CROSS – Capt. J. J. H Ferguson RAMC.	WRG
			One mule badly hurt in an accident by a French lorry evacuated to 52 Mob. Vet. Section.	
			RAMC OO No 53 received.	
	12.5.18		Weather fine – windy –	WRG
			ADMS No M21 ref. disposal of French troops admitted suffering from infectious cases	

D. D. & L., London, E.C. (A7883) Wt. W809/M1672 350,000 4/17 Sch. 52a Forms/C/2118/14

Instructions regarding War Diaries and Intelligence Summaries are contained in F. S. Regs., Part II. and the Staff Manual respectively. Title pages will be prepared in manuscript.

WAR DIARY
or
INTELLIGENCE SUMMARY.
(*Erase heading not required.*)

Army Form C. 2118.

VOL XVII Page 6

Place	Date	Hour	Summary of Events and Information	Remarks and references to Appendices
	13.5.18		Weather: Raining –	
		11 am	DDMS II Corps inspected MDS & DRS.	
			Lieut C.R. Wilkins RAMC left this unit to report for duty to 57 Div. in order to relieve Capt E.A. Lumley RAMC who will be taken on the strength of this unit.	WRG
			No 66997 Pte Garland A.E. appointed Acting Cpl (without pay) whilst clerk-in-charge in the Report Office.	
			S169 Map locations of Units & Transport lines 41 Div received.	
			Capt. J.J. H. Ferguson RAMC was evacuated to CCS suffering from "Tonsillitis"	
	14.5.18		Weather fine –	
			Capt L.W. Bain RAMC was taken on the strength of this unit.	WRG
			1 PB Man overstrength transferred to 139th Fd Amb^ce	
	15/5/18		Weather fine –	
			68305 A/Cpl Badcock RAMC transferred to 110 Fd Amb^ce	WRG
			Medical Defence Scheme No 4 received –	

D. D. & L., London, E.C.
(A7883) Wt. W809/M1672 350,000 4/17 Sch. 52a Forms/C/2118/14

Instructions regarding War Diaries and Intelligence Summaries are contained in F. S. Regs., Part II. and the Staff Manual respectively. Title pages will be prepared in manuscript.

WAR DIARY
or
INTELLIGENCE SUMMARY.
(Erase heading not required.)

Army Form C. 2118.

VOL. XVII Page 7

Place	Date	Hour	Summary of Events and Information	Remarks and references to Appendices
	16.5.18		Weather: fine & Warm.	
			Medical arrangements No 17 received.	WRG
	17.5.18		Weather fine & hot.	
			Re-engagement leave (18/5/18 to 15/6/18) to the United Kingdom granted to 19499 Pte Walker F.C. RA.M.C	WRG
	18.5.18		Weather fine & hot.	
			Re-engagement leave (19/5/18 to 16/6/18) to the United Kingdom granted to 84534 Pte Newbold R. J. RAMC	
			Capt. J. J. H. Ferguson MC RAMC, for Gallantry in the Field was granted the Bar to the Military Cross	WRG
			No 38368 Sgt Major Ratcliffe E. RA.MC, for Gallantry in the Field was granted the Distinguished conduct medal.	
			1st Amendmendment Medical Defence Scheme No 4 received.	

D. D. & L., London, E.C.
(A7883) Wt. W809/M1672 350,000 4/17 Sch. 52a Forms/C/2118/14

Army Form C. 2118.

Instructions regarding War Diaries and Intelligence Summaries are contained in F. S. Regs., Part II. and the Staff Manual respectively. Title pages will be prepared in manuscript.

WAR DIARY
or
INTELLIGENCE SUMMARY.
(Erase heading not required.)

Vol. XVII Page 8

Place	Date	Hour	Summary of Events and Information	Remarks and references to Appendices
	18.5.18 Cont^d	2 pm	A working party of three NCOs and 57 O.R. left this Field Ambulance to work in the Forward Area under the direction of OC 140 F^d Amb^ce.	
			The personnel of this F^d Ambulance now on detached duty is therefore as follows:	WLC

	NCOs	Other Ranks
Off Loading Post	1	3
40 Sanitary Section	1	2
Divisional Baths		1
II Corps Works B^n		1
D.D.M.S. Office		1
A.D.M.S. Office		2
Working Party	3	57
Total	5	67

D. D. & L., London, E.C. (A7883) Wt. W809/M1672 350,000 4/17 Sch. 52a Forms/C/2118/14

Army Form C. 2118.

Instructions regarding War Diaries and Intelligence Summaries are contained in F. S. Regs., Part II. and the Staff Manual respectively. Title pages will be prepared in manuscript.

WAR DIARY
or
INTELLIGENCE SUMMARY.
(Erase heading not required.)

VOL. XVII Page 9.

Place	Date	Hour	Summary of Events and Information	Remarks and references to Appendices
	19/5/18		Weather: fine & hot. The Commanding Officer attended a conference at the ADMS' office. Reinforcements: a party of 31 RAMC men reported from the 41st Divisional Wing for duty with this unit.	WRG
	20/5/18		Weather: fine & hot. Capt. E. A. Lumley RAMC reported back to this unit from the 57th Division and was taken on the strength of the unit. A copy of a special A.O. No 4 d 14/5/18 was received, which under the heading of "Act of Courage" highly commended the prompt & fearless action of No 51480 Staff Sergt V.D. Jones RAMC who on the 20th ult. succeeded in stopping some runaway mules. ADMS S21 d 20/5/18 received [illegible]	WRG

Instructions regarding War Diaries and Intelligence Summaries are contained in F. S. Regs., Part II. and the Staff Manual respectively. Title Pages will be prepared in manuscript.

WAR DIARY
or
INTELLIGENCE SUMMARY
(Erase heading not required.)

Army Form C. 2118

Vol. XVII Page 10.

Place	Date	Hour	Summary of Events and Information	Remarks and references to Appendices
	21/5/18		Weather very warm –	
			ADMS S178 Locations of Units & Transport lines 41 Div. received.	
		2 pm	Unit paid.	
		6 pm	Divisional Concert Party – the "Crumps" gave a performance in the Patients Recreation Room.	WRG
	22/5/18		Weather warm, windy –	
			ADMS S179 Corps medical arrangements in case of heavy fighting	WRG
			ADMS S180 Divisional Code names	
	23/5/18		Weather wet & stormy –	
			In the afternoon the DDMS II Corps inspected the Hospital –	
			An extra Nissen hut divided into four cubicles prepared for the reception of officer Patients thus making accommodation for 13 officers.	WRG
			The Court of Enquiry, which assembled on the 10th inst. to investigate an accident leading to the death of Mlle Messian, reassembled to make further investigations –	

Instructions regarding War Diaries and Intelligence Summaries are contained in F. S. Regs., Part II. and the Staff Manual respectively. Title Pages will be prepared in manuscript.

WAR DIARY
or
INTELLIGENCE SUMMARY
(Erase heading not required.)

Army Form C. 2118

Vol. XVII Page 11.

Place	Date	Hour	Summary of Events and Information	Remarks and references to Appendices
	24/5/18		Weather fine. Capt. G. La F. Lauder DSO. MC RAMC reported back to this unit from the United Kingdom and was taken on the strength of this unit. A Nissen Hut which was removed from the southern side of the camp was reerected next to the Officers ward – This hut will be used as a mess for the officer-Patients. 1st Amendment to 41st Divisional Medical Arrangements No 17 received O.C. 41 Divisional Train ASC. inspected the Transport of the unit.	WRG
	25/5/18		Weather fine ADMS 41 Divn visited the Hospital 2nd Amendment to 41 Divisional Medical Arrangements No 17 received ADMS S 185 Ref. A.D.S H12 a 44 received.	WRG
	26/5/18		Weather fine. In the afternoon a party of 61 Regimental Stretcher bearers arrived at this Dressing Station for a 6 days course of instruction on First Aid & Stretcher bearing. Programme of Training The following received: 3rd Amendment to Medical Arrangements No 17 –	WRG Appendix II

1875 Wt. W593/826 1,000,000 4/15 J.B.C. & A. A.D.S.S./Forms/C. 2118.

Army Form C. 2118

WAR DIARY
or
INTELLIGENCE SUMMARY
(Erase heading not required.)

Instructions regarding War Diaries and Intelligence Summaries are contained in F. S. Regs., Part II. and the Staff Manual respectively. Title Pages will be prepared in manuscript.

VOL. XVII Page 12

Place	Date	Hour	Summary of Events and Information	Remarks and references to Appendices
	27/5/18		Weather fine. Between 10 & 11 pm village of ROUSBRUGGE in neighbourhood of Hospital shelled with heavy shells. No casualties passed through this Dressing Station. Medical arrangements No 18 received.	WRG
	28/5/18		Weather fine. Between 10 & 11 am village of ROUSBRUGGE shelled with H.E. No casualties passed through this Dressing Station.	WRG
	29/5/18	10.15am	Weather fine. The Divisional Commander Major General Sir S.T.B Lawford K.C.B. visited the Units Transport Lines. Capt Brooks U.S.M.R.C. of the 307 U.S. Fd Ambulance 77 Div and four Sergeants from the same unit reported to this Field Ambulance for a few days training in the British methods of dealing with sick & wounded. The following was received. Operation Order 54 re relief of 140 Fd Ambulance by 139 Fd Ambulance on the 3rd Prox.	WRG

1875 Wt. W593/826 1,000,000 4/15 J.B.C. & A. A.D.S.S./Forms/C. 2118.

Army Form C. 2118

Instructions regarding War Diaries and Intelligence Summaries are contained in F. S. Regs., Part II. and the Staff Manual respectively. Title Pages will be prepared in manuscript.

WAR DIARY
or
INTELLIGENCE SUMMARY

(Erase heading not required.)

Place	Date	Hour	Summary of Events and Information	Remarks and references to Appendices
	30/5/18		Weather fine.	
		9.pm.	Immediate vicinity of Hospital (Eastern side) shelled for half an hour ~~with~~ High velocity shells – One shell landed in the camp near 140 Fd Ambulance Transport lines; no casualties or damage caused –	
			ADMS S192 new location of units 41 division received.	WRG
	31/5/18		Weather fine Capt. Brooks U.S.M.R.C. and the four sergeants from the 307 Fd Ambulance proceeded to 140 Fd Ambulance.	
			Capt. Armor U.S.M.R.C. with two NCOs and one man from the 307 U.S. Fd Ambce 77 Division – reported to this unit for instruction in DRS & MDS work.	WRG
		15pm.	Warning order No 55 received –	
			ADMS S199 received (OO No 54 in abeyance until further orders)	
			During the month of May 1602 patients have been admitted to this Field Ambulance, 388 of which were of other divisions. Of the 1214 patients from the 41st Division 784 were evacuated to CCS & 430 were discharged to duty. See appendices – III, IV, V, VI The health of the unit has been excellent during the last month as shown by the weekly health inspections where no sick were found. 7 cases out of this unit were evacuated to C.C.S.	WRG

Army Form C. 2118

Instructions regarding War Diaries and Intelligence Summaries are contained in F. S. Regs., Part II. and the Staff Manual respectively. Title Pages will be prepared in manuscript.

WAR DIARY
or
INTELLIGENCE SUMMARY
(Erase heading not required.)

VOL XVII Page 14.

Place	Date	Hour	Summary of Events and Information	Remarks and references to Appendices
			53 Reinforcements have been taken on the strength 9 Have been transferred to other units. 1 NCO and 2 men are away on leave. The strength of the unit is now as follows:	

	Officers	O.R.
RAMC	10	181
ASC HT	–	24
ASC MT	–	13
P.B. men	–	9
Total	10	227

The shortage is therefore 1 RAMC, 2 ASC HT, 1 PB man

The surplus: 1 officer.

The following is the distribution of personnel on detached duty:

Divl Baths	1
II Corps Works Bn	1
DDMS office	1
ADMS office	2
T.A.T. unloading Post	6
Working party	60
Sanitary inspectors	2
	73

WRG

1875 Wt. W593/826 1,000,000 4/15 J.B.C. & A. A.D.S.S./Forms/C. 2118.

Instructions regarding War Diaries and Intelligence Summaries are contained in F. S. Regs., Part II. and the Staff Manual respectively. Title Pages will be prepared in manuscript.

WAR DIARY
or
INTELLIGENCE SUMMARY
(Erase heading not required.)

Army Form C. 2118

VOL XVII Page 15.

Place	Date	Hour	Summary of Events and Information	Remarks and references to Appendices
			Transport.	
			Animals: Riders 8, H.D. 20, L.D. 15	
			Shortage: 2 L.D.	
			All vehicles are complete and in good repair. They were all thoroughly overhauled and painted.	
			The establishment of Motor ambulance Cars, motor cycles & cycles is complete.	
			31/5/18	
			A Ross Gardner Lt Colonel RAMC	
			D. C. 138th Field Ambulance	

1875 Wt. W593/826 1,000,000 4/15 J.B.C. & A. A.D.S.S./Forms/C. 2118.

Appendix II

SYLLABUS OF TRAINING REGIMENTAL STRETCHER BEARERS CLASS B MAY 26 to JUNE 2. 1918

	SUNDAY	MONDAY	TUESDAY	WEDNESDAY	THURSDAY	FRIDAY	SATURDAY	SUNDAY
8 to 10	BATH	STRETCHER DRILL 6 & 4 BEARERS	STRETCHER DRILL 3 BEARERS	STRETCHER DRILL 2 BEARERS	IMPROVISED CARRIAGE OF WOUNDED IN THE FIELD	DRESSING COLLECTING CARRIAGE OF WOUNDED IN THE FIELD	DRESSING COLLECTING CARRIAGE OF WOUNDED IN THE FIELD	BATH
10 to 11		DUTIES OF REGIMENTAL STRETCHER BEARERS NOTES ON BEARING DEMONSTRATION	WOUNDS BURNS SCALDS	CIRCULATION PRESSURE POINTS HAEMORRHAGE	FRACTURES DISLOCATIONS SPRAINS	RESPIRATION DROWNING GAS DEMONSTRATION	SHOCK LOSS OF CONSCIOUSNESS FITS. SUNSTROKE DEMONSTRATION	
11 to 12		PRINCIPLES OF FIRST AID IMPROVISATION	THE FIRST FIELD DRESSING THE SMALL DRESSING DEMONSTRATION	TOURNIQUETS DEMONSTRATION	SPLINTS AND THEIR APPLICATION DEMONSTRATION	TREATMENT OF SPECIAL CASES HEAD INJURIES ABDOMINAL INJ. DEMONSTRATION	THE LOUSE THE FLY	
2 to 3		SEPSIS ASEPSIS ANTISEPSIS	THE ROLLER BANDAGE DEMONSTRATION	TRENCH FOOT BLISTERS AND ABRASIONS OF FEET CARE OF FEET. DEMONSTRATION	IMPROVISED SPLINTS DEMONSTRATION	THE THOMAS' LEG SPLINT DEMONSTRATION	ORAL	
3 to 4		DRESSINGS DEMONSTRATION	THE TRIANGULAR BANDAGE DEMONSTRATION	PRACTICAL BANDAGING ROLLER & TRIANGULAR	PRACTICAL SPLINTING	PRINCIPLES OF SANITATION	EXAMINATION	

CHART SHOWING SICK AND WOUNDED EVACUATED TO C.C.S.

41ST DIVISION

Appendix IV

MAY 1918.

1	2	3	4	5	6	7	8	9	10	11	12	13	14	15	16	17	18	19	20	21	22	23	24	25	26	27	28	29	30	31
W	Th	F	Sat	Sun	M	Tu	W	Th	F	Sat	Sun	M	Tu	W	Th	F	Sat	Sun	M	Tu	W	Th	F	Sat	Sun	M	Tu	W	Th	F

50

40

30

20

10

0

WOUNDED —— To C.C.S.

SICK - - - - - To C.C.S.

138TH FIELD AMBULANCE

CHART SHOWING TOTAL ADMISSIONS AND EVACUATIONS ETC. IN DETAIL
41ST DIVISION (SICK)
Appendix V
MAY-1918.
1 Wed 2 Thur 3 Fri 4 Sat 5 Sun 6 Mon 7 Tues 8 Wed 9 Thur 10 Fri 11 Sat 12 Sun 13 M. 14 Tu 15 W 16 Th 17 F. 18 Sat 19 Sun 20 M 21 Tu 22 W. 23 Th 24 F. 25 Sat 26 Sun 27 M. 28 Tu 29 W 30 Th 31 F.
100 90 80 70 60 50 40 30 20 10
SICK (ONLY)
ADMISSIONS —
TOTAL EVACUATIONS DISCHARGES ETC. —
EVACUATED TO CCS —
DISCHARGED TO DUTY —
TRANSFERRED TO II CORPS SKIN DEPOT AND 139 FA
138TH FIELD AMBULANCE.

Appendix VI

CHART SHOWING RISE AND FALL OF ADMISSIONS. IN DETAIL 41ST DIVISION (SICK) 138TH FD. AMBCE.

Appendix VIII

War Diary

A.D.M.S.,

41st.Division.

REPORT on ACTION TAKEN concerning POINTS RAISED at

CONFERENCE held 19/5/18.

Para.	Subject	Action Taken
2	Increased Sick Rate	It is thought probable that the increased sick rate is due to living in gassed areas. So far, however, sufficient evidence has not been collected.
3	Regimental Stretcher Bearers Class	Syllabus submitted and amended in accordance with A.D.M.S.'s remarks.
4.	Dressings - Economy in use of.	An order has been issued re economy in the use of dressings etc.

W Ross Gardner

Lt.Colonel R.A.M.C.
O.C. 138th.Field Ambulance.

Appendix X

41st. D. R. S., M. D. S. & GAS CENTRE.

REPORT ON WORK CARRIED OUT 1/5/18 to 31/5/18

1. SANITATION

1. Latrines

(a) For Patients (other ranks) A covered in latrine was erected on the western side of the camp; type, bucket - fly proof: number of seats, 12: 2 for gassed cases: 2 for infectious cases: 2 for diarrhoea cases. In the case of the latter a special trap was devised so that the ward orderly could examine the stool.* Behind this latrine a covered in 2-seated bucket, fly proof was erected for senior N.C.O.s
Near the Officers' ward, a single seated bucket fly proof latrine was erected for Officers.

(b) For Personnel An open 7 seated bucket fly proof latrine was erected on the eastern side of the camp for men. A covered in 2 seated bucket fly proof latrine was erected behind the above for senior N.C.O.s

2. Urinals.

(a) For patients A gutter type urinal with pipe leading to urine pit was erected near patients' latrines.

(b) For all other urinals buckets which were periodically emptied into a urine pit near the camp incinerator were used.

(c) Night Urinals. 5 trays were made to be placed under the urine buckets used at night in the 5 big wards.

3. Ablution Shed.

An ablution shed with a bench (accommodation 20) was erected in the S.W. portion of the camp. Water laid on and connected to drainage system.

4. Baths.

In the southern portion of the campa hut was set aside for bathing gassed cases and a place for keeping several sets of complete clean clothing and underclothing was partitioned.off The bathing shed for patients and personnel situated in the portio of the camp occupied by the 18th. Field Ambulance and shared with them was inproved.

5. Disinfecting, delousing and degassing chamber.

This chamber about 12'x9'x 7q sunk 3' into the ground is being erected in the southern part of the camp as an experiment (the inner walls are made of corrugated iron sheeting sheeting and earth will be heaped up over the whole chamber. A stove will be lit inside and clothing to be deloused, disinfected or degassed will be hung up inside for periods of time which will be decided by experiment.

6. Refuse Binns. Four large dry refuse bins and 2 large wet refuse bins were constructed for the cookhouse and dining hall. A number of smaller tins were prepared, for wards, recreation room, etc.

7. Drainage. All open gulleys were periodically cleaned and edges trimmed up. Where necessary, several buried drains were cleaned out and extended. Grease traps had to be thoroughly overhauled and new perforated tin trays were fitted to these traps.

8. Bench for cleaning mess tins. To avoid patients and personnel washing mess tins in unauthorised places, a bench with tap and refuse bucket was erected near the dining hall.

2. COOKHOUSES

1. Oven. The large oven capable of roasting for 300 and also frying and boiling, was built.

/2. Soyer Stoves.

* See Appendix IX

2. COOKHOUSE. (continued)

2. Soyer Stoves. Extensions for the chimneys of these stoves were made.
3. Distemper. The walls of the whole cookhouse were distemp ered white.

3. DINING HALL.

1. Shelves were erected at one end of the hall.
2. Tables and forms were constructed and all the tables were covered with American cloth.
3. Distemper. The walls and ceiling of the dining hall were distempere white.

4. RECREATION ROOM.

1. Library. A cubicle at the western end of this room was erected for a library and store for games.
2. Newspaper Stand. was constructed.
3. Entrances. were altered and doors made where necessary.
4. Distemper. The walls and ceiling were distempered white.

5. ~~XXXXXX~~ PACKSTORE.

Rifle racks for 400 rifles and shelves for 400 sets of equipment were erected. A partition was made between this store and the Quartermaster Stores.

6. Q.M.Stores.

In one corner of this store a butcher's store was erected. Shelves for stores were put up.

7. WARDS.

1. Notice Boards. At the entrance of each ward and a large board showing the number of patientsin hospital, etc. were painted and erected
2. Partitions. A partition in the overflow ward and two partitions in the gas ward, were built.
3. Resuscitation.Beds. Iron cradles were fitted to 3 iron bedsteads, and tin cowls and pipes to lead the heated air from paraffin stovesto the foot of the beds, were constructed.
4. Heated Oxygen Apparatus. An apparatus for providing warm oxygen was constructed.
5. Haldane Oxygen Set. Obtained from the D.D.M.S., 2nd. Corps for gassed cases.
6. Moveable white barriers to indicate the line of separation between P.U.O. cases, Influenzal cases and other diseases were made and placed in one of the Medical Wards.

8. ACCOMODATION FOR OFFICERS.

1. A nissen Hut in the N.W. part of the camp was prepared for the reception of 8 to 10 Officers. It was distempered white and the floor lined with linoleum .
2. Another Nissen Hut divided up into four cubicles was also prepared for Senior or Staff Officers.
3. A Nissen Hut at the southern end of the camp was dismantled, re-erected next to the Officers' Ward, distempered, lined with linoleum for use as a mess and recreation room for sick Officers.
4. Cookhouse. A cookhouse and pantry for cooking for sick Officers were erected.

/ 9. TRANSPORT.

9. TRANSPORT.

A Harness Shed, a Forage Shed and a canvas water-trough were erected. A useful addition to the forage shed was a hay sifter which was constructed to save all small hay which is usually wasted on the ground. The night lines were rivetted.

10. MISCELLANEOUS.

1. The rivetting of all tents and huts has been going on continually and is now nearly completed.
2. Repairs to all roofs, windows and blinds had to be continuously effected.
3. Garden. The kitchen garden which required much weeding and transplantation, is now in very good order.
4. Fire Buckets. Twenty one additional fire buckets were prepared out of oil drums and disposed where necessary.
5. Posts and wires for hanging up blankets and clothing were erected in the western portion of the camp.

31/5/18.

W Ross Gardner.
Lt Col RAMC

APPENDIX IX.

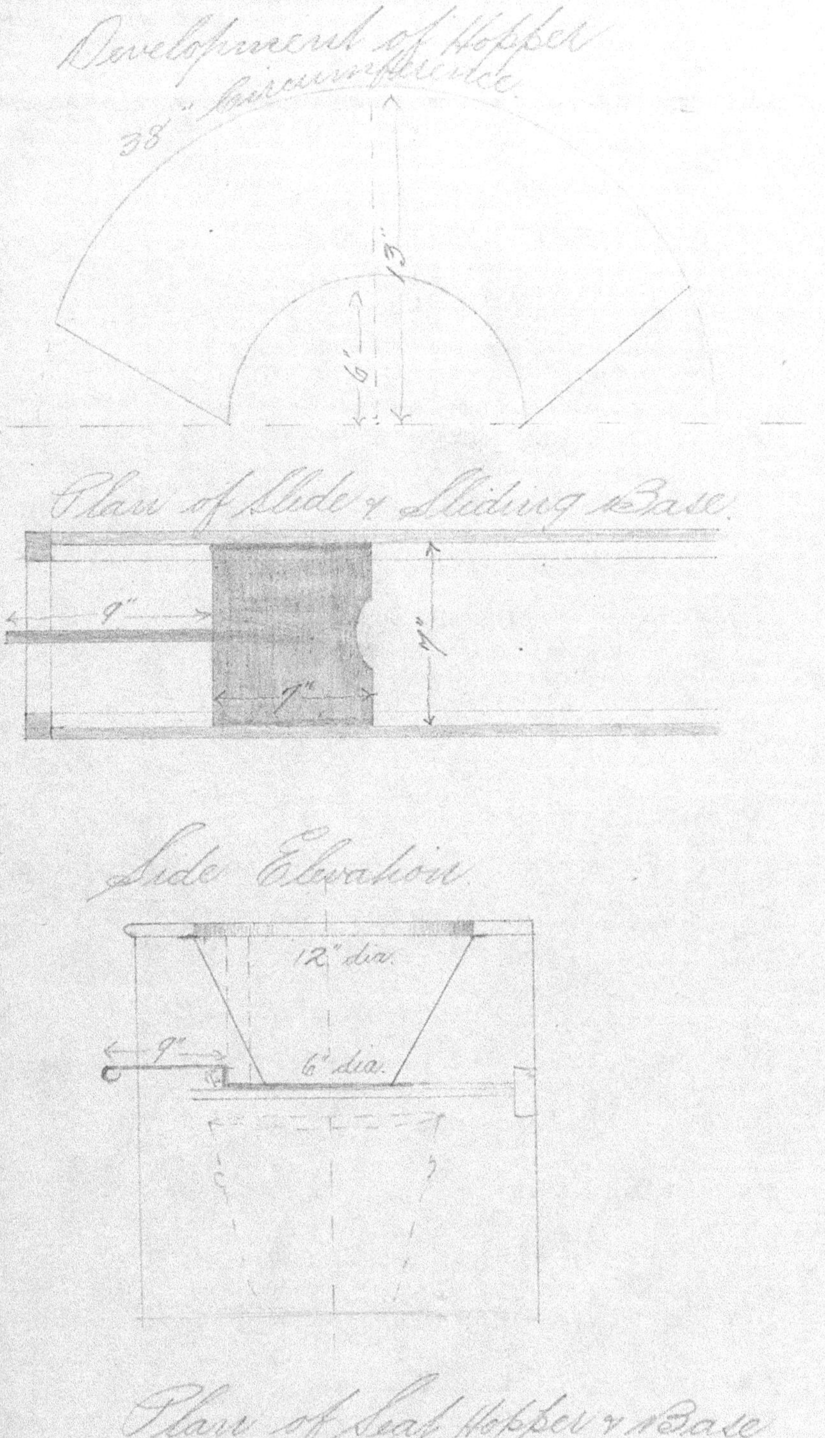

Rough Sketch of Latrine Seat to be used for the purpose of Detecting Malingerers – Diarrhoea Cases?

Development of Hopper

38" circumference

13"

6"

Plan of Slide & Sliding Base

9"

7"

7"

Side Elevation

12" dia.

9"

6" dia.

Plan of Seat, Hopper & Base

7"

7"

9"

Appendix I

LIST OF ARTICLES OF EQUIPMENT FORWARDED TO DIVISIONAL DUMP AT ST. OMER

MAY 6th.

1 pair	Field Surgical Panniers Nos. 1 & 2
1 pair	Field Medical Panniers Nos. 1 & 2
3	Field Fracture Boxes
3	Reserve Dressing Boxes
4	Tents, C.S.L.
3	Medical Comfort Panniers
1	Tent, Operating
1	Flag, Distinguishing and Poles (extending pole deficient)
2	Bags Entrenching (no tools)
18	Pans, Bed E.I.
1	Stools close F.A. nest (6 only)
60	Cases, Bolster, Tent
40 lbs.	Carbolised Tow
2	Mattresses, Operating Table
1	Box, Lantern, distinguishing, with 2 Lanterns
3	Balances, Spring, 100 lb.
20	Covers, Tin 6¼"
1	Set of Panniers G.S.
74	Sheets, Ground
24	Lanterns, Bulls Eye
3	Hooks, Reaping
3	Cans, Oil 5½ pts.
1	Can, Oil 9 pts.
8	Feeders

APPENDIX III

41st Division.

Table shewing disposal of Officers and Other Ranks who have passed through M.D.S., D.R.S. & GAS CENTRE.

	41st Division			
	To C.C.S.		To DUTY	
	OFFICERS	O.R's	OFFICERS	O.R's.
SICK	24	386	6	276
WOUNDED	6	368	1	147

	Other Formations			
	To C.C.S.		To DUTY	
	OFFICERS	O.R's	OFFICERS	O.R's.
SICK	7	256	NIL	38
WOUNDED	1	82	NIL	4

Appendix VII

Detached & filed

with Plans –

under

Main Dressing Stations

14

June 1918

CONFIDENTIAL.

Vol 26

140/3131

WAR DIARY

OF

138th FIELD AMBULANCE. R.A.M.C.

FROM JUNE 1st 1918. TO JUNE 30th 1918

(VOLUME XVIII.)

Instructions regarding War Diaries and Intelligence Summaries are contained in F. S. Regs., Part II, and the Staff Manual respectively. Title pages will be prepared in manuscript.

WAR DIARY
or
~~INTELLIGENCE SUMMARY.~~
(Erase heading not required.)

Army Form C. 2118.

VOL XVIII Page 1

Place	Date	Hour	Summary of Events and Information	Remarks and references to Appendices
ROUSBRUGGE SHEET 19 W17 c.o.4	1/6/18		Weather :- Fine	

STRENGTH

	OFFICERS	OTHER RANKS
R.A.M.C	10	181
ASC·HT	-	24
ASC·MT	-	13
P.B Men	-	9
TOTAL	10	227

PERSONNEL ON DETACHED DUTY

Div: Baths	1
II Corps Works Batt.	1
A.D.M.S' Office	2
D.D.M.S Office	1
T.A.T. Unloading Post	6
Working Party	60
Sanitary Inspectors	2
TOTAL	73

The following were received :-

A.D.M.S. S198 – List of Station Code Calls

" S197 – Re dry Weather Tracks

Lieut Col TAIT, U.S.M.O.R.C., 77th U.S.A. Division reported to this unit for instruction in the British methods of dealing with sick & wounded in the Field

W.E.G.

(A9475) Wt W2358/P360 600,000 12/17 D. D. & L. Sch. 52a. Forms/C2118/15.

Instructions regarding War Diaries and Intelligence Summaries are contained in F. S. Regs., Part II, and the Staff Manual respectively. Title pages will be prepared in manuscript.

WAR DIARY
or
~~INTELLIGENCE SUMMARY.~~
(Erase heading not required.)

Army Form C. 2118.

VOL XVIII Page II

Place	Date	Hour	Summary of Events and Information	Remarks and references to Appendices
ROUSBRUGGE	2/6/18		Weather :- Fine	
		11.0am	The Commanding Officer attended a conference at the ADMS' Office. In the afternoon the party of 61 Regimental Stretcher Bearers, having completed their course of instruction on First Aid & Stretcher Bearing returned to their respective units.	
			O.C. 1/2 West Riding Field Ambulance visited the Commanding Officer to make the necessary arrangements to take over the premises at 9.0am on the 4th inst.	WRG
			The following were received :- ADMS Wire reference impending move to 2nd Army Reserve Area. ADMS - S. 176, S 203, S 202 & S 125	
"	3/6/18		Weather :- Fine	
			Major C S C Rocke, MC, RAMC, proceeded to EPERLECQUES area as billeting officer with 2 N.C.O.s 2 O.R.s & 2 cycles - Billets were secured at LE COMMUNAL (Sht 27a J 24 B.8.0) and the above N.C.O.s & men left in charge.	WRG

(A9175) Wt W2358/P360 600,000 12/17 D. D. & L. Sch. 52a. Forms/C2118/15.

Instructions regarding War Diaries and Intelligence Summaries are contained in F. S. Regs., Part II, and the Staff Manual respectively. Title pages will be prepared in manuscript.

WAR DIARY
or
~~INTELLIGENCE SUMMARY.~~
(Erase heading not required.)

Army Form C. 2118.

Vol. XVIII Page 111

Place	Date	Hour	Summary of Events and Information	Remarks and references to Appendices
RAUSBRUGGE	3/6/18		One complete section from the 1/2 West Riding Field Ambulance arrived in the afternoon to take over part of the hospital. The working party, one sanitary inspector, 3 men from the Temporary Ambulance Train Unloading Point, the water cart & mules with the orderly and driver, reported back to this unit.	WRG
			Lieut. Colonel TAIT, U.S.M.O.R.C., Capt ARMOR, U.S.M.O.R.C. & his two N.C.O.s reported back to the 77th U.S.A. Division	
			The following were received :-	
			122 Inf Brigade Operation Order No 192	
			A.D.M.S. S. 204	
"	4/6/18		Weather :- Fine	
		8.30am	Major L.S.C. ROCHE, M.C. R.A.M.C. & Capt C.G.H. MOORE, R.A.M.C. moved off with the transport (less 2 horse ambulances) and halted for the night at BOLLEZEELE on their way to the EPERLECQUES Area. (One mule accidentally injured by a lorry was left in charge of a French	WRG

(A9475) Wt W2358/P360 600,000 12/17 D. D. & L. Sch. 52a. Forms/C2118/15.

Instructions regarding War Diaries and Intelligence Summaries are contained in F. S. Regs., Part II. and the Staff Manual respectively. Title pages will be prepared in manuscript.

WAR DIARY
or
~~INTELLIGENCE SUMMARY.~~
(Erase heading not required.)

Army Form C. 2118.

VOL XVIII Page IV

Place	Date	Hour	Summary of Events and Information	Remarks and references to Appendices
ROUSBRUGGE	4/6/18		farmer at ESQUELBECQUE.	
			Two horse ambulances with 1 N.C.O. & 4 O.R.s proceeded to 41st Divisional Artillery H.Q. to accompany the R.F.A. Brigades & D.A.C. to the Second Army Rest Area.	
			Capt E.A. LUMLEY, RAMC reported for temporary duty to the 41st D.A.C.	
			The remaining 3 men from the T.A.T. Unloading Post reported back to this unit.	WRG
		9.0am	The 1/2 W.R. Field Ambulance completed the taking over of all buildings and hospital stores.	
			One large ambulance car was detailed for duty ~~with~~ at PROVEN station during entrainment of the 122nd Infantry Brigade.	
		8.30pm	Capt L.W. BAIN, RAMC & Lieut. H. FARNCOMBE, RAMC with the personnel of this unit proceeded by march route to PROVEN where they entrained at 10.30pm.	
LE COMMUNAL SHEET 27a J 24 b 8 0.	5/6/18		Weather :- Fine	
		2.40am	Capt L.W. BAIN, RAMC & Lieut H. FARNCOMBE, RAMC with the personnel detrained	WRG

(A9475) Wt W2358/P360 600,000 12/17 D. D. & L. Sch. 52a. Forms/C2118/15.

Instructions regarding War Diaries and Intelligence Summaries are contained in F. S. Regs., Part II. and the Staff Manual respectively. Title pages will be prepared in manuscript.

WAR DIARY
or
~~INTELLIGENCE SUMMARY.~~
(Erase heading not required.)

Army Form C. 2118.

VOL XVIII Page V

Place	Date	Hour	Summary of Events and Information	Remarks and references to Appendices
LE COMMUNAL	5/6/18		at ST OMER & proceeded by march route to LE COMMUNAL where they arrived at 7.0 am.	
		8.0am	Major L.S.C. ROCHE, MC RAMC & Capt. C G H MOORE, RAMC with the horse transport moved off from BOLLEZEELE and arrived at LE COMMUNAL at 12 noon.	
			Cars were sent out to collect all sick of 122nd Infantry Brigade.	
			A hospital was opened – one barn for the dressing room and 20 patients, two operating tents for 20 patients & two bell tents making a total accommodation of 50 patients.	WRG
			The ADMS visited the unit.	
			One of the detached sanitary inspectors belonging this unit, returned	
"	6/6/18		Weather :- Fine	
		9.0am	Three horse ambulances and cars moved off to collect sick from all units of the 122nd Infantry Brigade.	WRG
			In the afternoon Lieut H FARNCOMBE, RAMC departed for temporary duty with the 23rd Middlesex Regt.	

(A9475) Wt W2358/P360 600,000 12/17 D. D. & L. Sch. 52a. Forms/C2118/15.

Army Form C. 2118.

Instructions regarding War Diaries and Intelligence Summaries are contained in F. S. Regs., Part II. and the Staff Manual respectively. Title pages will be prepared in manuscript.

WAR DIARY
or
INTELLIGENCE ~~SUMMARY~~
(Erase heading not required.)

VOL XVIII Page VI

Place	Date	Hour	Summary of Events and Information	Remarks and references to Appendices
LE COMMUNAL	6/6/18		A Kit Inspection by Officer i/c Sections was carried out.	
			Sanitary arrangements for this unit were completed, including a bathing installation for patients with heating arrangement	WRG
			The camps of the 18th Kings Royal Rifle Corps & the 15th Hampshire Regt were visited by one of the health inspectors of this unit	
"	7/6/18		Weather :- Fine	
			In the morning 3 horse ambulances were sent out to collect sick of the 122nd Infantry Brigade	
			All medical Equipment was checked	
			A Wheeler & Saddler from No 2 Coy. Div: Train reported to this unit to carry out necessary repairs	WRG
		2 pm	Unit paraded for Health Inspection	
			The A.D.M.S. visited the camp	
			The following was received :- S.1 - Location of Units.	
			Capt L.W. BAIN, RAMC reported for duty as temporary M.O to the 12th East Surrey Regt	

(A9475) Wt W2358/P360 600,000 12/17 D. D. & L. Sch. 52a. Forms/C2118/15.

Instructions regarding War Diaries and Intelligence Summaries are contained in F. S. Regs., Part II. and the Staff Manual respectively. Title pages will be prepared in manuscript.

WAR DIARY or ~~INTELLIGENCE SUMMARY.~~

(Erase heading not required.)

Army Form C. 2118.

VOL XVIII Page VII

Place	Date	Hour	Summary of Events and Information	Remarks and references to Appendices
LE COMMUNAL	8/6/18		Weather :- Fine In the morning the sick of 122nd Infantry Brigade & Divisional artillery were collected In the afternoon Capt F P JOSCELYNE, MC RAMC gave a lecture on Sanitation to the Officers & N.C.O.s of the 15th Hants Regt A Unit Canteen was opened Two more bell tents were pitched for hospital patients Medical Arrangements No 19 were received from the ADMS The 2 Horse Ambulances on duty with the Div. Artillery reported back to this unit	WRG
	9/6/18		Weather :- Fine The Sick were collected as usual 160 men of this unit were bathed. Capt F P JOSCELYNE, M C, RAMC gave a lecture on Sanitation to the Officers & N C O's of the 18th Kings Royal Rifle Corps	WRG

(A9475) Wt W2358/P360 600,000 12/17 D. D. & L. Sch. 52a. Forms/C2118/15.

Instructions regarding War Diaries and Intelligence Summaries are contained in F. S. Regs., Part II, and the Staff Manual respectively. Title pages will be prepared in manuscript.

WAR DIARY
or
~~INTELLIGENCE SUMMARY.~~
(Erase heading not required.)

Army Form C. 2118.

Vol XVIII — Page VIII

Place	Date	Hour	Summary of Events and Information	Remarks and references to Appendices
LE COMMUNAL	9/6/18	(cont)	The following were received :-	
			Warning Order No. 38 from 122 Inf Brigade	WRG
			Wire from A D M S reference 9 hours notice for the Division to move	
			Fourteen relief runners were appointed	
"	10/6/18		In addition to the usual sick round, the 41st Machine Gun Battn & the 19th Middlesex Regt (who arrived in this area on the 9th inst) were visited	
			This unit began a weeks Course of Training (See App).	
			The following distinctive marks were adopted for Runners & personnel of the pioneer section of this unit.	WRG
			Runners :- Red arm band, 1" in depth on the outer half of left sleeve	
			Pioneers :- Blue Band ½" in depth on the outer edge of both epaulettes.	
			The Locations of the Divisional Artillery Units were received.	
			Capt F P JOSCELYNE, MC RAMC delivered a lecture on Sanitation to the Officers & NCOs of the 12th East Surrey Regt.	

(A9175) Wt W2358/P360 600,000 12/17 D. D. & L. Sch. 52a. Forms/C2118/15.

Instructions regarding War Diaries and Intelligence Summaries are contained in F. S. Regs., Part II. and the Staff Manual respectively. Title pages will be prepared in manuscript.

Army Form C. 2118.

WAR DIARY
or
~~INTELLIGENCE SUMMARY.~~
(Erase heading not required.)

VOL. XVIII Page IX.

Place	Date	Hour	Summary of Events and Information	Remarks and references to Appendices
LE COMMUNAL	11/6/18		Weather :- Fine	
			Sick collected as on previous day	
			Announcement was made of "Mentions in Despatches" by Gen Sir H.C.O. PLUMER, G.C.B., C.M.G., G.C.V.O., A.D.C. of the undermentioned :-	WRG
			T4 041952 S/Sgt. Major, Matthews, C.E. (ASC)	
			74102 Sgt. Moody, W.J. (RAMC)	
"	12/6/18		Weather :- Fine.	
			Sick collected as on previous day.	
		10.0am	A.D.M.S. inspected the Hospital.	WRG
			The following were received :- ADMS - S 212 and S 213.	
			Capt F.P. JOSCELYNE M.C. RAMC gave a lecture on Sanitation to the 228th Field Coy, R.E.	
"	13/6/18		Weather :- Fine	
			All the Hospital Tents were transferred to a more suitable field	WRG

(A9475) Wt W2358/P360 600,000 12/17 D. D. & L. Sch. 52a. Forms/C2118/15.

Instructions regarding War Diaries and Intelligence Summaries are contained in F. S. Regs., Part II. and the Staff Manual respectively. Title pages will be prepared in manuscript.

WAR DIARY
or
~~INTELLIGENCE SUMMARY~~
(Erase heading not required.)

Army Form C. 2118.

VOL XVIII Page X

Place	Date	Hour	Summary of Events and Information	Remarks and references to Appendices
LE COMMUNAL	13/6/18	(cont)	next to the old one. Moreover, an improvised tent to hold 20 cases and two more bell tents were erected.	
			This extra accommodation was necessary owing to a high admission rate produced by an outbreak of mild Influenza in this Division.	WRG
		9.0am	The usual Sick round carried out	
		10.0am	A D M S held a Medical Board with this unit	
			Medical Arrangements No 20 received from A.D.M.S.	
"	14/6/18		Weather :- Fine & windy.	
			Sick collected as on previous day.	
			Major J LA F. LAUDER, D.S.O. MC, RAMC, CAPT & QM J. STARKIE, MC, RAMC, & Sgt Major E. RATCLIFFE, D.C.M, proceeded to a demonstration of Field Cookery at LUMBRES.	WRG
			Two more bell tents and a marquee were erected, bringing up the total accommodation to 150.	

(A9175) Wt W2358/P360 600,000 12/17 D. D. & L. Sch. 52a. Forms/C2118/15.

Instructions regarding War Diaries and Intelligence Summaries are contained in F. S. Regs., Part II, and the Staff Manual respectively. Title pages will be prepared in manuscript.

WAR DIARY or ~~INTELLIGENCE SUMMARY.~~

(Erase heading not required.)

Army Form C. 2118.

Vol XVIII Page XI

Place	Date	Hour	Summary of Events and Information	Remarks and references to Appendices
LE COMMUNAL	14/6/18	(cont)	Four reinforcements arrived	WRG
			Capt. H M GODFREY, RAMC. departed from this unit for temporary duty as M.O. to the 15th Hants. Regt.	
"	15/6/18		Weather: Fine	
			Sick collected as on previous day	
			Capt F.P. JOSCELYNE, MC RAMC proceeded under A.D.M.S' instructions to 41st Div. Reception Camp at NOIR CARME as Medical Officer i/c - one N.C.O, one Batman & one ASC MT. Driver accompanied him. One Sunbeam Ambce Car & some Med. Surgical Equipment were taken.	WRG
			The same morning under instructions from ADMS. Capt C.G.H MOORE, RAMC, with a Tent Sub Division (2 NCOs & 17 other ranks) proceeded to No 18 CCS. EBBLINGHEM for temporary duty.	
			The following were received from ADMS - S217 & S218	
			Lieut. H FARNCOMBE, RAMC was posted as permanent Medical Officer i/c 23rd Middlesex Regt & struck off the strength of this unit	

(A9475) Wt W2358/P360 600,000 12/17 D. D. & L. Sch. 52a. Forms/C2118/15.

Army Form C. 2118.

Instructions regarding War Diaries and Intelligence Summaries are contained in F. S. Regs., Part II. and the Staff Manual respectively. Title pages will be prepared in manuscript.

WAR DIARY
or
~~INTELLIGENCE SUMMARY.~~
(Erase heading not required.)

VOL XVIII Page XII

Place	Date	Hour	Summary of Events and Information	Remarks and references to Appendices
LE COMMUNAL	16/6/18		Weather :- Fine	
			Sick Collected as usual	MRG
			From 9 0 am to 2 0 pm a Ford Car was stationed in NORDAUSQUES' village to evacuate any casualties which might result from a Div. Artillery Shoot on the Artillery Ranges S. of NORDAUSQUES.	
			The following were received from the ADMS :- S219 S220	
"	17/6/18		Weather :- Cool & Windy	
			Sick collected as usual	MRG
			1 Reinforcement arrived	
			Nothing of further importance to report	
"	18/6/18		Weather :- Fine	
			Sick Collected as usual	MRG
			Nothing further to report	
"	19/6/18		Weather :- Fine in the morning - showery later	
			Sick Collected as usual	MRG
		9 am/12 noon	Route March	

(A9475) Wt W2358/P360 600,000 12/17 D. D. & L. Sch. 52a. Forms/C2118/15.

Instructions regarding War Diaries and Intelligence Summaries are contained in F. S. Regs., Part II, and the Staff Manual respectively. Title pages will be prepared in manuscript.

WAR DIARY
or
~~INTELLIGENCE SUMMARY.~~
(Erase heading not required.)

Army Form C. 2118.

VOL XVIII Page XIII

Place	Date	Hour	Summary of Events and Information	Remarks and references to Appendices
LE COMMUNAL	19/6/18	4pm	Personnel paraded for Inspection of Box Respirators, &c	WRG
		2/2.30	A.S.C. M.T. paraded with Animals for Inspection.	
		4pm	One Water Cart + RAMC orderly detailed for temporary duty with 41st DIV Reception Camp	
	20/6/18		Weather: Cool & windy	
			Usual Sick were collected.	
		8 am	Major J LA F. LAUDER, DSO, MC RAMC proceeded i/c one section with one Horse Ambulance & one A.D.S. Limber to EPERLECQUES Forest to take part in practice operations in conjunction with the 122nd Infantry Brigade, returning at 2.0pm.	WRG
"	21/6/18		Weather: Dull.	
			Usual sick were collected.	WRG
		2 pm	The Commanding Officer inspected the RAMC personnel of this unit paraded in Full Marching Order.	
		2.30pm	Health Inspection of the unit was carried out.	
"	22/6/18		Weather: Fine	WRG

(A9175) Wt W2358/P360 600,000 12/17 D. D. & L. Sch. 52a. Forms/C2118/15.

Army Form C. 2118.

Instructions regarding War Diaries and Intelligence Summaries are contained in F. S. Regs., Part II, and the Staff Manual respectively. Title pages will be prepared in manuscript.

WAR DIARY
or
~~INTELLIGENCE SUMMARY.~~
(Erase heading not required.)

VOL XVIII Page XIV

Place	Date	Hour	Summary of Events and Information	Remarks and references to Appendices
LE COMMUNAL	22/6/18	9 a.m.	Sick collected as on previous day	
			S 219a was received from the A.D.M.S.	WRG
			There is nothing else of importance to report	
"	23/6/18		Weather :- Showery	
			Sick collected as on previous day.	WRG
			Capt E.A. LUMLEY, MC, RAMC reported back to this unit from the 41st Div Ammunition Column	
		4pm	NCO departed from this unit to give a Course of Instruction in Stretcher Bearing - 5th Labour Group	
"	24/6/18		Weather :- Fine	
			Sick collected as on previous day	
			With reference to the impending move of the Division to the RUBROUCK area, the following were received :-	WRG
			S 223, S 225 from the ADMS : BM 936, + 937 + O.O. 193 from the 122nd Brigade	
			Capt L.N. BAIN, MC, RAMC reported back from the 12th East Surrey Regt.	
			Owing to the move of the Field Ambulance to the new area, all cases	

(A9475) Wt W2358/P360 600,000 12/17 D. D. & L. Sch. 52a. Forms/C2118/15.

Army Form C. 2118.

WAR DIARY
or
~~INTELLIGENCE SUMMARY.~~
(Erase heading not required.)

Instructions regarding War Diaries and Intelligence Summaries are contained in F. S. Regs., Part II, and the Staff Manual respectively. Title pages will be prepared in manuscript.

Vol XVIII Page XV

Place	Date	Hour	Summary of Events and Information	Remarks and references to Appendices
LE COMMUNAL	24/6/18	(cont)	unable to march had to be evacuated to No 36 C.C.S. 200 cases (mostly of Influenza) were evacuated from 11.0pm to 4.30am next morning with the help of 10 Ambulance Cars from No 5 M.A.C.	WRG
			A Horse Ambulance was sent to the 41st Div Artillery to follow the Brigades on the line of march the next day.	
"	25/6/18		Weather :- Fine	
		7 am	Three Ambulance Cars went to collect the sick of the 122nd Infantry Brigade & 41st Div: Artillery	
		8 am	Four Ambulance Cars from No 5 M.A.C. reported to take 28 convalescent cases to the 41st Div. Reception Camp	
		9 am	The personnel & transport of the unit, the Commanding Officer in charge & Major LAUDER proceeded by march route to RUBROUCK where	WRG
RUBROUCK	"		they arrived at 2.0pm (Map Ref. Sht 27. H 8. d 8.4.)	
Map Ref:- (H.8.d.8.4.) Sheet 27.			A rear party consisting of one Officer, one N.C.O. & 6 other ranks & 3 cars were left at LE COMMUNAL to evacuate the remaining patients	

(A9175) Wt W2358/P560 600,000 12/17 D. D. & L. Sch. 52a. Forms/C2118/15.

Instructions regarding War Diaries and Intelligence Summaries are contained in F. S. Regs., Part II. and the Staff Manual respectively. Title pages will be prepared in manuscript.

WAR DIARY
or
~~INTELLIGENCE SUMMARY.~~
(Erase heading not required.)

Army Form C. 2118.

VOL XVIII Page XVI

Place	Date	Hour	Summary of Events and Information	Remarks and references to Appendices
RUBROUCK	25/6/18		to clear up the camp. They rejoined the main body at RUBROUCK at 4.30pm	
			Locations of 122 Inf. Bde. Units were received & Cars sent out to collect the sick	WRG
			The following were received :- Secret 226 from ADMS: O.O. 194, BM. D48 from 122 Inf Bde.	
RUBROUCK	26/6/18	8.30am	The personnel & transport, the Commanding Officer i/c, with these officers proceeded by march route to the ZERMEZEELE area. They arrived	
RIETVELD. Map Ref:- (Sht 27: I4 b8.6)	"		at 3.45pm at RIETVELD (Map Ref. Sht 27 I4 b 8.6) accommodation for 50 cases was provided in barns)	WRG
			One officer, one NCO & 4 O.R. were left to evacuate the sick with 3 Cars, and to clear up the Camp.	
			One Horse Ambulance followed the Brigade to its billeting area. Later on in the evening two Ambce Cars were sent out to collect sick	

(A9475) Wt W2358/P360 600,000 12/17 D. D. & L. Sch. 52a. Forms/C2118/15.

Instructions regarding War Diaries and Intelligence Summaries are contained in F. S. Regs., Part II. and the Staff Manual respectively. Title pages will be prepared in manuscript.

WAR DIARY
or
~~INTELLIGENCE SUMMARY.~~
(Erase heading not required.)

Army Form C. 2118.

VOL XVIII Page XVII

Place	Date	Hour	Summary of Events and Information	Remarks and references to Appendices
RIETVELD	27/6/18		Weather :- Fine.	
			Under instructions from the A.D.M.S. a Collecting Post was formed at 122nd Infantry Bde. H.Q. at Sht 27 K 3 d. Capt L.W. BAIN, MC, RAMC & Capt E.A. LUMLEY, MC, RAMC & 19 other ranks with the necessary equipment and 2 Sunbeam Ambulance Cars from this unit proceeded to the above post at 2 opm.	WRS
		6pm	Commanding Officer attended a conference at the ADMS Office	
		8pm	The horse ambulance which accompanied the Div: artillery reported back to this unit.	
"	28/6/18		Weather :- Fine in the morning - then stormy	
			The Commanding Officer visited the proposed site for a D.R.S. at RYVELD now occupied as a Corps Rest Station by the French.	WRS
			The following were received from the A.D.M.S :- S 230 Location of units of the Division & S 232 - Wastage Return.	
			Surplus Transport & 16 O.R. reported to this unit for temporary attachment (from 139 F.A).	

(A9475) Wt W2355/P360 600,000 12/17 D. D. & L. Sch. 52a. Forms/C2118/15.

Instructions regarding War Diaries and Intelligence Summaries are contained in F. S. Regs., Part II, and the Staff Manual respectively. Title pages will be prepared in manuscript.

WAR DIARY
or
~~INTELLIGENCE SUMMARY.~~
(Erase heading not required.)

Army Form C. 2118.

VOL XVIII Page XVIII

Place	Date	Hour	Summary of Events and Information	Remarks and references to Appendices
RIETVELD	29/6/18		Weather :- Fine	
			A party of one runner & 4 bearers from this unit reported to M.O. i/c 15th Hants. Regt for duty while the above moved to the Forward area - On arrival these men were to report for duty to the nearest RAMC post occupied by 139th Field Ambulance	WRG
		2.0pm	An advance party, 2 NCOs & 39 other ranks moved by march route to the site of the French XIV Corps Rest Station to be taken over by this unit (Map. Ref: Sht. 27 J24 b.3.2.)	
			The following were received :- S 233/1 (41st DIV Administrative Instructions No 35) RAMC Operation Order No 56	from ADMS
			Operation Order 195 from the 122nd Inf. Bde.	
	30/6/18		Weather :- Fine & hot	
RYVELD J24 b.3.2 (Sheet 27)		9.30am	The personnel & transport of this unit, Major L.S.C. ROCHE, MC, RAMC in charge, proceeded by march route from the ZERMEZEELE area to the site of the French XIV Corps Rest Station, arriving at 11-30 am (Map ref. Sht 27 J24 b.3.2)	WRG

(A9475) Wt W2358/P360 600,000 12/17 D. D. & L. Sch. 52a. Forms/C2118/15.

Instructions regarding War Diaries and Intelligence Summaries are contained in F. S. Regs., Part II, and the Staff Manual respectively. Title pages will be prepared in manuscript.

WAR DIARY
or
INTELLIGENCE SUMMARY.
(Erase heading not required.)

Army Form C. 2118.

VOL XVIII Page XIX

Place	Date	Hour	Summary of Events and Information	Remarks and references to Appendices
RYVELD.	30/6/18		Two Operating Tents & 3 Bell Tents were erected to house the 122nd Inf. Bde & Artillery Sick.	
			Parties of one runner & four Bearers from this unit reported to the Medical Officers i/c 18 K.R.R. Corps & 12th East Surrey Regt. to accompany them to the Forward Area. These runners and bearers were to report for duty to the nearest RAMC post occupied by 139 Fld Ambce on completion of duty with the 122nd Infantry Brigade.	WEG
			A party of one NCO & 21 other ranks from this unit reported to O.C. 139 Fld Ambce at WIPPENHOECK for duty.	
			Motor Cyclist with Cycle also reported for duty to the 139 Fld Ambce.	
			46840 Cpl Mann W.T. 106603 Cpl Fairweather, C.F. (Sanitary Inspectors) reported to O.C. 140th & 139th Field Ambces respectively, for sanitary supervision in Forward Area.	
			6 Stretcher Carriages (with stretchers) were also sent to 139 Fld Ambce.	
		4pm	ADMS visited the Camp.	

Instructions regarding War Diaries and Intelligence Summaries are contained in F. S. Regs., Part II. and the Staff Manual respectively. Title pages will be prepared in manuscript.

WAR DIARY
or
~~INTELLIGENCE SUMMARY.~~
(Erase heading not required.)

Army Form C. 2118.

Vol XVIII Page XX

Place	Date	Hour	Summary of Events and Information	Remarks and references to Appendices
RYVELD	30/6/18		**STRENGTH**	

	OFFICERS	O RANKS
RAMC	9	181
ASC. HT.		24
ASC. MT.		12
P.B. men		9
TOTAL	9	226

PERSONNEL ON DETACHED DUTY

	OFF.	O.R.s	CARS &c
139 F.A.		46	6 Wheeled Stretcher Carriages, 1 motor Cycle
18 CCS	1	19	
C. P	2	23	2 Ambce Cars
5th Labour Group		1	
41st Rec Camp	1	6	1 Car, 1 Water Cart, 2 Horses
A D M S		4	
190 Bde, R.F.A.		1	
Div Baths		1	
15th Hants	1	–	
Leave		5	
Sanitary Inspectors –		2	
	5	102	

WRG

(A9475) Wt W2358/P360 600,000 12/17 D. D. & L. Sch. 52a. Forms/C2118/15.

Instructions regarding War Diaries and Intelligence Summaries are contained in F. S. Regs., Part II. and the Staff Manual respectively. Title pages will be prepared in manuscript.

WAR DIARY
or
~~INTELLIGENCE SUMMARY.~~
(Erase heading not required.)

Army Form C. 2118.

Place	Date	Hour	Summary of Events and Information	Remarks and references to Appendices
			Resumé. The points of note during the previous month are:-	
		(1)	Movements. (i) The unit proceeds from the line to the 2nd Army Rest area in one stage, moving brigades with the affiliated Inf. Bde. Group & having medical charge Artillery Bdes. & Ammunition Column.	
			(ii) Movement from the Rest area in three stages to the sector occupied by 7th French Div. (15th Corps d'Armée) moving by brigades on occupation of DRS. by this Fld. Amb.	WRG
		(2)	Occupation of DRS on site of a Infirmerie du 5me Corps	
		(3)	Health. Affiliated Inf. Bde. Group became seriously affected with an epidemic of Influenza, see app.	app. 2
		(4)	Instruction of runners & other Ambulance personnel. See appx.	
		(5)	Disposition. Reduction in strength of unit by detachment of men & officers to C.C.S. & Div. Reception Camp, & later by establishment of a Fld. Amb. Cp. in forward area & attachment of 37 R.A.M.C. bearers by Fld. Amb. in line	

30/6/18

W. Ross Gardner Lt Col RAMC
O.C. 138th Field Ambulance

(A9165) Wt W2358/P300 600,000 12/17 D. D. & L. Sch. 52a. Forms/C2118/15.

APPENDIX – 2

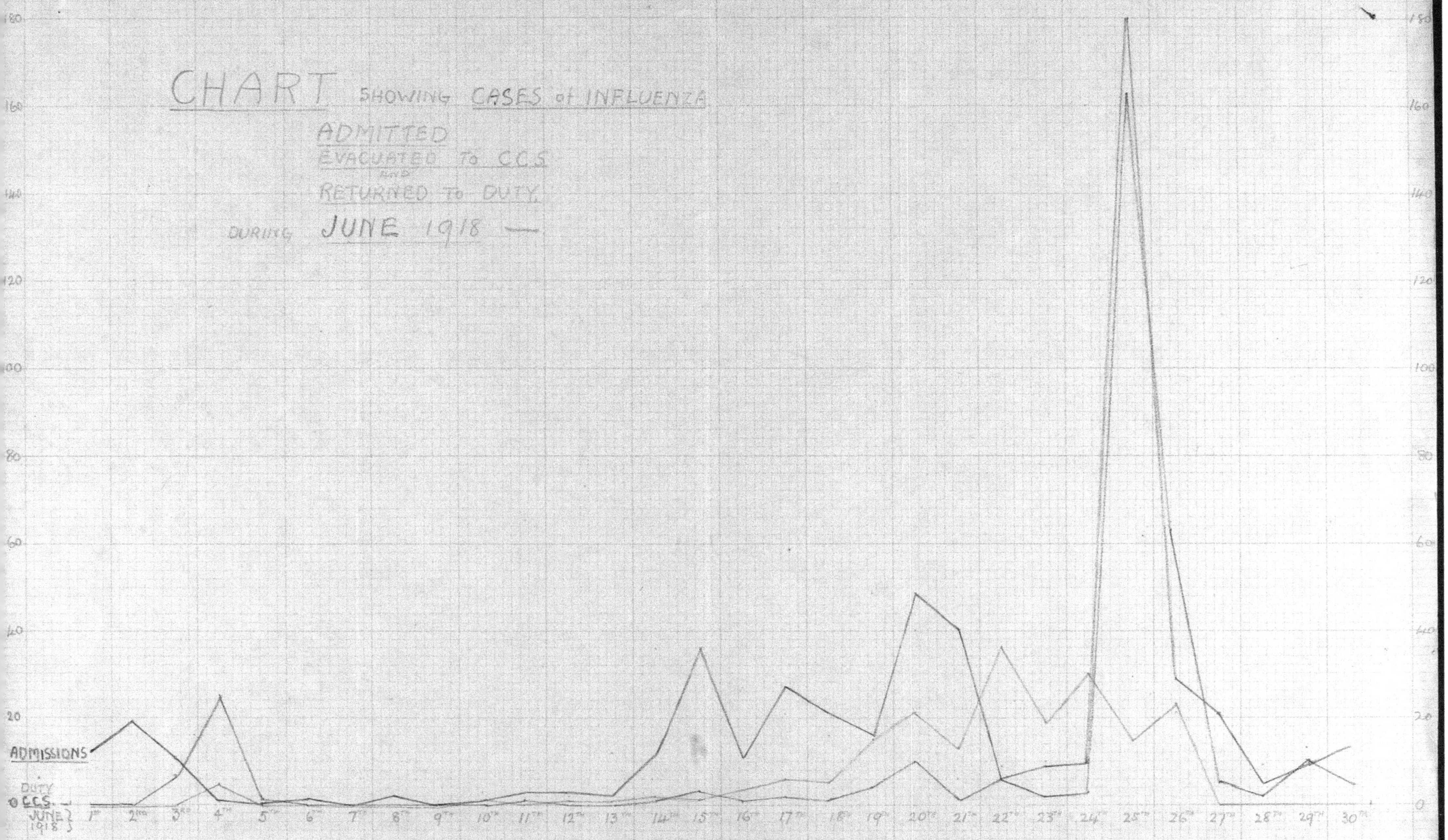

CHART showing CASES of INFLUENZA

ADMITTED
EVACUATED TO C.C.S.
AND
RETURNED TO DUTY
DURING JUNE 1918 —

ADMISSIONS
DUTY
C.C.S.

0 20 40 60 80 100 120 140 160 180

JUNE 1918: 1st 2nd 3rd 4th 5th 6th 7th 8th 9th 10th 11th 12th 13th 14th 15th 16th 17th 18th 19th 20th 21st 22nd 23rd 24th 25th 26th 27th 28th 29th 30th

APPENDIX — 1

138th Field Ambulance.

Syllabus of Training.

TIME	MONDAY	TUESDAY	WEDNESDAY	THURSDAY	FRIDAY	SATURDAY.
6 to 7 am	PHYSICAL DRILL					
8.0 to 9.0 am	SQUAD DRILL	LOADING & UNLOADING AMBULANCE WAGONS	SQUAD DRILL	LOADING & UNLOADING AMBULANCE WAGONS.	FIELD DAY. ESTABLISHMENT OF:- 2 C.P.s — 1 A.D.S — B & C SECTIONS A. AT A DISTANCE OF 5 MILES. (AREA & SITES UNKNOWN)	TENT PITCHING AND STRIKING (BY SECTIONS)
9.0 am to 10.0 am	LECTURE. BANDAGING AND SPLINTS.	LECTURE. ACTIVITIES OF FIELD AMBULANCES IN OPEN WARFARE.	LECTURE. FIRST AID BANDAGING.	CARRYING WOUNDED OVER TWO MILES OF OPEN COUNTRY		LECTURE. 1 DUTIES OF BEARER N.C.O.s 2 RUNNERS (TRENCH OR OTHER) MAPS 3 PIONEERS' SECTION 4 MAINTENANCE OF CONCENTRATION
10.0 am to 12 noon	PITCHING AND EQUIPPING OPERATION TENT. CARRIAGE OF WOUNDED.	DEMONSTRATION. A.D.S. LIMBER AND PACKING.	CARRIAGE OF WOUNDED OVER OPEN COUNTRY.	MARCH OUT OF 3 MILES ↓		ROUTE MARCH WITH TRANSPORT.
2.0 pm to 4.0 pm	COLLECTION OF WOUNDED EXTENDED ORDER.	ESTABLISHMENT OF A.D.S. & C.P.s & RAPID RETIREMENT ON FORMER FROM LATTER	CARRIAGE OF WOUNDED AND IMPROVISED METHODS OF TRANSPORTATION (e.g. G.S. WAGON, CONVERTED)	ESTABLISH A.D.S. & COLLECT WOUNDED & RETURN.		

List of appendices accompanying War Diary for month of June, 1918.

APPENDIX NO.	SUBJECT.
1	Syllabus of Training.
2	Chart showing Cases of Influenza admitted, evacuated and returned to duty during June, 1918.

W Ross Gardner

Lieut. Colonel, R.A.M.C.,

O.C.,138th. Field Ambulance.

July 1918

WR 27

140/3200.

CONFIDENTIAL

WAR DIARY

OF

138TH FIELD AMBULANCE

FROM JULY 1ST TO JULY 31ST, 1918.

(VOLUME XIX).

Army Form C. 2118.

Instructions regarding War Diaries and Intelligence Summaries are contained in F. S. Regs., Part II, and the Staff Manual respectively. Title pages will be prepared in manuscript.

WAR DIARY
or
INTELLIGENCE SUMMARY.
(Erase heading not required.)

VOL XIX Page 1

Place	Date	Hour	Summary of Events and Information	Remarks and references to Appendices
RWELD (Sheet 27 b 2.2) Station with Div^l Rest	1/7/18		Weather v. hot	
			ADMS visited the station this morning. Final decision made as regards future plan of permanent situation of Div^l R.S.	[illegible]
			Question of water given serious consideration, & decision taken to sink our well to a further depth of 15'	
	2/7/18		Weather wind & much cooler	
			Capt E.A. LUMLEY MC RAMC reported for temporary duty to OC 13th Fld. Amb. (FA in the line)	[illegible]
			Capt L.W. Bain MC RAMC & 9 OR returned to DRS for duty	
			RAP temporarily established at Sh 27 R.2.a.4.4 given up all the units, including our dressing station, that had 'staged' having moved into forward area E. of WATOU – GODEWAERSVELDE Rd.	
			One large Sunbeam Car reports to OC. 134 FA. for duty in forward area	

(A9475) Wt W2358/P360 600,000 12/17 D. D. & L. Sch. 52a. Forms/C2118/15.

Instructions regarding War Diaries and Intelligence Summaries are contained in F. S. Regs., Part II. and the Staff Manual respectively. Title pages will be prepared in manuscript.

WAR DIARY
or
INTELLIGENCE SUMMARY.
(Erase heading not required.)

Army Form C. 2118.

VOL XIX – Page 2

Place	Date	Hour	Summary of Events and Information	Remarks and references to Appendices
RWELA	2/7/18		Weather has become much cooler	
			R.R.S. now open to receive sick.	
			Method of evacuation to this station from forward area is from	
			M.D.S. (140 Fld Amb.) Remy Siding (Sh 27 L22 a 1.1.) by Corps (15th Corps)	
			Light Railway to detraining point at WINNEZEELE, Sh 27 J17 c 2.7,	
			thence by Motor Amb. to this station.	
			This unit assumed medical charge of 557 Army Troops RE.	
			15 Hospital marquees drawn from No 58 C.C.S. LONGUENESSE	
			Location of units of 41st Div. No.	
			5.239 (Location of units of Div. received from ADMS.)	

Instructions regarding War Diaries and Intelligence Summaries are contained in F. S. Regs., Part II. and the Staff Manual respectively. Title pages will be prepared in manuscript.

WAR DIARY
or
INTELLIGENCE SUMMARY.
(Erase heading not required.)

Army Form C. 2118.

VOL XIX Page 3

Place	Date	Hour	Summary of Events and Information	Remarks and references to Appendices
AWELD	4/7/18		Weather fine & warm	
			Capt J.J.H. FERGUSON M.C. RAMC reported for duty	
			Capt L.W. BAIN M.C. RAMC reported for temporary duty as	[initials]
			41st Div Reception Camp in relief of Capt F.P. JOSCELYNE M.C. RAMC	
			Capt H.M. GODFREY RAMC returned back from temporary duty	
			with 15th Hants & proceeded to 19 Middlesex Regt as temp.	
			M.O. in relief of Capt S.S. CROSSE M.C. RAMC proceeding on leave	
			S.240 Corps Cable Div received from ADMS	
	5/7/18		Weather dull but warm	
			RE commenced work on erection of Nissen huts	
			ADMS visited DRS. Corps Commander visited Camp	[initials]
			S.752 Location of units 41 Div Recd.	
			S.241 from ADMS DRS Corps recd	
			S.242 Location of units transport lines recd	

(A9175) Wt W2358/P360 600,000 12/17 D. D. & L. Sch. 52a. Forms/C2118/15.

Instructions regarding War Diaries and Intelligence Summaries are contained in F. S. Regs., Part II. and the Staff Manual respectively. Title pages will be prepared in manuscript.

WAR DIARY
or
INTELLIGENCE SUMMARY.
(*Erase heading not required.*)

Army Form C. 2118.

VOL XIX Page 4

Place	Date	Hour	Summary of Events and Information	Remarks and references to Appendices
RWELA	6/7/18		Weather fine & warm	
			1st Lt [illegible] Fiess US [illegible] reported for duty	
			Work proceeding satisfactorily in erection of huts	[initials]
	7/7/18		Weather fine & warm	
			Div H.Q. closed at LE LINGUE sheet 27 [illegible] at 10 am & reopened at Sh 27 [illegible]	
			Capt [illegible] Joscelyne [illegible] reported back for duty with ADMS 4th Div	[initials]
			ADMS visited Camp.	
	8/7/18		Weather much cooler	
			Capt Joscelyne reported for duty to ADMS 4th Div	
			1 [illegible] hut for reception of patients ready (Capacity [illegible])	[initials]

(A9475) Wt W2358/P360 600,000 12/17 D. D. & L. Sch. 52a. Forms/C2118/15.

Instructions regarding War Diaries and Intelligence Summaries are contained in F. S. Regs., Part II. and the Staff Manual respectively. Title pages will be prepared in manuscript.

WAR DIARY
or
INTELLIGENCE SUMMARY.
(*Erase heading not required.*)

Army Form C. 2118.

VOL XXX Page 5

Place	Date	Hour	Summary of Events and Information	Remarks and references to Appendices
RWELD	9 7/18		Weather much cooler	
			1 Marquee was erected & completed by means of double slips	[illegible]
	10 7/18		Weather fine but cool. Stormy during afternoon & evening	
			Nothing of importance to record	[illegible]
			Further tentage 3 Hospital marquees erected for patients	
	11 7/18		Weather cooler	
			Second marquee hut completed	
			Further tentage erected to accommodate large convoy of patients	[illegible]
			Nothing further to report.	

(A9475) Wt W2358/P360 600,000 12/17 D. D. & L. Sch. 52a. Forms/C2118/15.

Instructions regarding War Diaries and Intelligence Summaries are contained in F. S. Regs., Part II. and the Staff Manual respectively. Title pages will be prepared in manuscript.

WAR DIARY
or
INTELLIGENCE SUMMARY.
(Erase heading not required.)

Army Form C. 2118.

Vol XIX Page 6

Place	Date	Hour	Summary of Events and Information	Remarks and references to Appendices
[illegible]	12/9/18		Weather windy with rain	
			A.D.M.S. visited camp	[illegible]
			Erection of a Bath House has been commenced	
			Otherwise nothing to report	
	13/9/18		Weather much warmer	
			A.D.M.S. visited camp	[illegible]
			Otherwise nothing to note	
	17/9/18		Weather showery & much cooler	
			Arrangements made to complete & put into use a Dining	[illegible]
			hall for personnel & patients	

(A9475) Wt W2358/P360 600,000 12/17 D. D. & L. Sch. 52a. Forms/C2118/15.

Instructions regarding War Diaries and Intelligence Summaries are contained in F. S. Regs., Part II. and the Staff Manual respectively. Title pages will be prepared in manuscript.

WAR DIARY
or
INTELLIGENCE SUMMARY.
(*Erase heading not required.*)

Army Form C. 2118.

VOL XIX Page 7.

Place	Date	Hour	Summary of Events and Information	Remarks and references to Appendices
	15/7/18		Weather v. hot	
			Lt Col W Ross Gardner R.A.M.C. granted leave 16/7/18 – 15/8/18	[illegible]
			D.D.M.S. XIX Corps visited & inspected Hospital & Camp	
	16/7/18		Weather much cooler & gusts of rain	
			Dining Hall completed & now in use for Patients	[illegible]
			A/O.C. attended a conference at A.D.M.S.' office 3.30 pm	
	17/7/18		Weather v. hot & close: storm threatening.	
		3.30pm	Major J. [illegible] A/O.C. attended a Conference at A.D.M.S.' office & subject matter of 41st Div. Medical Defence Scheme & that of XIX Corps considered.	[illegible]
			S.M.S. 252 recd. (XIX Corps Med. Arrangements No 10 – for active operations. Amendment to S 250 41st Div. Defence Scheme recd.	
			Temp Sub. Div. O/c Capt [illegible] R.A.M.C. recalled from No 15 C.C.S.	

(A9475) Wt W2358/P360 600,000 12/17 D. D. & L. Sch. 52a. Forms/C2118/15.

Army Form C. 2118.

Instructions regarding War Diaries and Intelligence Summaries are contained in F. S. Regs., Part II. and the Staff Manual respectively. Title pages will be prepared in manuscript.

WAR DIARY
or
INTELLIGENCE SUMMARY.
(*Erase heading not required.*)

VOL XIX Page 8

Place	Date	Hour	Summary of Events and Information	Remarks and references to Appendices
RWELD	8/7/18		Weather fine	
			Location of units of Div. recd from ADMS	
			Amendment to Corps medical arrangements recd	
			71 Cases (other formations) transferred to Hospice ARNEKE 2/1 E. Lancs Fd Amb. under instructions from DDMS.	
			Reserve of 100 stretchers & 200 blankets received from 2/1 E Lancs Fd Amb.	
			Progress of work in erection of permanent structures in Camp good being	
			3 large Nissen huts (capacity 40 lying cases)	
			1 large French hut (" 35 lying cases)	
			Cook house annexe	[initials]

(A9475) Wt W2358/P360 600,000 12/17 D. D. & L. Sch. 52a. Forms/C2118/15.

Instructions regarding War Diaries and Intelligence Summaries are contained in F. S. Regs., Part II, and the Staff Manual respectively. Title pages will be prepared in manuscript.

WAR DIARY
or
INTELLIGENCE SUMMARY.
(*Erase heading not required.*)

Army Form C. 2118.

VOL XIX Page 9

Place	Date	Hour	Summary of Events and Information	Remarks and references to Appendices
RWBLR	19/2/18		Weather fine; much wind after noon	
			Station Cards Cables rec'd from A.D.M.S.	
			S.25g rec'd from A.D.M.S. (in connexion with conveyance of walking wounded)	
			A.D.M.S. visited & inspected Camp.	[initials]
			3 large Hospital Marquees struck	
	20/2/18		Weather boisterous	
			S.25g (as above) re. lorries for conveyance of W. wounded)	
			Arrangements made to improve water supply to Camp.	[initials]
	21/2/18		Weather fine	
			Saw the A.D.M.S. (Col.) re.? inspection & attack [illegible]	
			Otherwise nothing to note.	[initials]

(A9475) Wt W2358/P360 600,000 12/17 D. D. & L. Sch. 52a. Forms/C2118/15.

Instructions regarding War Diaries and Intelligence Summaries are contained in F. S. Regs., Part II, and the Staff Manual respectively. Title pages will be prepared in manuscript.

WAR DIARY
or
INTELLIGENCE SUMMARY.
(Erase heading not required.)

Army Form C. 2118.

VOL XIX Page 10

Place	Date	Hour	Summary of Events and Information	Remarks and references to Appendices
RWELD	22/9/18		Weather fine	
			Seven Hospital marquees returned to 53 C.C.S. & replaced by 7 small marquees.	[initials]
			G.O.C. 41st Div. visited & inspected Camp.	
			Further hut (French type) for dispensary & Dressing Room.	
			Location of transport lines 41st Div. recd.	
	23/9/18		Weather v. wet	
			Otherwise nothing to note.	[initials]
	24/9/18		Weather wet	
			Camp becoming seriously cut up. All traffic, wheeled, through Camp suspended.	
			S.2252 Location of units recd.	
			7 O.Rs. from this unit transferred to 36 C.C.S. in exchange for same number of O.Rs. now fit for front line duty.	[initials]

(A9475) Wt W2358/P360 600,000 12/17 D. D. & L. Sch. 52a. Forms/C2118/15.

Instructions regarding War Diaries and Intelligence Summaries are contained in F. S. Regs., Part II, and the Staff Manual respectively. Title pages will be prepared in manuscript.

WAR DIARY
or
INTELLIGENCE SUMMARY.
(*Erase heading not required.*)

Army Form C. 2118.

VOL XIX Page II

Place	Date	Hour	Summary of Events and Information	Remarks and references to Appendices
RAVELO.	25/7/18		Weather fine Work proceeding satisfactorily. 1 L.D. [illegible] drawn	
	26/7/18		Weather showery. otherwise nothing of note	
	27/7/18		Weather - v. wet Protection of [illegible] against being cut up taken in hand - track boards & corduroy huts. Ground v. heavy after recent rain & work being seriously delayed 1st Lt. R.K. First US Engrs struck off strength [illegible] Posts Camp.	

(A9475) Wt W2358/P360 600,000 12/17 D. D. & L. Sch. 52a. Forms/C2118/15.

Instructions regarding War Diaries and Intelligence Summaries are contained in F. S. Regs., Part II. and the Staff Manual respectively. Title pages will be prepared in manuscript.

WAR DIARY
or
INTELLIGENCE SUMMARY.
(Erase heading not required.)

VOL XIX Page 12 Army Form C. 2118.

Place	Date	Hour	Summary of Events and Information	Remarks and references to Appendices
RWELD	28/7/18		Weather v. wet	
			Capt. H.M. Cooper, RAMC posted for duty with 1?? F.A.	[illegible]
RWELD	29/7/18		Weather fine & bright & v. warm	
			8 Hospital marquees struck	
			Officers ward – [illegible] now complete	[illegible]
	30/7/18		Weather hot	
			5 double Hospital marquees collected & returned to 55 CCS	
			& replaced by 8 single Hosp marquees	[illegible]
	31/7/18		Weather fine & bright	
			1 Party of 55 Patients & 5 OR RAMC proceeded to 4 Army Rest	
			Camp for 14 days.	

(A9475) Wt W2358/P360 600,000 12/17 D. D. & L. Sch. 52a. Forms/C2118/15.

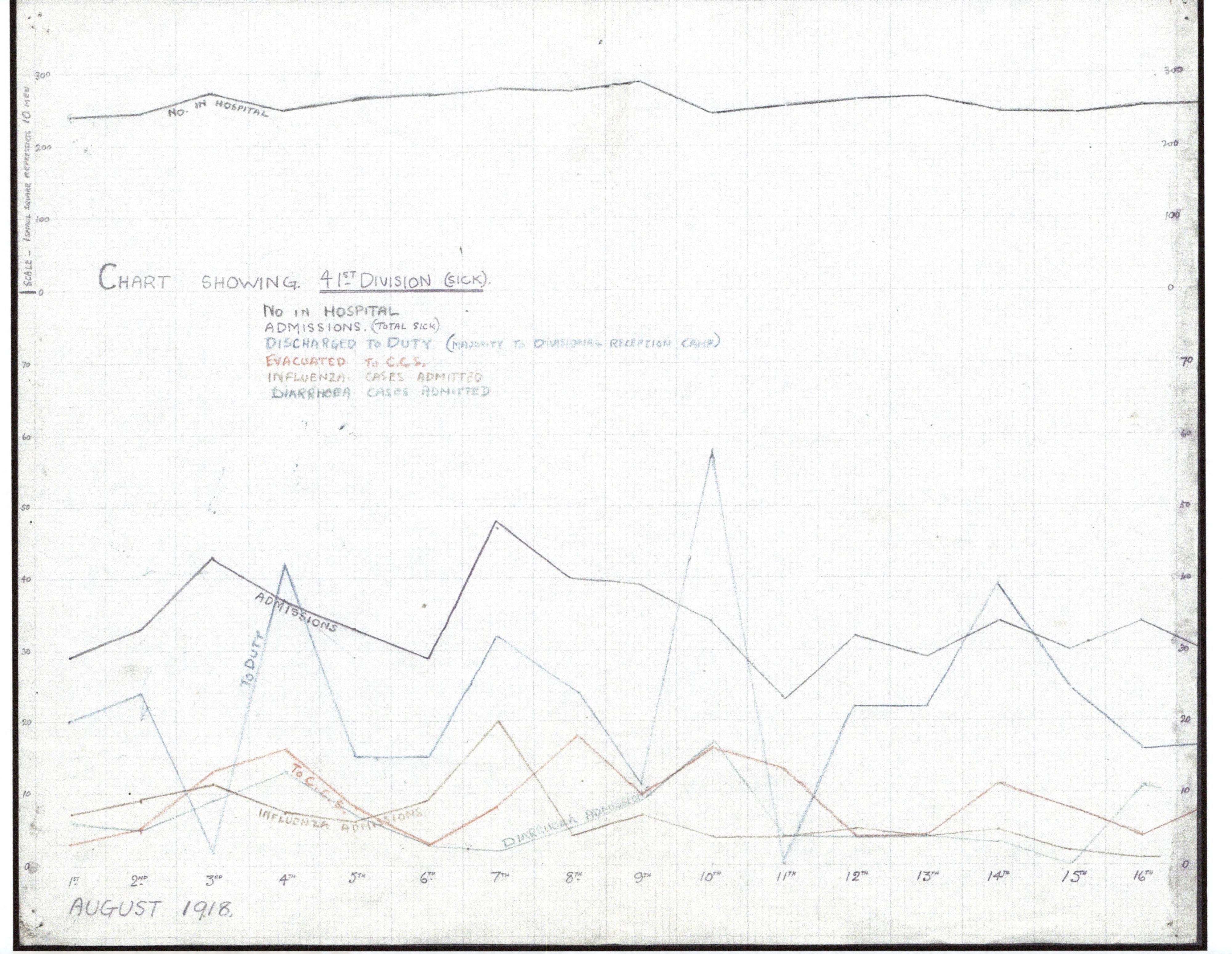
Chart showing 41st Division (sick).
No in Hospital
Admissions. (Total sick)
Discharged to Duty (Majority to Divisional Reception Camp)
Evacuated to C.C.S.
Influenza cases admitted
Diarrhoea cases admitted
Scale – 1 small square represents 10 men
No. in Hospital
Admissions
To Duty
To C.C.S.
Influenza Admissions
Diarrhoea Admissions
300
200
100
0
70
60
50
40
30
20
10
0
1st
2nd
3rd
4th
5th
6th
7th
8th
9th
10th
11th
12th
13th
14th
15th
16th
August 1918.

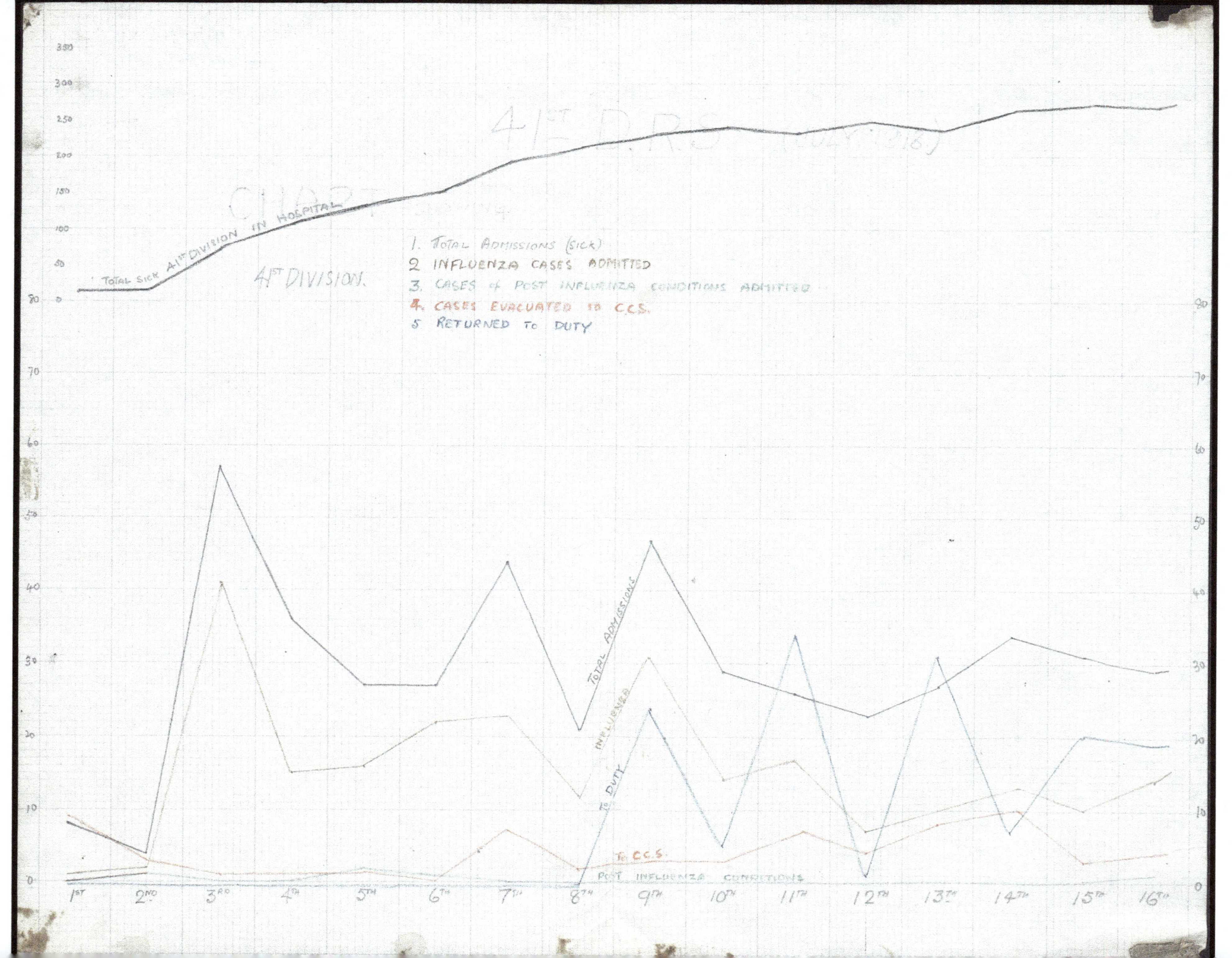

41st D.R.S
CHART
41st DIVISION.
TOTAL SICK 41st DIVISION IN HOSPITAL
1. TOTAL ADMISSIONS (SICK)
2 INFLUENZA CASES ADMITTED
3. CASES of POST INFLUENZA CONDITIONS ADMITTED
4. CASES EVACUATED to C.C.S.
5 RETURNED to DUTY
TOTAL ADMISSIONS
INFLUENZA
To DUTY
To C.C.S.
POST INFLUENZA CONDITIONS
0
50
100
150
200
250
300
350
0
10
20
30
40
50
60
70
80
1st
2nd
3rd
4th
5th
6th
7th
8th
9th
10th
11th
12th
13th
14th
15th
16th

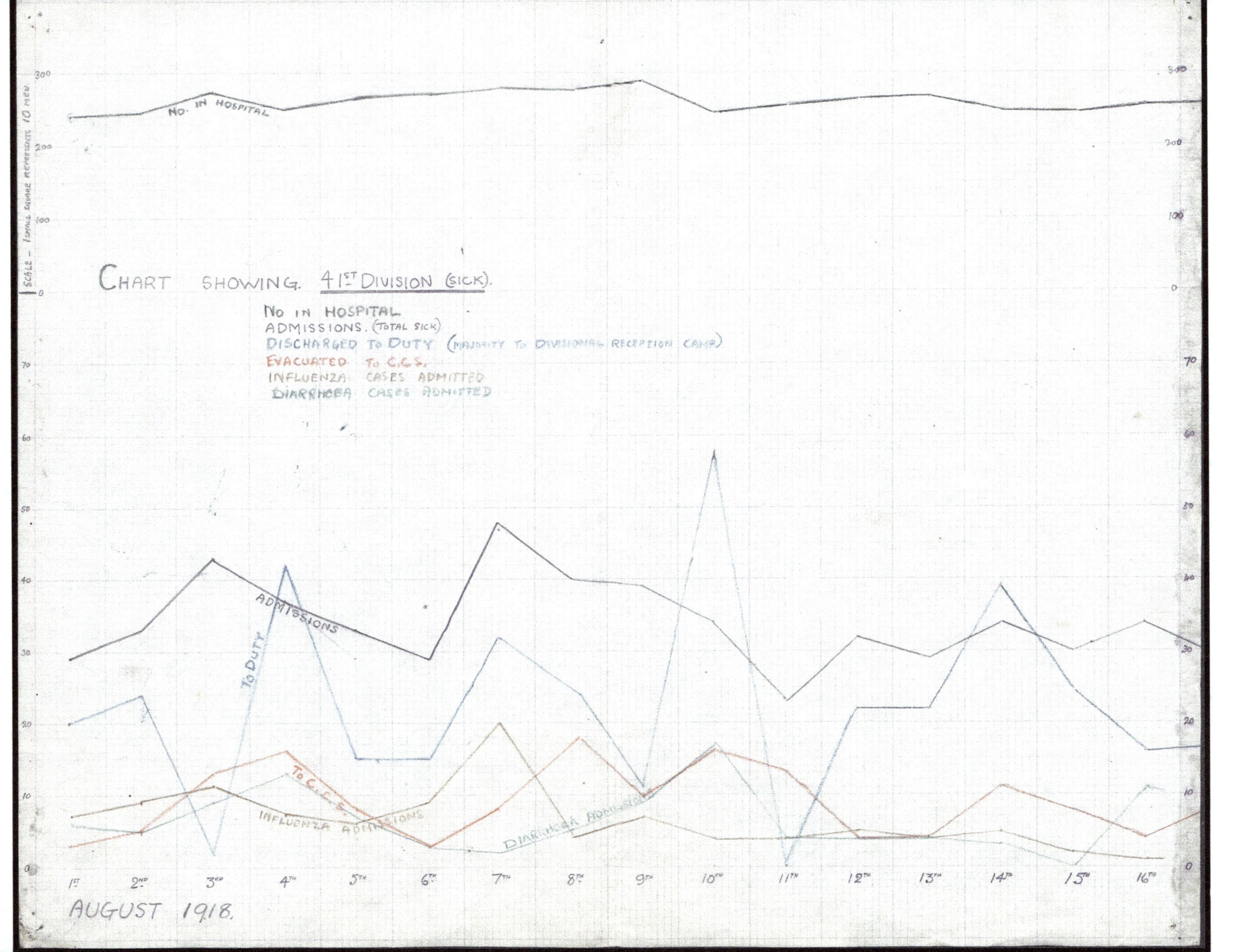

CHART SHOWING 41ST DIVISION (SICK).
No IN HOSPITAL
ADMISSIONS. (TOTAL SICK)
DISCHARGED TO DUTY (MAJORITY TO DIVISIONAL RECEPTION CAMP)
EVACUATED TO C.C.S.
INFLUENZA CASES ADMITTED
DIARRHOEA CASES ADMITTED
SCALE – 1 SMALL SQUARE REPRESENTS 10 MEN
NO. IN HOSPITAL
ADMISSIONS
TO DUTY
TO C.C.S.
INFLUENZA ADMISSIONS
DIARRHOEA ADMISSIONS
300
200
100
0
70
60
50
40
30
20
10
0
1ST 2ND 3RD 4TH 5TH 6TH 7TH 8TH 9TH 10TH 11TH 12TH 13TH 14TH 15TH 16TH
AUGUST 1918.

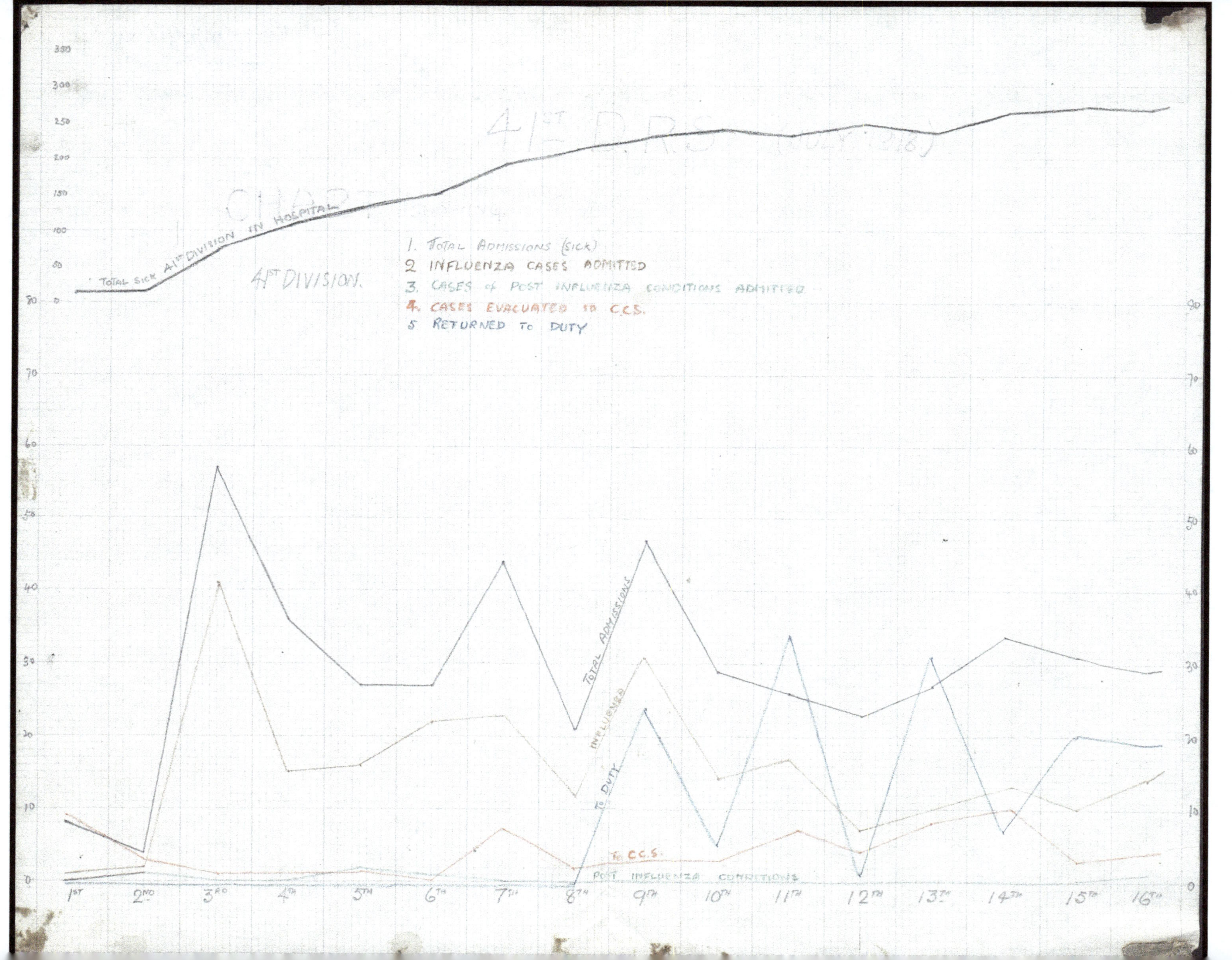
41st D.R.S. (JULY 1918)
CHART
41st DIVISION.
TOTAL SICK 41st DIVISION IN HOSPITAL
1. TOTAL ADMISSIONS (SICK)
2 INFLUENZA CASES ADMITTED
3. CASES of POST INFLUENZA CONDITIONS ADMITTED
4. CASES EVACUATED to C.C.S.
5 RETURNED To DUTY
TOTAL ADMISSIONS
INFLUENZA
To DUTY
To C.C.S.
POST INFLUENZA CONDITIONS
1st
2nd
3rd
4th
5th
6th
7th
8th
9th
10th
11th
12th
13th
14th
15th
16th

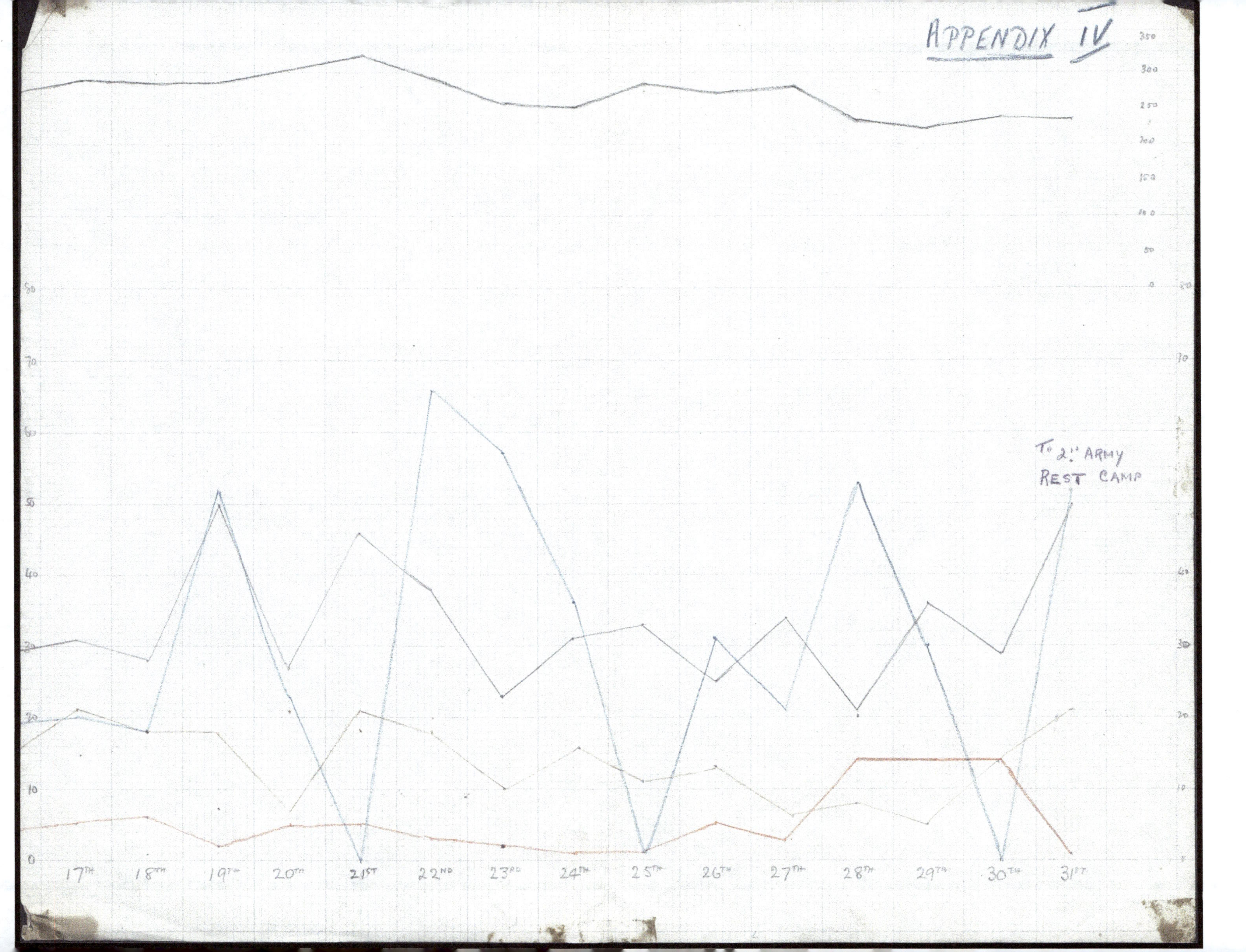

APPENDIX IV
350
300
250
200
150
100
50
0
80
70
60
50
40
30
20
10
0
17TH
18TH
19TH
20TH
21ST
22ND
23RD
24TH
25TH
26TH
27TH
28TH
29TH
30TH
31ST
To 2nd ARMY
REST CAMP

Orders for Patients proceeding to Baths APP 1

1. Hand in A.F. W.3118.
2. Put Valuables in dorothy bag – inventory to be taken in duplicate, patient to sign the original & place same in bag with valuables – tie bag up with numbered disc. A second disc bearing same number to be worn round neck.
3. Undress –
4. Hand in Boots, Great Coat & Cap. Place these together with change of uniform & underclothing in Dressing Room under corresponding seating number in Dressing Room.
5. Bath – you will receive soap & scrubbing brush.
6. Dressing Room – Feet will be inspected & dealt with here after bathing – dress
7. Receive valuables on handing in disc (worn round the neck) & then sign duplicate inventory which is filed.
8. Given back Field Card, after same has been endorsed "Bath" (in small letters) under treatment & initialled by N.C.O. i/c
9. Uniform will be labelled – giving Ward No. Regtl No. Rank, Name &c
10. Uniform will be returned the following day before noon.
11. Pyjamas to be handed in to Ward store upon receipt of uniform.
12. Uniform unfit for further wear will be condemned by Capt & Q M J Starkie, MC RAMC – NCO i/c will notify this to the NCO i/c Ward on same slip.

[signature] Lt Col RAMC

APP 2

Admissions

1. Patients on admission are "up" or "bed" (letter "B" to be put in top right hand corner of A.F. W 3118).
2. "UP" Patients – bath & clean change of underclothing & loan of uniform (at Baths) immediately on admission and prior to admission to Wards.
3. Indicate in top left hand corner of A F W 3118, no. of Ward
4. Bed Patients – pyjamas, socks & slippers (Ward Store) & bath as soon as fit. – extra issue of 3 blankets.
5. All Patients to retain boots, great coat & cap.
6. Uniforms of patients bathed to be returned before noon the following day & the loaned uniforms to be returned to Bath Store.
7. Above inapplicable to Scabies, impetigo & other infectious skin diseases, (Special Instructions for these cases).
8. Bath again 5 days after first bath, according to Bath Time Table
9. No 1 Ward is far as possible to be reserved for BED cases – thence to other wards. No 2 Ward – recently bathed cases.
10. Establishment of clothing, &c to Wards :-

No. 1 Ward	Other Wards
Pyjamas	
Slippers	
Socks	

11. "Bed" Patients on bathing receive underclothing as under para 2 – Pyjamas returned by N C O i/c Baths to Ward Patients then become "Up Patients" unless otherwise indicated.
12. Change of Ward – Number of new Ward will be recorded by discharging ward on A F W 3118 as per para 3.
13. A F W 3118 will accompany patients to Bath House & the word "bath" (small) will be written on A F W 3118 under treatment, giving date & initials of Bath N.C.O.
14. Ward Orderly will verify instructions in para 13.
15. All N C Os i/c Wards will notify Receiving Room by 12 noon of all vacancies in Wards.
    Ward No. 1 – This includes discharges from this to other Wards of any cases being transferred on that day.
16. Blanket Issue :- Bed Patients :- 3.
    Up Patients in Pyjamas :- 2.
    Up " excused duty :- 1
    Light Duty Patients :- –

[signature] Major
O.C. [illegible] Field Amb.

(1251) Wt. 4028/618 100m Pads 1/18. A. W. & Co. (2486).

Army Form C348
(Pads).

MEMORANDUM.

From
O.C. 138 Field Amba

Date 1 - 8 1918.

To
A D M S
41st Div.

Appendices to War Diary July 1918

1/ Orders for patients proceeding to Baths

2/ Admissions

3/ Diagram shewing disposal

4/ Chart shewind admission & discharges during month.

ORDERLY ROOM
No. 2460/18
DATE
138th FIELD AMBULANCE

[signature] Major
O/C 138th Field Ambulance.

19

VR 28

140/3324

CONFIDENTIAL

28-7-5/18
3/9/18.

Aug. 1918

WAR DIARY

OF

138TH FIELD AMBULANCE

FROM AUGUST 1ST TO AUGUST 31ST, 1918.

(VOLUME - XX)

Instructions regarding War Diaries and Intelligence Summaries are contained in F. S. Regs., Part II. and the Staff Manual respectively. Title pages will be prepared in manuscript.

WAR DIARY
or
INTELLIGENCE SUMMARY.
(Erase heading not required.)

Army Form C. 2118.

VOLUME XX (Page I)

Place	Date	Hour	Summary of Events and Information	Remarks and references to Appendices
RWELD (41 W.H.R.S.) Sh 27 J27 b3.2	1/8/18		Weather v. wet Constructional work proceeding satisfactorily. Hutting accommodation now for 250 patients (5 huts 12.4 Nissen & 2 French type huts) Arrangements made to disinfect blankets (100 blankets daily means day) this with baths & change of underclothing, it is considered should 'delouse' the Hospital in one week. Attention being given particularly to cookhouse where arrangements are being made, ovens, dixie stands etc. to deal with 300 patients in one 'shift'; similarly with Dining Hall. { Admissions – 33 { C.C.S. – 5 { R.T.R. – 24	[signature]
	2/8/18		Weather showery but bright P.259 location of medical units 2nd Army recd from ADMS S.250 Code names American units at 41st Div recd Dining Hall completed seating accommodation for 250. { Admissions – 43 { CCS 13 { [illegible] 2	[signature]

D. D. & L., London, E.C.
(1034) Wt W5300/P713 750,000 3/15 B 2688 Forms/C2118/16

Instructions regarding War Diaries and Intelligence Summaries are contained in F. S. Regs., Part II. and the Staff Manual respectively. Title pages will be prepared in manuscript.

WAR DIARY
or
INTELLIGENCE SUMMARY.
(Erase heading not required.)

Army Form C. 2118.

VOLUME XX Page II

Place	Date	Hour	Summary of Events and Information	Remarks and references to Appendices
Div. R. S.	3/4/18		Weather still showery but owing to complete system of surface drainage & duck-boarding, camp has remained relatively dry. Hospital now divided into the following distinct sections: { Med. & Surgical Officers Sergeants Infectious [illegible] } { Admissions - 37 E.C.S. [illegible] - 16 R.T.R. - 42 }	[illegible]
	4/4/18		Weather fine camp drying up [illegible] Conference at D.D.M.S. Office re attack by 15th [illegible] & medical arrangements in connection with same. S291 recd. (re visit of H.M. the King to Corps area) Lt. Col. G.B. MASSON [illegible] reported for 3 days instruction in running of [illegible]. 1st Lt R.G. MAUGER U.S.M.O.R.C. posted to this unit (at present on detached duty at XIX Corps H.Q.)	[illegible]

D. D. & L., London, E.C.
(1034) Wt W5300/P713 750,000 3/15 E 2688 Forms/C2118/16

Instructions regarding War Diaries and Intelligence Summaries are contained in F. S. Regs., Part II. and the Staff Manual respectively. Title pages will be prepared in manuscript.

WAR DIARY
or
INTELLIGENCE SUMMARY.
(*Erase heading not required.*)

Army Form C. 2118.

VOL XX PAGE 111

Place	Date	Hour	Summary of Events and Information	Remarks and references to Appendices
Camb	4/8/18		Admissions 33 — 33 C.C.S. 7 R.T.Do. 16 } 23 (9 same as remaining in Hosp.)	
	5/8/18		Weather again showery. S R 26716 Location of Med Unit 2nd Army Sec. Baths at this station now operating, capacity 200 per hour. System in connexion with Baths being complete change of underclothing, ironing & brushing of uniform. Pyjamas for 1st night in Hosp. & uniform issued following morning. H.R.H. inspected camp. Admissions 25 . 25 C.C.S. 4 R.T.D. 15 } 19 (Remaining 10)	[illegible]

D. D. & L., London, E.C.
(1034) Wt W3300/P713 750,000 3/15 E 2688 Forms/C2118/16

Instructions regarding War Diaries and Intelligence Summaries are contained in F. S. Regs., Part II. and the Staff Manual respectively. Title pages will be prepared in manuscript.

WAR DIARY
or
INTELLIGENCE SUMMARY.
(Erase heading not required.)

Army Form C. 2118.

VOL XX – PAGE IV

Place	Date	Hour	Summary of Events and Information	Remarks and references to Appendices
	6/8/[illegible]		Weather fine & bright	
			Disinfection of faeces now satisfactory, [illegible] with 1 2 [illegible] employed)	
			S.254 Evacuation of units 41st Div.) Recd from ADMS	
			Station Cmdt. Cable recd from ADMS	[signature]
			Admissions . 48 - 45	
			C.C.S. . 8	
			R.T.D. . 32 > 40 (Sick [illegible] 8, remaining [illegible])	
	7/8		Weather fine	
			ADMS inspected Camp	
			S. 252 Recd (Medical scheme for evacuation of wounded 41st Div.)	
			Admissions - 35 - 35	
			C.C.S. . 14	
			R.T.D. . 4 > 22 (Sick [illegible] 17, remaining)	[signature]

D. D. & L., London, E.C.
(10341) Wt W3300/P713 750,000 3/15 E 2688 Forms/C2118/16

Instructions regarding War Diaries and Intelligence Summaries are contained in F. S. Regs., Part II. and the Staff Manual respectively. Title pages will be prepared in manuscript.

WAR DIARY
or
INTELLIGENCE SUMMARY.
(Erase heading not required.)

Army Form C. 2118.

VOL. XX PAGE V

Place	Date	Hour	Summary of Events and Information	Remarks and references to Appendices
	8/8/18		Weather fine. Officers Sect of Hospital Camp [illegible], accommodation for 10 officers a further extension - 4 cubicles, and small [illegible] hut, for officers of Field rank. Admissions - 40 [illegible] C.C.S. - 11 R.T.D. - 11 7 [illegible] (gain of 18)	[initials]
	9/8/18		Weather good Nothing to report Admissions - 35 [illegible] (gain of 7) C.C.S. - 16 R.T.D. - 5 & 58 to 27 Army Rest Camp. Average number of cases to Hospital, with Diarrhoea, is 28	[initials]
	10/8/18		Weather - v. warm 5,255 Amendment to Divl Code names Recd. Admissions : 23 C.C.S. : 13 R.T.D. : –	[initials]

D. D. & L., London, E.C.
(1034?) Wt W5300/P713 750,000 5/15 E 2088 Forms/C2118/16

Instructions regarding War Diaries and Intelligence Summaries are contained in F. S. Regs., Part II. and the Staff Manual respectively. Title pages will be prepared in manuscript.

WAR DIARY

or

INTELLIGENCE SUMMARY.

(Erase heading not required.)

Army Form C. 2118.

VOL XX PAGE VI

Place	Date	Hour	Summary of Events and Information	Remarks and references to Appendices
	11/4/18		Weather fine 1 NCO & 2 OR proceeded to Church Parade TERDEGHEM & at march past HM the King. ADMS visited Camp Location of Div. units recd from ADMS Admissions - 32 CCS - 5 RTD - 22	[illegible]
	12/4/18		Weather fine Nothing of note to report Admissions - 35 CCS 4 RTD 23 Remaining in Hospital 25	[illegible]
	13/4/18		Weather fine & warm Report office & Reception Room altered Sulphur Dioxide apparatus installed for treatment of scabies & impetigo. Admissions - 37 CCS 11 RTD 35	[illegible]

D. D. & L., London, E.C.
(1034-) Wt W5300/P713 750,000 3/15 B 2688 Forms/C2118/16

Army Form C. 2118.

WAR DIARY
or
INTELLIGENCE SUMMARY.
(Erase heading not required.)

Instructions regarding War Diaries and Intelligence Summaries are contained in F. S. Regs., Part II. and the Staff Manual respectively. Title pages will be prepared in manuscript.

VOL XX PAGE VII

Place	Date	Hour	Summary of Events and Information	Remarks and references to Appendices
	14/8/18		Weather still continued good. Medical arrangements XIX Corps in case of heavy casualties recd from A.D.M.S. 400 gallon water tank recd from Corps water supply officer. Camp water supply (basis for bathing) as follows 3 water carts 2 refillings each = 330 gallons Water tank lorry (3 journeys) = 400 gallons Wells in camp about = 200 " Total = 930 or 3 gallons per man all purposes cooking, washing, bathing. (In addition Fd. Amb. personnel 230) Admissions = 33 C.C.S. = 8 R.T.D. = 25	[illegible initials]
	15/8/18		Weather, fine Lt Col W. Ross Gardner D.S.O. [illegible] returned from leave Admissions = 35 C.C.S. = 5 R.T.D. = 16	[illegible initials]

D. D. & L., London, E.C. (1034) Wt W5300/P713 750,000 3/15 E 2688 Forms/C2118/16

Instructions regarding War Diaries and Intelligence Summaries are contained in F. S. Regs., Part II. and the Staff Manual respectively. Title pages will be prepared in manuscript.

WAR DIARY
or
INTELLIGENCE SUMMARY.
(*Erase heading not required.*)

Army Form C. 2118.

VOL XX PAGE VIII

Place	Date	Hour	Summary of Events and Information	Remarks and references to Appendices
RWELD (DRS)	16/8/18	-	Weather fine and warm. One Nissen Hut collected for erection at DRS. Admissions 31 C.C.S. 11 R.T.D. 20	[illegible]
	17/8/18	-	Change in weather: dull and cooler. ADMS visited D.R.S. 1 HD Horse received Admissions 44 CCS 4 RTD. 17	[illegible]
	18/8/18	-	Fine. G.O.C. inspected DRS. Admission 47 CCS. 10 RTD 30	[illegible]

D. D. & L., London, E.C.
(1034) Wt W5300/P713 750,000 3/15 E 2688 Forms/C2118/16

Instructions regarding War Diaries and Intelligence Summaries are contained in F. S. Regs., Part II. and the Staff Manual respectively. Title pages will be prepared in manuscript.

WAR DIARY
or
INTELLIGENCE SUMMARY.
(Erase heading not required.)

Army Form C. 2118.

VOL. XX PAGE IX

Place	Date	Hour	Summary of Events and Information	Remarks and references to Appendices
RWELD (DRS)	19/8/18	-	Fine. Medical arrangements Second Army operation No 25a rec^d from ADMS. Instructions received to collect sick of Artillery Units of Division. Two mules injured by bolting evacuated. Admissions 49 CCS 10 RTD 29	[signature]
	20/8/18	-	Fine ADMS inspected DRS. DMS Army inspected DRS. Admissions 47 CCS 28 RTD 33	[signature]
	21/8/18	-	Fine - very warm Lt Col W. Ross Gardner, RAMC - acting ADMS. Admissions 43 CCS 12 RTD. 32	[signature]

D. D. & L., London, E.C.
(1034) Wt W3500/P713 750,000 3/12 E 2688 Forms/C2118/16

Instructions regarding War Diaries and Intelligence Summaries are contained in F. S. Regs., Part II. and the Staff Manual respectively. Title pages will be prepared in manuscript.

WAR DIARY
or
INTELLIGENCE SUMMARY.
(Erase heading not required.)

Army Form C. 2118.

VOL XX PAGE X

Place	Date	Hour	Summary of Events and Information	Remarks and references to Appendices
RWELD (ARS)	22/8/18	–	Fine. very warm. Secret communications received :– No 322 Cancelling Divisional Code Names. 324. Ref: Model of Divisional Front. 325 Areas administered by Sanitary Sections. Admissions 65 CCS 13 RTD 30	[illegible]
	23/8/18	–	Fine – cooler. Admissions 59 CCS 12 RTD 55	[illegible]
	24/8/18	–	Fine Received from ADMS. No S 332 Location of Units. Admissions 44 CCS 20 RTD. 1	[illegible]

D. D. & L., London, E.C.
(1034) Wt W5300/P713 750,000 3/15 E 2688 Forms/C2118/16

Instructions regarding War Diaries and Intelligence Summaries are contained in F. S. Regs., Part II. and the Staff Manual respectively. Title pages will be prepared in manuscript.

WAR DIARY
or
INTELLIGENCE SUMMARY.
(Erase heading not required.)

Army Form C. 2118.

VOL XX PAGE XI

Place	Date	Hour	Summary of Events and Information	Remarks and references to Appendices
RWELD (5R1)	25/8/18	-	Fine. Thunder storm in the evening OO No 58 received from ADMS (Ref Brigade relief) Admissions 50 CCS 12 RTD 3	[signature]
	26/8/18	-	Weather showery. Admissions 88 CCS 6 RTD 36	[signature]
	27/8/18	-	Showery S. 339 received (Location of Div. Units) OO. 59 received. Move of Division to Rest Area. Admissions 58 CCS 142 RTD. 159	[signature]

D. D. & L., London, E.C.
(10341) Wt W5300/P713 750,000 3/15 E 2688 Forms/C2118/16

Instructions regarding War Diaries and Intelligence Summaries are contained in F. S. Regs., Part II. and the Staff Manual respectively. Title pages will be prepared in manuscript.

WAR DIARY
or
INTELLIGENCE SUMMARY.
(Erase heading not required.)

Army Form C. 2118.

VOL XX. PAGE XII

Place	Date	Hour	Summary of Events and Information	Remarks and references to Appendices
RWELD (DRS)	28/8/18	-	Rain. Heavy downpour about noon.	
		5. am	Major L S C Roche RAMC and 2 ORs proceeded as Billeting party to HALLINES.	
		12 noon	Parties working in forward Area returned to HQ (DRS)	
		2. pm	Transport under Capt. C G H Moore RAMC proceeded by March route to Rest Area: billeted night 28/29 at RENESCURE: arrived LA WATTINE 29/8/18 at 3 pm.	
		4 30 pm	Advance party left and arrived HALLINES 6·30 pm.	
			All Stores, equipment &c handed over to 102 Field Ambulance and relief completed by 6 pm. One Tent Sub division under Captain J J H Ferguson RAMC remained at DRS until 31/8/18.	
		9 0 pm	Main body marched out and proceeded by march route to embussing point: Arrived HALLINES 4 30 am 29/8/18.	
			S/343/4 (41 Div A1 No 40) received 2 pm. This Unit to collect sick of 122 and 124 Brigades. Admission 35, CCS 18, RTD 38	[signature]
HALLINES SHEET 36D F1. d 8.8.	29/8/18	-	Fine.	
		10 am	Major J. La F Lauder RAMC proceeded with 2 ORs as billeting party to LA WATTINE	
		2 pm	Main body left and proceeded by march route to LA WATTINE. Arrived 5 30 pm Location of 122 Bde Unit received and sick collected.	[signature]

D. D. & L., London, E.C.
(1034) Wt W5300/P713 750,000 3/15 E 2688 Forms/C2118/16

Instructions regarding War Diaries and Intelligence Summaries are contained in F. S. Regs., Part II. and the Staff Manual respectively. Title pages will be prepared in manuscript.

WAR DIARY
or
INTELLIGENCE SUMMARY.
(Erase heading not required.)

Army Form C. 2118.

VOL XX PAGE XIII

Place	Date	Hour	Summary of Events and Information	Remarks and references to Appendices
LA WATTINE SHEET 27A P 32. d 5.0.	30/9/18	-	Fine.	
			Orders received to send holding party back to HALLINES to secure billets: 1 N.C.O and 17 ORs proceeded.	[signature]
HALLINES SHEET 36D F2. d 4.6.	31/8/18	-	Fine	
		10 am	Main body with Transport marched out and arrived HALLINES 12 noon	
			Tent Sub Division arrived HALLINES 4 pm from DRS RWELD	[signature]
			S345 received. (Brigade to return to Dickebusch Area)	

for [signature] Major R.A.M.C.
O.C. 133th Field Ambulance.

D. D. & L., London, E.C.
(1834?) Wt W5300/P713 750,000 3/18 E 2688 Forms/C2118/16

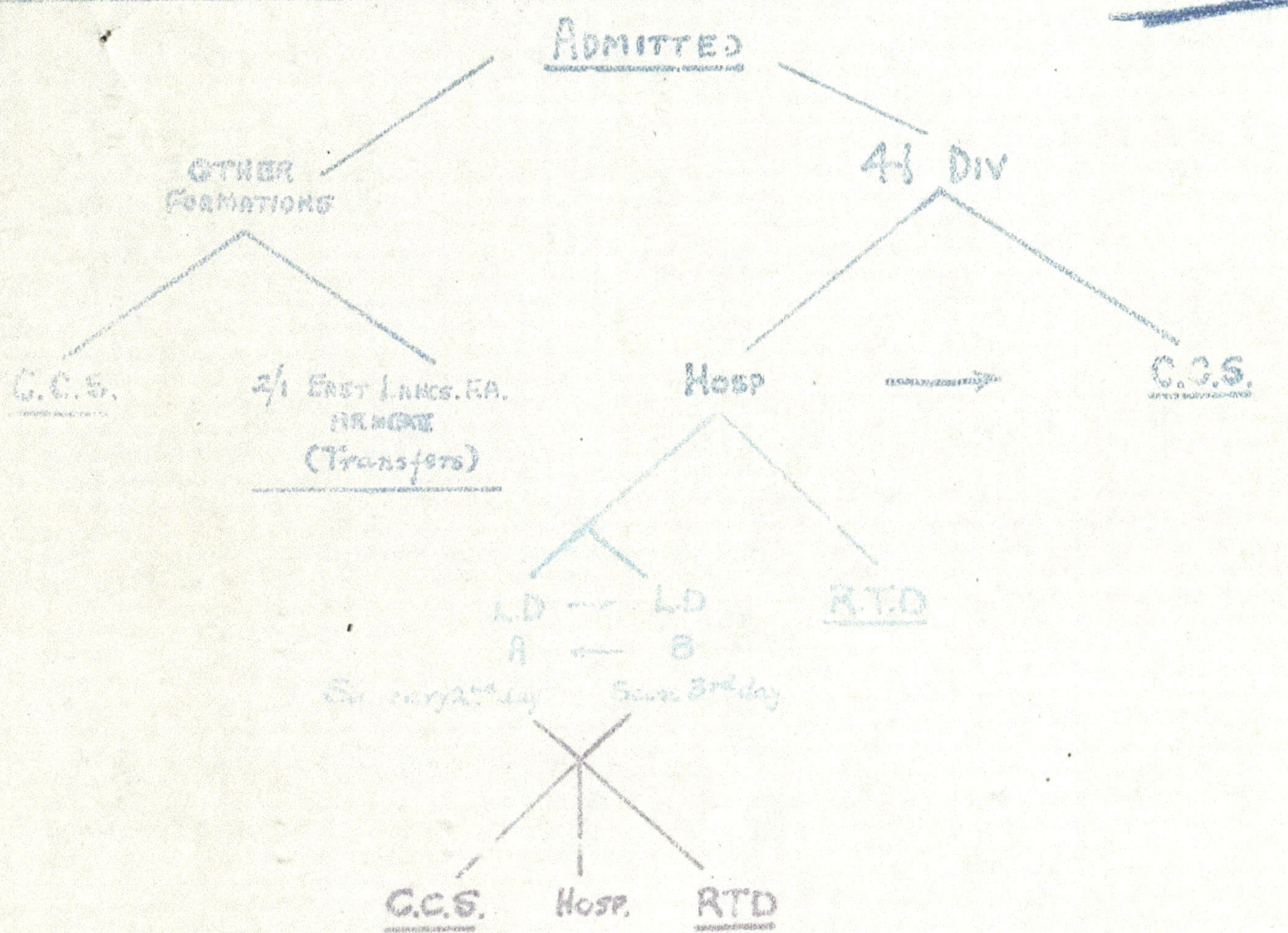

DISPOSAL
APP 3
ADMITTED
OTHER FORMATIONS
41 DIV
C.C.S.
2/1 EAST LANCS. F.A.
(Transfers)
HOSP
C.C.S.
L.D
L.D
A
B
R.T.D
C.C.S.
HOSP.
RTD

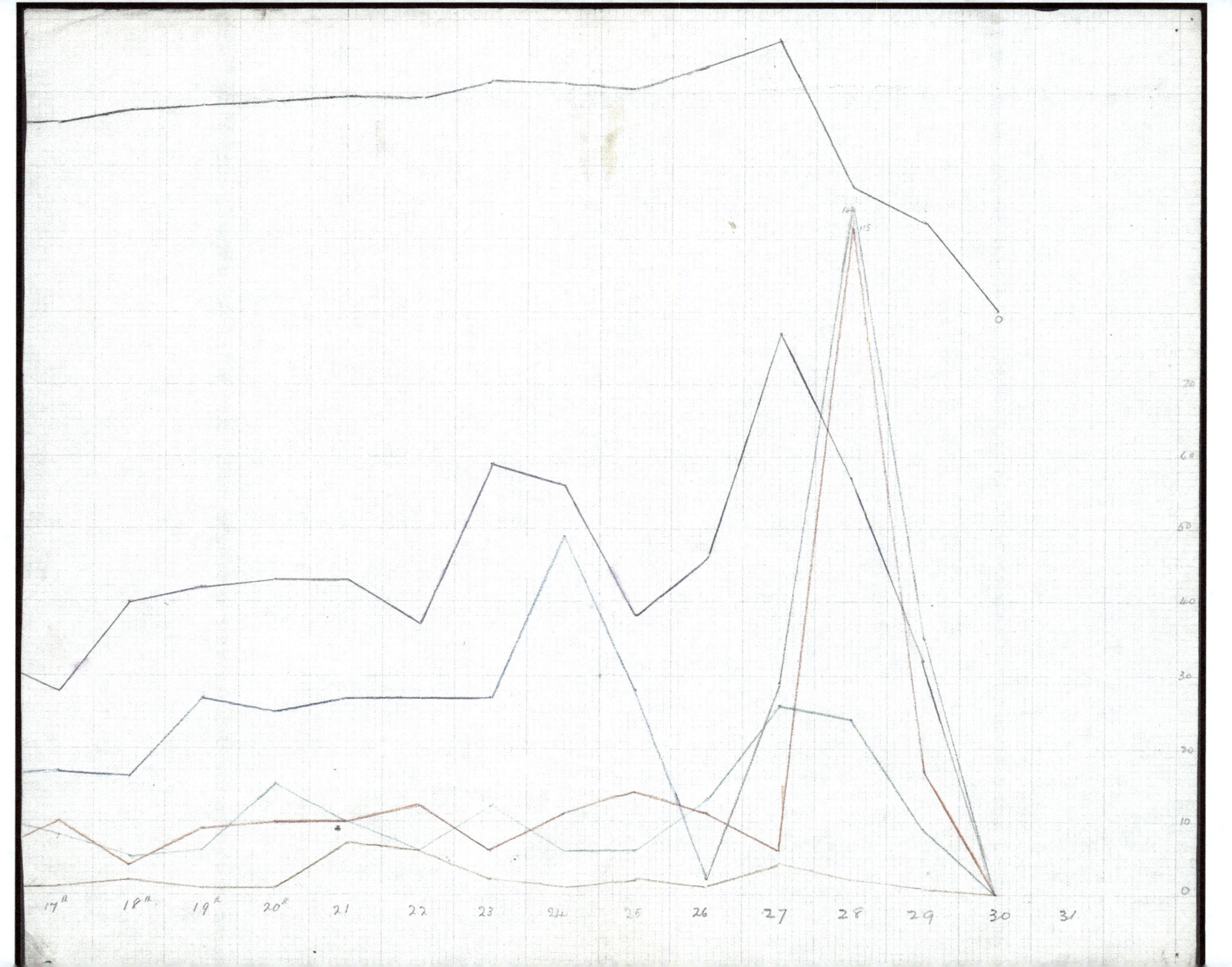
70
60
50
40
30
20
10
0
17th
18th
19th
20th
21
22
23
24
25
26
27
28
29
30
31

28031 W3125/M2250 1000m 6/17 M.R.Co.,Ltd. (1367) Forms W3091

Army Form W.3091.

Vol 29

14/34/01

Cover for Documents.

Sept 1918

Nature of Enclosures.

CONFIDENTIAL

WAR DIARY

OF

138th FIELD AMBULANCE

FROM 1/9/18 TO 30/9/18

(VOLUME XXI)

3

Notes, or Letters written.

Sept 1918

Instructions regarding War Diaries and Intelligence Summaries are contained in F. S. Regs., Part II. and the Staff Manual respectively. Title pages will be prepared in manuscript.

WAR DIARY
or
~~INTELLIGENCE SUMMARY.~~
(Erase heading not required.)

Army Form C. 2118.

VOLUME XXI Page 1

Place	Date	Hour	Summary of Events and Information	Remarks and references to Appendices
HALLINES	1/9/18	1 am	122 Bde O.O. 222 received.	
		6.30 am	Transport moved off under Capt C.G. Moore, RAMC and proceeded by march route to ABEELE area; arriving 6.0 pm	
		7.0 am	Main body moved off under Capt J.J.H Ferguson, RAMC and proceeded by march route to LUMBRES entrained there 10.0 am and arrived ABEELE area 5.0 pm Billeted for night REMY SIDING. Weather fine. ADMS. No 1332 (Lectures on application of Thomas' Splints for fractured femurs) received.	WRG
REMY SIDING (Sheet 27. L 23. a 4 7)	2/9/18	-	Weather fine. Major J. La F. Lauder, DSO, RAMC reconnoitred the forward area to locate suitable sites for ADSs. H.Q. of Field Ambulance established at REMY SIDING.	
		2 pm	Major L.S.C Roche, RAMC with one bearer sub-division, 3 large cars and 1 Ford proceeded to ST DUNSTANS (Sheet 28. H.22. b 8.3) to establish there Left Sub Sector A.D.S Capt J.J.H. Ferguson, MC. RAMC, with one bearer sub division, 2 large cars and 1 Ford proceeded to LONGBARN (Sheet 28. G.30. d. 6.8) to establish there Right Sub. Sector A.D.S. One Officer, two bearer sub divisions, 6 Stretcher carriages, and 4 Ambulance Cars reported from 140 Field Ambulance for duty.	WRG
— " —	3/9/18	-	Capt C G H. Moore, RAMC and 2 tent sub divisions proceeded to take over from 133 Field Ambulance, the Advanced Army Dysentry Centre at HILLHOEK: party reinforced later by 6 additional O Ranks. One Officer, 37 OR, RAMC and 6 wheeled stretcher carriages reported for duty from 139 Fd Amb. Captain Mitchell, RAMC relieved Captain Ferguson, RAMC at Longbarn. Captain Ferguson posted as temporary M O 12th East Surrey Regt, vice Captain Christie evacuated "gassed". (Contd)	WRG

D. D. & L., London, E.C.
(10341) Wt W5300/P713 750,000 3/18 B 2188 Forms/C2118/16

Instructions regarding War Diaries and Intelligence Summaries are contained in F. S. Regs., Part II. and the Staff Manual respectively. Title pages will be prepared in manuscript.

WAR DIARY
or
~~INTELLIGENCE SUMMARY.~~
(*Erase heading not required.*)

Army Form C. 2118.

VOLUME XXI Page 2.

Place	Date	Hour	Summary of Events and Information	Remarks and references to Appendices
REMY (HQ)	–	–	(Continued) 2 OR, RAMC, personnel of Field Ambulance, evacuated "gassed". Warning Order of impending offensive received from Division 9 pm: Confirmed 11 pm	WRG
— " —	4/9/18	–	Weather fine. Reported for duty:– 1 Officer 16 O Ranks RAMC from 139 Field Amb 1 –"– 26 — " — " 140 " " 3 lorries for evacuation of walking wounded. Personnel at each ADS augmented to 72 O Ranks. Ambulance cars at LONGBARN 7 ST DUNSTANS 6 + Casualties. LONGBARN Lying 88 Sitting 358 } Total 463 ST DUNSTANS " 17 " 50 OOs received in connection with operations. No 224 from 122 Inf Bde No 226 " 123 " " No 214 " 124 " " A.A Dysentery Centre. Admissions 21. Discharges 84 Relief of bearers: half relieved 7 pm: remainder 7 am 5/9/18. ADS established at VIJVERHOEK (H 29 c 3 6) instead of ST DUNSTANS. Latter post now Car Exchange	WRG + See app 2 } See appendix I
— " —	5/9/18	–	Weather fine. One bearer sub division from each ADS returned to HQ. 2 lorries returned to depot. Received:– From 122 Bde OO No 225: General situation on Brigade front " 122 " OO " 226 } " 123 " OO " 215 } Relief of Brigades in line by 123 Bde " 124 " OO " 227 } (Continued)	WRG

D. D. & L., London, E.C.
(1034) Wt W5300/P713 750,000 3/15 E 2188 Forms/C2118/16

Instructions regarding War Diaries and Intelligence Summaries are contained in F. S. Regs., Part II. and the Staff Manual respectively. Title pages will be prepared in manuscript.

WAR DIARY
or
~~INTELLIGENCE~~ SUMMARY.

(Erase heading not required.)

Army Form C. 2118.

VOLUME XXI Page 3.

Place	Date	Hour	Summary of Events and Information	Remarks and references to Appendices
			(Continued) Casualties NOON - NOON. LONGBARN Lying 16 Sitting 153 } Total 209. VIJVERHOEK " 23 " 17 Road DICKEBUSCH - CAFE BELGE clear and passable by large cars Road CAFE BELGE - ST DUNSTANS passable by Ford cars only - by day. AADC. Admissions 17. Discharges 82.	WRS
REMY (HQ)	6-9-18	-	Weather fine during day: thunder storm in evening. Remaining lorry returned to Depot. Received from ADMS S 356 Situation Medical Units 2/Army. S 357 Location of Units 41/Div. Casualties to NOON. LONGBARN Lying 22 Sitting 31 } Total 72. VIJVERHOEK " 3 " 16 Road CAFE BELGE - ST DUNSTANS now clear + passable by all traffic night + day. AADC. Admissions 29 Discharges 2	WRS
"	7-9-18	-	Weather - morning fine: afternoon, thunderstorm - heavy rain. ADMS and O.C Field Ambulance visited ADSs. Received S. 358 ref. relief of Div. Artillery. Casualties LONGBARN Lying 6 Sitting 34 } Total 79 VIJVERHOEK " 6 " 30 23 "gassed" cases were evacuated from 124 Bde HQ during night 6-7/9/18. ST DUNSTANS Car Exchange post with stores taken over by a 35/Div Inf Bde HQ. LA LAITERIE taken over by Field Amb. A.ADC Admissions 7 Discharges 39	WRS —

D. D. & L., London, E.C.
(1034) Wt W5300/P713 750,000 3/15 E 2688 Forms/C2118/16

Army Form C. 2118.

WAR DIARY
or
~~INTELLIGENCE SUMMARY.~~
(Erase heading not required.)

Instructions regarding War Diaries and Intelligence Summaries are contained in F. S. Regs., Part II. and the Staff Manual respectively. Title pages will be prepared in manuscript.

VOLUME XXI Page 4.

Place	Date	Hour	Summary of Events and Information	Remarks and references to Appendices
REMY HQ.	8/9/18	–	Weather showery. Handing over of ST DUNSTANS to 35/Div. completed 9 am. Holding party, Field Amb. occupied LA LAITERIE. DICKEBUSCH. Casualties. LONGBARN. Lying 6 Sitting 47 } Total 62. VIJVERHOEK. " 5 " 4 } A.A.D.C Admissions 17. Discharges 21. Shelling VIERSTRAAT - HALLEBAST Rd about 5 pm H.E.	WRS
— — —	9/9/18	–	Weather still showery. Constructive work at ADSs commenced. 20 Rame 1 NCO RE + 3 sappers reported LONGBARN. – Six elephant shelters to be erected. 20 " 1 " " 3 " " VIJVERHOEK { Propping + improving overhead protection sandbagging etc. 10 " 1 " " 3 " " LA LAITERIE for Camouflage work under XIX Corps Camouflage Offr. Casualties. LONGBARN. Lying 4 Sitting 28 } Total 37. VIJVERHOEK. " 5 " 4 } A A D C Admissions 21 Discharges 12. Received. From ADMS. S 362. Forecast of Brigade Relief. S 361 Location Medical Units 2/Army. S 364. Location Transport Lines. Shelling morning Scottish Wood. 1.30 pm to 2.30 pm. H 27. 28. 4 pm to 5 pm H 26.	WRS

D. D. & L., London, E.C.
(10341) Wt W3300/P713 750,000 3/15 B 2188 Forms/C2118/16

Instructions regarding War Diaries and Intelligence Summaries are contained in F. S. Regs., Part II. and the Staff Manual respectively. Title pages will be prepared in manuscript.

Army Form C. 2118.

WAR DIARY
or
~~INTELLIGENCE SUMMARY.~~
(Erase heading not required.)

VOLUME XXI Page 5

Place	Date	Hour	Summary of Events and Information	Remarks and references to Appendices
REMY HQ	10/9/18	–	Weather fine. Showery. OC Field Amb and Major Lander inspected the feet of men of 'D' Co 23/MDX. Hospital treatment recommended for officers & men of whole Coy (ration strength 105). ADMS visited HQ Field Amb. 75 OR 23/MDX admitted Field Amb & treated for trench feet. Arrangements being made for treating feet of all 122 Inf. Bde prior to returning into the line. HOPOUTRE Baths selected: treatment to take place 13th & 14th. 100 men – working party from Support Battalion – reported LONGBARN for removing dung heap. Construction work at ADSs proceeded with. 2 Shelters completed at LONGBARN. Casualties LONGBARN Lying – Sitting S. 49 W 7 VIJVERHOEK – – S 7 W – } Total 63. Very busy night with sick: chief causes Diarrhoea & Pyrexia. Several cases Bronchitis. also cases of Trench feet. 11/Queens sent largest number cases. A.A.D.S. Admissions 18. Discharges 19. 5 Reinforcements reported for duty. Shelling at H. 35 about 4 pm H. 28 29 night. Machine Gun was shooting up WYTSCHAETE–VIERSTRAAT Road (I.S. No6)	WRS
– – –	11/9/18	–	Heavy rain. Dull. Continuous rain making roads and tracks bad. OC Field Amb and Major Lander prospected for suitable site for Trench Foot Preparation Centre. Baths being erected at ADS Longbarn. Clearing and construction work progressing at ADSs. Road from CAFE BELGE up to H. 23 c 0 1 badly in need of repair owing to rain. ADMS visited HQ Field Amb. CASUALTIES LONGBARN { Lying S. 1 W 13 Sitting S. 30 W 6 VIJVERHOEK { Lying S. – W – Sitting S 6 W 1 } Total 57 A fairly busy night on Right Sub Sector (Longbarn). A working party of 20 DLI caught by shelling in VIERSTRAAT Area. A number of bad stretcher cases. Shelling:– VIERSTRAAT Area 11 pm – 1 am 12/9/18 H.E DICKEBUSCH Area 9 am to 3 pm (desultory. HE) CAFE BELGE Area 10 pm – 2 am 12/9/18 desultory 5.9 AADS Admissions 6 Discharges 4 (Continued)	WRS ✓

D. D. & L., London, E.C.
(1034) Wt W3300/P713 750,000 3/15 B 2688 Forms/C2118/16

Army Form C. 2118.

Instructions regarding War Diaries and Intelligence Summaries are contained in F. S. Regs., Part II. and the Staff Manual respectively. Title pages will be prepared in manuscript.

WAR DIARY
or
~~INTELLIGENCE SUMMARY.~~
(Erase heading not required.)

VOLUME XXI. Page 6.

Place	Date	Hour	Summary of Events and Information	Remarks and references to Appendices
			(Continued) Central Medical Inspection Room opened at (Sheet 28) G 21 a 7 2 for inspection of Battalion Sick under Capt. Bain. RAMC.	WRG
REMY HQ	12/9/18	–	Weather continues dull and stormy. Heavy rains. ADMS and OC Field Amb visited forward area. Received from ADMS. Location of Divisional Units " " 122 Inf Bde. OO No 227. (9 pm) " " 123 " " OO " 231 (12 midnight) 10 RAMC of working party transferred from Right to Left Sub Sector; and 7 returned to HQ. C.R.E. visited LONGBARN and recommended structural alterations. CASUALTIES. LONGBARN Lying S. 3 W 3 Sitting S. 31* W 4 } Total 56. VIJVERHOEK Lying S. – W 1 Sitting S. 12 W 2 * Includes 3 personnel of 140 Field Amb. SHELLING. H.35 a. H.29.c 6 pm to 4 am. (13/9/18) DICKEBUSCH – CAFE BELGE 5.9. 4.2. HE. H 28 a + b 2.45 pm to 3.30 pm 5.9 8? H.E AADS. Admissions 26 Discharges 6.	WRG
—.—	13/9/18	– 7 am	Weather fine. 10 OR RAMC commenced treatment of the feet of all men of 122 Inf Bde for prevention of Trench Feet at HOPOUTRE Baths: to be treated at the rate of 150 per hour. 7 OR RAMC proceeded to Baths at G 24. d. 2 0 to establish there a Trench foot preparation + prevention Centre. 813 men of 122 Bde treated at HOPOUTRE Baths. Casualties. LONGBARN Lying S. 8 W 2 Sitting S 93 W 3 } Total 111. VIJVERHOEK Lying S – W – Lying S 4 W 1 (Continued)	WRG

D. D. & L., London, E.C.
(1034.) Wt W5300/P713 750,000 5/15 E 2188 Forms/C2118/16

Instructions regarding War Diaries and Intelligence Summaries are contained in F. S. Regs., Part II. and the Staff Manual respectively. Title pages will be prepared in manuscript.

WAR DIARY
or
~~INTELLIGENCE SUMMARY.~~
(Erase heading not required.)

Army Form C. 2118.

VOLUME XXI. Page 7.

Place	Date	Hour	Summary of Events and Information	Remarks and references to Appendices
			(Continued) Dvr E. Roach, ASC. MT wounded in the back with shrapnel about 8.30 pm whilst his Ford Car which was out of action was being towed back to ADS LONGBARN. Car damaged to slight extent. Driver Roach evacuated to CCS. No 4 RAP now being evacuated via track along narrow gauge line from GORDON FARM to HALLEBAST - VIERSTRAAT RD. SHELLING. On road opposite ADS VIJVERHOEK H.29 c.2.8 thence along to H.28 b. with H.E.* morning continuously: afternoon intermittently. Shrapnel between ADS & Lake. Cross Roads N.10.b.9.5 with 5.9 4.30 to 5.30 pm. VIERSTRAAT. BARDENBURG RD. Shrapnel 5.30 - 6.30 pm CAFE BELGE - DICKEBUSCH 5.9 Gas. 5.0 pm to 3.0 am. A.ADS. Admissions 26. Discharges 24. Received. From 122 Bde. Defence Scheme. " S.366 Move of 124 Bde to LICQUES Area " OO 217 from 124 Bde ref. move.	* Intelligence reports 15 cm How: WRG
REMY HQ.	14/9/18	-	Fine. Showery. Balance of men of 122 Inf Bde treated at HOPOUTRE BATHS. Working party of 100 men withdrawn from LONGBARN. Casualties LONGBARN. Lying S. W. 1, Sitting S. 16 W. - } Total 25. VIJVERHOEK Lying S. W. : Sitting S. 3 W. 5* } * Includes Pte Proctor, RAMC, 139 Field Amb "Bearer" Collections & evacuations from line now all proceeding through LONGBARN A.DS. (except walking wounded) Madden at LONGBARN now cleared out. SHELLING. VIJVERHOEK 1.30 to 2 pm. Mixed Gas & HE. VIJVERHOEK, CAFE BELGE, DICKEBUSCH } throughout evening & night at intervals } Gas & HE. Red Cross Flag pole brought down by shell at 6 pm. 1. OR RAMC slightly gassed - evacuated. H 26.d. Gas Shells. A.A.D.S. Admissions 75. Discharges 16.	WRG

D. D. & L., London, E.C.
(10341) Wt W5300/P713 750,000 3/15 E 2188 Forms/C2118/16

Instructions regarding War Diaries and Intelligence Summaries are contained in F. S. Regs., Part II. and the Staff Manual respectively. Title pages will be prepared in manuscript.

WAR DIARY
or
~~INTELLIGENCE SUMMARY.~~
(Erase heading not required.)

Army Form C. 2118.

VOLUME XXI. Page 8.

Place	Date	Hour	Summary of Events and Information	Remarks and references to Appendices
REMY HQ	15/9/18	–	Fine. Warm. Roads drying up well. Casualties LONGBARN Lying S. 3 W. 3 Sitting S. 19 W. 2 } Total 37. VIJVERHOEK Lying S. – W. – Sitting S. 10 W. – } Collections from No 4 RAP to bearer relay post, thence to ADS VIJVERHOEK. No Shelling reported from ADSs. Capt H M Godfrey Rame returned from leave: reported ADS LONGBARN for duty. Secret 369 received from ADMS. ADMS notify that No 62 CCS. 2/Canadian CCS and No 10 CCS are returning to their old site at REMY SIDING. AADS. Admissions 24 Discharges 19. A report of work done at this Centre for the week ending Sept 14. is attached.	WRS
REMY HQ.	16/9/18	–	Fine. bright + sunny. ADMS + OC Field Amb visited new site of Field Amb HQ at HOOGGRAAF, and holding party sent to new HQ. to repair roof to. Casualties LONGBARN Lying S. – W. 1 Sitting S. 22 W. 4 } Total 37. 2 OR personnel of 140 F. Amb evacuated gassed (slightly) VIJVERHOEK Lying S. – W. 1 Sitting S. 5 W. 4 } Evacuations from line now all through ADS LONGBARN. Working party (Infantry) reinstated at LONGBARN. No Shelling reported. Received: Secrets No 370 371. 372 + Medical Scheme (provisional) 41/Div: Thunderstorm with heavy rain during night. AADS Admissions 30. Discharges 29	WRS

D. D. & L., London, E.C.
(10341) Wt W3300/P713 750,000 3/15 B 2488 Forms/C2118/16

Instructions regarding War Diaries and Intelligence Summaries are contained in F. S. Regs., Part II. and the Staff Manual respectively. Title pages will be prepared in manuscript.

WAR DIARY
or
~~INTELLIGENCE SUMMARY.~~
(Erase heading not required.)

Army Form C. 2118.

VOLUME XXI Page 9.

Place	Date	Hour	Summary of Events and Information	Remarks and references to Appendices
REMY HQ	17/9/18	–	Fine. HQ transferred to HOOGGRAAF. (Sheet 28. G 26 c. 44) Roof retiled new HQ by holding party. Casualties LONGBARN Lying S. 15 W. 2 Sitting S. 7 W. 4 } Total 33. VIJVERHOEK Lying S. – W. – Sitting S. 4 W. 1 No 3 RAP. hit by shell about 10 am. One Regimental stretcher bearer wounded: Ford car damaged. New position of RAP on same side road. 20 yards NW of old position. 100 working party of 11/Queens and 10 REs working at LONGBARN. Arrangements made for erecting 2. 18' cupola dugouts at 3 RAP and later 2. 18' cupola dugouts at N4 b 38. 25 RAMC OR and 3 RE working party under OC 228 Field Co. commenced work 1 pm. Stores (surplus) transferred from VIJVERHOEK to LONGBARN. Water tins refilled at BUSSEBOOM water point. Shelling. N. 10 b 37 HV. 10 am. ADS VIJVERHOEK and CAFE BELGE Rd } 9 pm to 5 am. HE + Gas. OO 228 received. Battalion reliefs. AADS. Admissions 7 Discharges 25.	WRG
HOOGGRAAF Sheet 28. (G26. c 44)	18/9/18	–	Fine. 3. GS Wagons and RAMC OR working party sent to LONGBARN to salve Nissen huts. ADMS visited HQ Field Amb.	WRG

(Continued)

D. D. & L., London, E.C.
(1034.) Wt W5300/P713 750,000 3/18 E 2188 Forms/C2118/16

Instructions regarding War Diaries and Intelligence Summaries are contained in F. S. Regs., Part II. and the Staff Manual respectively. Title pages will be prepared in manuscript.

WAR DIARY
or
~~INTELLIGENCE SUMMARY.~~
(Erase heading not required.)

Army Form C. 2118.

VOLUME XXI Page 10

Place	Date	Hour	Summary of Events and Information	Remarks and references to Appendices
			(Continued) Casualties. LONGBARN Lying S. – W. 1 Sitting S. 28 W. 10; VIJVERHOEK Lying S. – W. – Sitting S. 2 W. – } Total 41.	
			Shelling. Cafe Belge Road + Vicinity 8 pm to 6 am (19-9-18) HE + Gas. Vicinity LONGBARN ADS 6 am (19-9-18) H.V. 5.9	
			GOC XIV Div. visited LONGBARN ADS. Major Barton Rame 46 F Amb XIV Div. visited LONGBARN ADS.	WRG
			AADS. Admissions 5 Discharges 29	
			Secret 374 received: Location of Units. Secret 375 " XIV Division to take over VIJVERHOEK ADS + LAITERIE	
HOOGGRAAF HQ.	19/9/18	–	Fine. Showery. XIV Division took over VIJVERHOEK ADS and LAITERIE. Surplus Stores handed over and personnel returned to HQ.	WRG
			Casualties LONGBARN Lying S. – W. 4 Sitting 18, 2 } 24.	
			Shelling Ouderdom 10-11 pm HV. HE. Bardenburg (No 3 RAP) 12.30 to 2 pm HE 5.9 4.2	
			The working party of 50 men at RAP No 3 was heavily shelled and ordered by an Officer of 19/MAX to withdraw. They reported back to ADS Longbarn.	
			ADMS visited HQ Field Amb.	
			AADS. Admissions 3 Discharges 14	

D. D. & L., London, E.C. (10341) Wt W5300/P713 750,000 3/18 E 2688 Forms/C2118/16

Instructions regarding War Diaries and Intelligence Summaries are contained in F. S. Regs., Part II. and the Staff Manual respectively. Title pages will be prepared in manuscript.

WAR DIARY
or
~~INTELLIGENCE SUMMARY.~~
(*Erase heading not required.*)

Army Form C. 2118.

VOLUME XXI Page 11

Place	Date	Hour	Summary of Events and Information	Remarks and references to Appendices
HOOGGRAAF HQ.	20/9/18	-	Fine. Major L.S.C. Roche, RAMC proceeded on leave. Capt C.W.B. Littlejohn, RAMC i/c ADS LONGBARN. Working party 36 OR RAMC reported LONGBARN. Casualties. LONGBARN. Lying S 3, W 2; Sitting 10, 4 } Total 19. No shelling reported. Received S. 379. Light Railway Service from REMY to DAN SIDING ceased. Cases for D.R.S to be evacuated by arrangement with No 2 MAC. S. 384 Location of Div. Units. S. 381 " . Med. Units 2/Army. A.A.D.C. Admissions 9. Discharges 17.	WCL
HOOGGRAAF HQ.	21/9/18	-	Fine. OC Field Ambulance visited LONGBARN + forward Area. Working party 23 Mdx at LONGBARN. Casualties. Lying S 1, W -; Sitting 5, 2 } Total 8. Shelling. - No shelling reported by ADS 4 pm. About 6 - HE shells in vicinity of HQ. Field Amb. Casualties from 23/Mdx. A.A.D.C. removed from HILLHOEK to 139 Field Ambulance. O.C. 139 Field Amb. now responsible for administration of this Centre. Received S. 385 Medical Arrangements XIX Corps: (Operations on a large scale entailing heavy casualties)	WCL

D. D. & L., London, E.C.
(1034 1) Wt W5300/P713 750,000 3/15 E 2688 Forms/C2118/16

Instructions regarding War Diaries and Intelligence Summaries are contained in F. S. Regs., Part II. and the Staff Manual respectively. Title pages will be prepared in manuscript.

WAR DIARY
or
~~INTELLIGENCE SUMMARY.~~
(Erase heading not required.)

Army Form C. 2118.

VOLUME XXI Page 12

Place	Date	Hour	Summary of Events and Information	Remarks and references to Appendices
HOOGGRAAF HQ.	22/9/18	-	Fine. Showery. Car Post at BRICK HOUSE withdrawn 33 OR. Rame returned to 139 F.Amb. also 4 Wheeled Stretchers and 1 Sunbeam Car. Casualties. S. W. Sitting 5 Lying 1 } Total 6. No shelling reported by ADS.	WRG
HOOGGRAAF HQ.	23/9/18	-	Fine. Showery. Remainder of personnel of 139 Field Amb. returned to their Unit. Personnel and 6 Stretcher Carriages returned to 140 Field Amb. Personnel withdrawn from AADC and ADS LONGBARN. ADMS 41 Div. visited HQ. Field Amb. Received from ADMS. Secret 388. Copy of OO issued by this Unit 6/17 " 389 Location Units 122 Inf Bde. " 390. Location of Units. " 384 Situation Med. Units 2/Army. " 386 2/Army Special Centres.	WRG

D. D. & L., London, E.C.
(1034) Wt W3300/P713 750,000 3/15 E 2688 Forms/C2118/16

Instructions regarding War Diaries and Intelligence Summaries are contained in F. S. Regs., Part II, and the Staff Manual respectively. Title pages will be prepared in manuscript.

WAR DIARY
or
~~INTELLIGENCE SUMMARY.~~
(Erase heading not required.)

Army Form C. 2118.

VOLUME XXI. Page 13.

Place	Date	Hour	Summary of Events and Information	Remarks and references to Appendices
HOOGGRAAF HQ.	24/9/18	-	Fine. O.C. Field Amb. attended conference at 122 Inf Bde HQ. RAMC runners attached to 187 and 190 Bde RFA. Capt J. J. H. Ferguson. RAMC returned to HQ for duty, from 12 East Surrey Regt. Received from ADMS. Secret No 392 (41 Div Ad. Instructions No 46) Instructions drawn up for guidance of Battalion runners. Lecture by Major Lauder RAMC to Battalion runners of this Unit.	WRG
HOOGGRAAF HQ.	25/9/18	-	Fine. showery. BM 410 received from 122 Inf Bde re manoeuvres to be held on 26/9/18. Received from ADMS. Secret 393. Amendments to Medical Arrangements. 395 XIX Corps Admin. Instructions. Traffic Control. 396. Amendment to 41 Div: Admin: Instructions. No 46. 394. Amendments to locations. Runners posted to Battalions of 122 Inf. Bde.	WRG
HOOGGRAAF HQ.	26/9/18	-	Fine. Light Echelon of Field Ambulance took part in Brigade Manoeuvres. Conference ADMS Office 5.30 pm. Received from ADMS Secret 398 Location Medical Units 2/Army Received from 122 Inf. Bde. Secret Admin: Instructions Nos 1 + 2.	WRG

D. D. & L., London, E.C.
(1034) Wt W3300/P713 750,000 3/18 E 2688 Forms/C2118/16

Instructions regarding War Diaries and Intelligence Summaries are contained in F. S. Regs., Part II. and the Staff Manual respectively. Title pages will be prepared in manuscript.

WAR DIARY
or
~~INTELLIGENCE SUMMARY.~~
(Erase heading not required.)

Army Form C. 2118.

VOLUME XXI Page 141

Place	Date	Hour	Summary of Events and Information	Remarks and references to Appendices
HOOGGRAAF	27/9/18	–	Fine. Capt C G Moore, RAMC Capt + QM J Starkie RAMC One tent sub division, with transport stores and equipment not required for active operations moved by route march to HILLHOEK DRS established there. Received from ADMS Secret MP 47 " " Secret 400 Received from 122 Inf Bde Secret SCG 81 " " " Secret 435 " " " Secret Admin Instructions Nos 3 and 4	WRG
HOOGGRAAF	28/10/18	– 5.40 am 6.30 am 1.30 pm 8.0 pm	Dull with heavy rain. Capt J J H Ferguson, RAMC and 3 OR RAMC proceeded as billeting party to G 22 b 2 3 Main body Field Ambulance moved off to G 22 b 23 with remainder of transport. Moved off to new site H 15 d 5 3 Moved off and proceeded by route march to SWAN CHATEAU I 19 c 5 7. Arrived 10 pm and billetted there for the night. Received from 122 Inf Bde Secret Instructions No 5. 123 Bde will be attacking through 124 Bde at 7.30 am 122 Inf Bde will move into reserve 138 Field Ambulance will move to vicinity of VERBRANDEN MOLEN	WRG

D. D. & L., London, E.C.
(1034 ?) Wt W5300/P713 750,000 3/15 E 2688 Forms/C2118/16

Instructions regarding War Diaries and Intelligence Summaries are contained in F. S. Regs., Part II. and the Staff Manual respectively. Title pages will be prepared in manuscript.

WAR DIARY
or
~~INTELLIGENCE SUMMARY.~~
(Erase heading not required.)

Army Form C. 2118.

VOLUME XXI Page 15

Place	Date	Hour	Summary of Events and Information	Remarks and references to Appendices
SWAN CHATEAU 28/I 19 c 5.4	29/9/18	–	Fine. Rain latter part of day.	
		10 am	Field Ambulance moved off by route march to VERBRANDEN MOLEN I 28 d 6.6, and occupied vacated German dugouts under Railway embankment. Transport proceeded as far as condition of roads would permit to vicinity of dugouts. Bearer squads sent to 122 Brigade Battalions and Relay posts of 140 Field Amb. Bearers assisted with evacuation of patients from ADS of 140 Field Amb at VERBRANDEN [illegible] owing to rain which rendered evacuation difficult. [illegible] Road in very bad condition owing to rain [illegible] stretchers could not be used. Stretcher cases carried to Horse Ambulances about a Kilometre distance on main road.	[illegible]
VERBRANDEN MOLEN 28/I 26 a 6.6	30/9/18	–	Rain.	
		5.0 am	Party of 10 OR RAMC repaired bridge over stream in order that ADS limbers could proceed to new site and cars.	
		5.30 am	One tent sub division (W. Estes) proceeded to new site at KORTEWILDE 28/P.14.a.3.9 and established A.D.S. there. Casualties received & evacuated wounded 8 Sick 3. Bearers continued with evacuations at VERBRANDEN MOLEN and 1 NCO and 8 bearers under Lieut Manger M O R C remained behind to assist with evacuations, while remainder of Ambulance with transport proceeded to new ADS at KORTEWILDE and billetted there for the night.	[illegible]

[illegible signature]
Lt Col RAMC
[illegible] 138th F.A.

D. D. & L., London, E.C.
(1034.) Wt W5300/P713 750,000 5/15 E 2188 Forms/C2118/16

ADVANCED ARMY DYSENTRY CENTRE *App 1*

138 FIELD AMBULANCE — SEPTEMBER 1918

DATE	ADMISSIONS	DISCHARGES: DUTY	CORPS REST STATION	64 CCS	ORDINARY CCS	102 FA	NZ STAT.	14 DRS	34 DRS	35 DRS	63 [illegible]	TOTAL DISCHARGES
3	24	-	26	6	1							33
4	21	1	50	18	15							84
5	17	1	19	8	54							82
6	29	-	-	2	-							2
7	7	-	14	8	17							39
8	17	3	7	3	8							21
9	21	-	9	-	3							12
10	18	-	8	7	4							19
11	6	-	-	-	4							4
12	26	-	-	-	-	6						6
13	26	-	12	5	1				6			24
14	75	1	6	-	-		2	1	5	1		16
15	24	-	2	-	1	6	8	2	-			19
16	30	-	7	-	-	-	7	4	9	2		29
7	7	-	7	-	-	10	8	[illegible]	-	-		25
18	5	1	9	-	-	-	-	10	2	-	7	29
19	3	-	1	-	1	-	-	3	5		4	14
20	9	1	5	-	-	-	-	2	9	-	-	17
21												
22	From 21/9/18 139 Field Ambulance											
23	took over A.A.D. Centre.											
24												
25												
26												

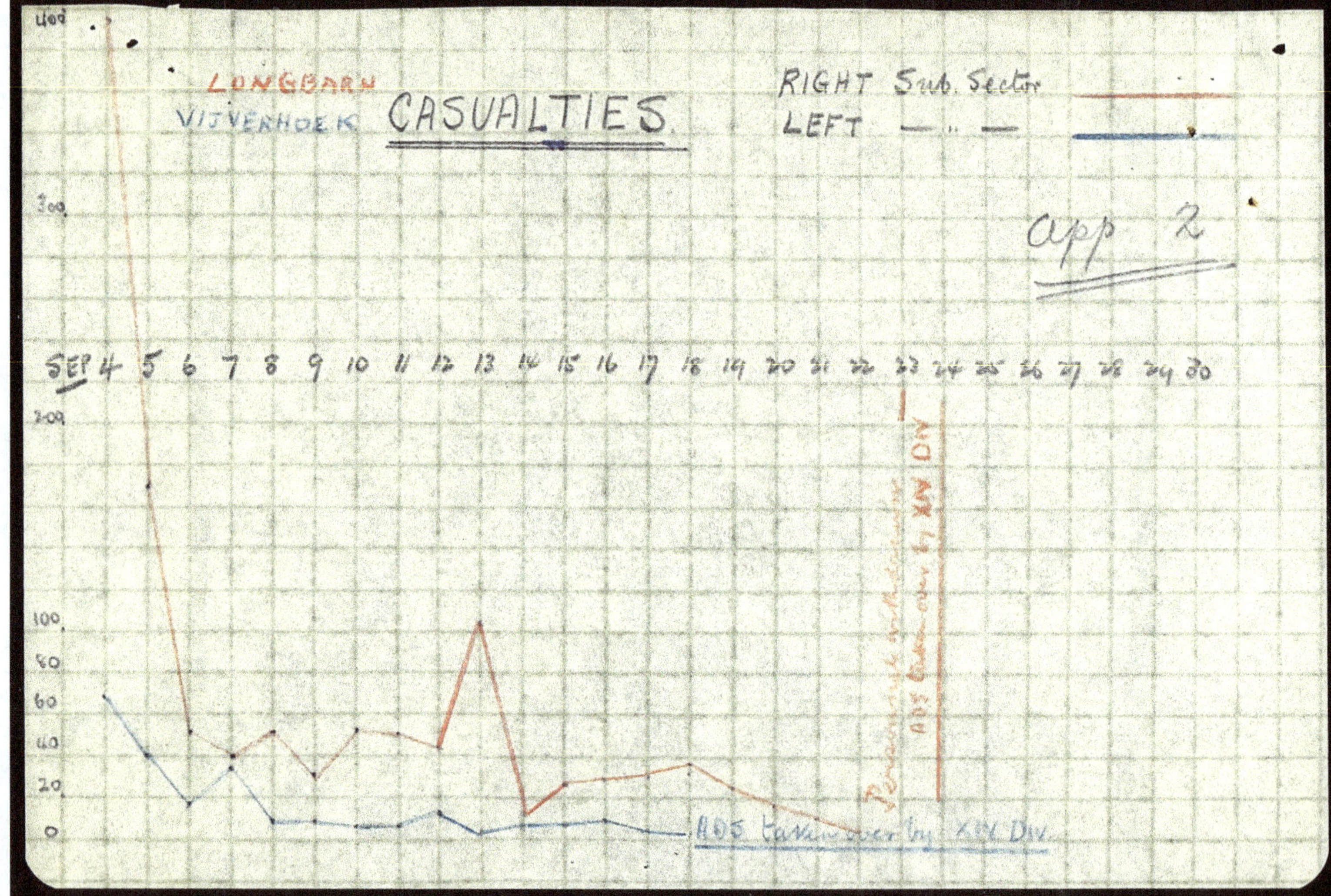
LONGBARN
VIJVERHOEK
CASUALTIES
RIGHT Sub. Sector
LEFT — " —
App 2
400
300
200
100
80
60
40
20
0
SEP 4 5 6 7 8 9 10 11 12 13 14 15 16 17 18 19 20 21 22 23 24 25 26 27 28 29 30
ADS taken over by XIV DIV
ADS taken over by XIV Div.

~~Jan 1919~~ Oct. 1918 26

140/36/10

Vol 30

CONFIDENTIAL

WAR DIARY

OF

138TH FIELD AMBULANCE.

OCTOBER 1ST TO 31ST 1918.

(VOLUME XXII)

Instructions regarding War Diaries and Intelligence Summaries are contained in F. S. Regs., Part II. and the Staff Manual respectively. Title pages will be prepared in manuscript.

WAR DIARY
or
~~INTELLIGENCE SUMMARY.~~
(Erase heading not required.)

Army Form C. 2118.

VOLUME XXII Page 1

Place	Date	Hour	Summary of Events and Information	Remarks and references to Appendices
KORTEWILDE 28/P. 14. a. 3. 9	1/10/18	–	Fine. Rain in the evening	
		6.30 am	Field Ambulance moved off to new site at P. 24. b. 5. 6. and established A.D.S. at Pill Box at road side. Area heavily shelled by hostile artillery during the whole day and night. Numerous casualties received from roads in vicinity of ADS. Bearers from RAPs subjected to heavy shell fire and machine gun fire. Evacuation by Horse ambulance and Ford car to 35 Div. ADS and 140 F. Amb ADS. Total Casualties received & evacuated Sick 9 Wounded 48 RAMC personnel casualties ~~included above~~ 1 Killed. 5 Wounded.	WRG
ADS. Pill box at 28/P 24 b. 5. 6.	2/10/18	–	Fine. 1 NCO and 8 OR remained at Pillbox to carry on evacuations while remainder of personnel and transport moved to new site at J. 36. c. 7. 3. Hostile shell fire encountered while Ambulance was arranging to establish ADS there resulting in casualties amongst personnel (RAMC 1 Killed 4 wounded ASC MT 1 wounded) ADS established 1 bell tent. 1 operating tent. Evacuations by Sunbeam & Ford Cars Total casualties. Sick 5 Wounded 63 1 ~~[illegible]~~ RAMC personnel wounded in addition to those mentioned above. Area intermittently shelled throughout the day: heavily shelled and bombed during night Received from ADMS Secret No 407	WRG

D. D. & L., London, E.C.
(1034 ?) Wt W5300/P713 750,000 3/15 B 2488 Forms/C2118/16

Instructions regarding War Diaries and Intelligence Summaries are contained in F. S. Regs., Part II, and the Staff Manual respectively. Title pages will be prepared in manuscript.

WAR DIARY
or
~~INTELLIGENCE SUMMARY.~~
(Erase heading not required.)

Army Form C. 2118.

VOLUME XXII Page 2

Place	Date	Hour	Summary of Events and Information	Remarks and references to Appendices
ADS J 36 c 7 3	3/10/18	-	Fine Ambulance relieved for 24 hours by Ambulance of 34/Division. Intermittent shelling during day Heavy shelling and bombing throughout the night. Several casualties received off the road and evacuated. ADMS 41 instructions. The Field Ambulance to be responsible for evacuation from forward area near Divisional front. Suitable site for combined ADS to be selected near GHELUVELT and to be prepared in such a way to be capable of being converted into MDS if situation permits. 100 OR Infantry will be supplied for carriage of cases across bad section of YPRES-MENIN Rd. Light Railway to be completed as far as GHELUVELT for use of Walking wounded.	WRG
J 36 c 7 3.	4/10/18	-	Fine Field Ambulance moved off and established ADS at GHELUVELT J 21 b 1.5 on YPRES-MENIN RD relieving 88 Field Ambulance. Relief completed by 10 a.m. Reserve and Line Car posts established Labour Companies working on construction of light railway. No shelling in vicinity. Casualties Sick 73 Wounded 5. Bombing by hostile planes during night.	WRG

D. D. & L., London, E.C.
(10341) Wt W5300/P713 750,000 3/15 E 2688 Forms/C2118/16

Instructions regarding War Diaries and Intelligence Summaries are contained in F. S. Regs., Part II. and the Staff Manual respectively. Title pages will be prepared in manuscript.

WAR DIARY
or
~~INTELLIGENCE SUMMARY.~~
(Erase heading not required.)

Army Form C. 2118.

VOLUME XXII Page 3

Place	Date	Hour	Summary of Events and Information	Remarks and references to Appendices
GHELUVELT 28/J 21 b.1.5 A.D.S. (Forward HQ)	5/10/18	-	Rain. Weather dull Work on light railway continued. Railroad completed to A.D.S Constructive work carried out at ADS and adjoining dugouts. Total casualties. Sick 36 Wounded 29	WRG
GHELUVELT ADS	6/10/18	-	Weather dull. Winter time commenced. Clocks put back 1 hour at 1 am. 2 Bearer sub divisions (one as working party) and 1 tent sub division, with 2 Officers of 106 Field Ambulance reported for duty at ADS in combination with this Field Ambulance. Capt H M Godfrey RAMC posted as permanent MO to 41/Div M.E. Battn. 122 Infantry Bde moved into Busseboom Rest Area. Total Casualties Sick 29 Wounded 7 Constructive work continued at ADS	WRG
GHELUVELT ADS.	7/10/18	-	Weather fine. Rain towards evening. 122 Inf Bde relieved by 123 Inf Bde, move into Hillhoek Rest area. Report on roads in forward area in relation to their condition for Ambulance transport sent to ADMS 41/Div. Divisional Rest Station + Scabies Hospital at HILLHOEK administered by this Field Ambulance to close down at 23.59 hours. Patients and surplus stores to be transferred to White Farm REMY on 8th inst. Personnel of this Ambulance to report to the ECOLE (HQ 140 Field Amb). Capt Ch Moore RAMC to report on completion of move to GHELUVELT. Total casualties. Sick. 32 Wounded 17. Constructive + protective work continued.	WRG

D. D. & L., London, E.C.
(1034) Wt W3300/P713 750,000 3/15 E 2688 Forms/C2118/16

Instructions regarding War Diaries and Intelligence Summaries are contained in F. S. Regs., Part II. and the Staff Manual respectively. Title pages will be prepared in manuscript.

WAR DIARY
or
~~INTELLIGENCE SUMMARY.~~
(Erase heading not required.)

Army Form C. 2118.

VOLUME XXII Page 4

Place	Date	Hour	Summary of Events and Information	Remarks and references to Appendices
GHELUVELT A.D.S.	8/10/18	-	Weather Fine Total Casualties Sick 23 Wounded 18. Capt C. G. Moore, Capt + QM J Starkie with personnel of this Ambulance transport, stores &c from Hillhock arrived at the ECOLE MDS (28/I 9.c) 19 OR. RAMC reinforcements arrived at ADS for duty Constructive work - accommodation for personnel &c - carried on. Major LSC Roche reported back from leave to the ADS.	WRG
GHELUVELT ADS	9/10/18	-	Fine Total Casualties Sick 23 Wounded 23. Evacuation of patients from ADS siding by light railway to YPRES commenced. Constructive work still in progress. Two shelters for patients awaiting evacuation by train, erected.	WRG
GHELUVELT A.D.S.	10/10/18	-	Fine. Working party of 1 officer 3 NCOs + 48 bearers reported for duty in forward area from 107 F. Amb. Total Casualties Sick 29 Wounded 26. Light Railway Service running from ADS twice daily at 08.00 hours and 22.00 hours. Work on shelters continued: three more to be erected. Investigation carried out and report made on old wells, pumps, streams &c in the area with view to discovery of water supplies. Working party of 1 NCO + 10 men attached to REs for construction of RAP at J.29.b.7.4. ADMS 41/Div visited and inspected ADS.	WRG

D. D. & L., London, E.C.
(1034.) Wt W5300/P713 750,000 3/18 E 2188 Forms/C2118/16

Instructions regarding War Diaries and Intelligence Summaries are contained in F. S. Regs., Part II, and the Staff Manual respectively. Title pages will be prepared in manuscript.

WAR DIARY
or
~~INTELLIGENCE~~ SUMMARY.
(Erase heading not required.)

Army Form C. 2118.

VOLUME XXII Page 5.

Place	Date	Hour	Summary of Events and Information	Remarks and references to Appendices
GHELUVELT ADS.	11/10/18	-	Weather dull + showery. Section NCO Commanders with runners made tour of inspection of forward area with a view to selecting sites for RAPs. Dump of stretchers and blankets left at selected sites. Received from ADMS. Booklets SS 455 Preventive measures against lice. Total casualties. Sick 23 Wounded 16. Sandbagging of shelters + dugouts carried out	WRG
GHELUVELT ADS.	12/10/18	-	Fine Showery afternoon + evening ADMS 41/Div: visited ADS. Bearer Officers from 139 + 140 Field Amb. consulted with OC this Ambulance. Three shelters erected. Total casualties Sick 45. Wounded 49.- (includes 1 ASC MT personnel)	WRG
GHELUVELT ADS.	13/10/18	-	Raining. Capt + QM J Starkie proceeded on leave to UK. 2 Bearer sub divisions reported from 139 Field Amb } for work in forward area. 2 " " " " 140 " " } Capt C. G. Moore reported to ADS for duty from ECOLE. Major J.h.a.F. Lauder and Major LSC Roche proceeded to STONE DUMP Collecting Post. Bearer divisions posted in forward area. Total Casualties. Sick 28 Wounded 23. See "Medical Scheme of Evacuation". Posts established in forward area in accordance with same.	WRG

D. D. & L., London, E.C.
(1034) Wt W5300/P713 750,000 3/15 E 2688 Forms/C2118/16

Instructions regarding War Diaries and Intelligence Summaries are contained in F. S. Regs., Part II. and the Staff Manual respectively. Title pages will be prepared in manuscript.

WAR DIARY
or
~~INTELLIGENCE SUMMARY.~~

(Erase heading not required.)

Army Form C. 2118.

VOLUME XXII Page 6.

Place	Date	Hour	Summary of Events and Information	Remarks and references to Appendices
GHELUVELT ADS.	14/10/18	-	Fine. Mist early morning.	
		05.30	Attack by 132 Inf Bde. 05.30 hours.	
		07.15	Wounded began to arrive at ADS 07.15 hours. Evacuations by light railway, lorries and cars from ADS.	
		11.50	Roads in forward area in bad condition owing to yesterdays rain. Collecting Post being established at K 34 d. 10.0. Total Casualties to noon - 400.	WRG
		18.00	Collecting Post K 35. a. 1.1. Car Post. L 31. a. 1.6. 122 + 124 Inf Bde. All clear. 123 Inf Bde very few casualties. GHELUWE too badly shelled to utilize for evacuation purposes. Considerable difficulty being experienced in moving cars forward owing to bad condition of roads. Casualties so far total 800. Prisoners of War utilized to assist in evacuation at ADS, &c.	
		24:00	Total casualties received and evacuated 850: includes about 270 stretcher cases. Deaths at ADS. 2 officers. 9 OR (including 2 PofW.) Weather continued fine during whole day and no difficulty experienced in evacuating from ADS.	
GHELUVELT ADS.	15/10/18	-	Fine. Total Casualties Sick 65. Wounded 88. RAMC Corps visited ADS. 9 Civilian Refugees passed through ADS. from WEVELGHEM.	WRG

D. D. & L., London, E.C.
(1034) Wt W3300/P713 750,000 3/15 E 2688 Forms/C2118/16

Army Form C. 2118.

Instructions regarding War Diaries and Intelligence Summaries are contained in F. S. Regs., Part II. and the Staff Manual respectively. Title pages will be prepared in manuscript.

WAR DIARY
or
~~INTELLIGENCE SUMMARY.~~

(Erase heading not required.)

VOLUME XXII Page 7.

Place	Date	Hour	Summary of Events and Information	Remarks and references to Appendices
GHELUVELT ADS	16/10/18	–	Raining	
		15.30	Personnel moved off by lorries – followed by transport, and proceeded to MOORSEELE Sheet 28/L 23 b 5.7 in relief of Ambulance of 36/Div: Field Ambulance occupied Convent and established ADS and HQ there.	
			ADS at GHELUVELT taken over by 106 Field Amb.	WRG
			Arrived MOORSEELE about 18.30 hours.	
			Roads shelled in vicinity causing casualties amongst 15/Hants; received at ADS.	
			Capt J J H Ferguson RAMC evacuated to CCS & struck off strength of the Amb.	
MOORSEELE 28/L 23 b 5.7 ADS. HQ.	17/10/18	–	Fine	Sheet 29 { Collecting Post G21. c 3.6
			Civilians arriving all day from COURTRAI. Many sick attended to at ADS.	
			Evacuation: general procedure; seriously wounded cases evacuated by cars to DADIZEELE thence by MAC to CCS. Slightly wounded & sick retained at ADS.	Car Post G23 d.3.4 }
			Personnel and transport from MDS ECOLE arrived at this ADS.	
			Total casualties treated Sick 60 Wounded 30 (includes civilians Sick 10 wounded 3)	WRG
MOORSEELE ADS. HQ	18/10/18	–	Fine	
			MDS established by 140 F. Amb at DADIZEELE. Party of 30 OR from this Amb sent to assist in preparation of same. All cases for evacuation now sent to this MDS.	
			Refugees still coming in from Courtrai. Casualties on road caused by Artillery shelling.	
			Total casualties dealt with	WRG
			Military Sick 44 Wounded 106 (includes 50 gassed cases)	
			Refugees " 39 " 24 (evacuated Sick 26 wounded 18)	
			Included in above 2 personnel RAMC wounded.	

D. D. & L., London, E.C.
(1034) Wt W5300/P713 750,000 3/15 E 2688 Forms/C2118/16

Instructions regarding War Diaries and Intelligence Summaries are contained in F. S. Regs., Part II. and the Staff Manual respectively. Title pages will be prepared in manuscript.

WAR DIARY
or
~~INTELLIGENCE~~ SUMMARY.
(Erase heading not required.)

Army Form C. 2118.

VOLUME XXII Page 8

Place	Date	Hour	Summary of Events and Information	Remarks and references to Appendices
MOORSEELE ADS HQ	19/10/18	–	Fine Casualties. Sick 66 Wounded 34. Included in wounded were 29 cases caused by one enemy shell on road in vicinity – pioneer battn North'd Fus. Civilian refugees treated 8 Sick 6 wounded.	WRG
MOORSEELE ADS HQ	20/10/18	6.30 10.30	Fine. Field Amb. marched off by route march with transport leaving holding party behind until arrival of 140 Field Amb. to take over as MDS. HQ + ADS established at Infantry Barracks. COURTRAI 29/H. 31. d. 2. 4. Evacuations by car to pontoon bridge M. 5. c. 2. 2. thence across bridge by horse ambulance. MAC cars take up cases other side of bridge + convey to MDS. MOORSEELE Car Post established at H 33. c. 5. 9 Total casualties 35 Div: S. 2 W 78 41 Div: S. 12. W 7. ADMS visited ADS.	WRG
ADS + HQ COURTRAI H 31 d. 2. 4. Sheet 29.	21/10/18	– 14.00	Raining. Evacuations now by cars direct to MDS. Ambulance moved off by route march with transport. ADS established at Hospice, SWEVEGHEM 29/O. 1 d. 1. 9. Heavy shelling in vicinity. One shell struck building in which ADS was established – no casualties. ADS moved to Tobacco Factory O. 1. c. 8. 3. Total Casualties Sick 39 Wounded 111 (mostly 18/KRRC) (Personnel wounded 2 RAMC 1 ASC HT att) ADS at Courtrai taken over by 140 F Amb and MDS established there. This F. Amb left holding party to carry on until their arrival.	Collecting Post. N. 18 d. 1. 9 Forward Car Post. U. 5. b. 8. 8. WRG

D. D. & L., London, E.C. (1034) Wt W5300/P713 750,000 3/15 E 2888 Forms/C2118/16

Instructions regarding War Diaries and Intelligence Summaries are contained in F. S. Regs., Part II. and the Staff Manual respectively. Title pages will be prepared in manuscript.

WAR DIARY
or
~~INTELLIGENCE SUMMARY.~~
(Erase heading not required.)

Army Form C. 2118.

VOLUME XXII Page 9.

Place	Date	Hour	Summary of Events and Information	Remarks and references to Appendices
SWEVEGHEM ADS + HQ. 29/O 1 c 8 3	22/10/18	–	Fine morning. Rain later in day. Relay post with wheeled stretchers 29/O. 15. d. 3. 8 for evacuating 122 Bde. Car post N. 18. d. 8. 2 (123 Bde) Car post O. 14. b. 6. 7 (10 Queens) Car post O. 32 b 6. 0 (26 RF. 20 DLI) Total casualties, mostly of 12 E Surreys + 15 Hants and including 1 Officer + 2 other ranks of 22 Inf Reg. (German Prisoners of War) Sick 49 wounded 169.	See locations RAPs WRG
SWEVEGHEM. ADS + HQ.	23/10/18	–	Dull – misty. For the evacuation of 123 Bde a canal carry party has been established at O 16 c 2 8. This house is also the advanced RAP of 23 Mdx. Cases are carried from there across the foot bridge by RAMC bearers to the main 23 Mdx RAP or to the Ford Car Post O 15 d. 6. 9 and from there to the Sunbeam Car Post O. 14. b. 5. 5 thence to ADS. Total Casualties Sick 22 wounded 20. 12 Civilians treated (10 gassed or wounded 2 sick) MDS at COURTRAI transferred to Convent H 33 a. 7. 9.	See locations RAPs WRG
SWEVEGHEM ADS & HQ.	24/10/18	–	Fine. Car + collecting Posts at O. 14. b 6. 7. O. 2. b 8 2. O 9 b 8. 7. Ambulances can run direct to ADS via Lock 6; the bridge here being now completed. Total Casualties – mostly 123 + 124 Bde – Sick 67 wounded 54. 7 RAMC 140 Field Amb gassed (3 died) 106 Field Ambulance to detail bearer personnel for duty in the event of 106 Bde going into action (see appendix) Bearers reported to this ambulance in accordance with above.	See location RAPs 35/Div Instructions ref: 106 Bde Med scheme of evacuation WRG

D. D. & L., London, E.C. (10341) Wt W5390/P713 750,000 3/15 E 2188 Forms/C2118/16

Instructions regarding War Diaries and Intelligence Summaries are contained in F. S. Regs., Part II. and the Staff Manual respectively. Title pages will be prepared in manuscript.

WAR DIARY
or
INTELLIGENCE SUMMARY.
(Erase heading not required.)

Army Form C. 2118.

VOLUME XXII Page 10

Place	Date	Hour	Summary of Events and Information	Remarks and references to Appendices
SWEVEGHEM ADS & HQ	25/10/18	-	Fine. Capt L W Bain RAMC reported to 20 DLI for duty. 123 (Right Bde) and 124 (Left Bde) in action. Collecting post established at Convent P25 c 4 7. Car posts at O 6 c 9.0 (RFus) and O 11 a 9.1 (20 DLI + 10 Queens) RAPs of 10 Queens + 20 DLI are cleared via KNOKKE RFus RAP cleared by road running from O 6 a to Lock 6 as there is considerable shelling between RFus Aid Post + Car post. Total Casualties received and evacuated at ADS. Sick / Wounded 41 Div: 31 / 296 Others 10 / 49 Total 41 / 345 All RAPs clear at 16 30 hours when visited by OC Field Amb + ADMS Corps. ADS clear of cases at 20.00 hours.	See Location RAPs. WRG WRG
SWEVEGHEM ADS & HQ	26/10/18	-	Fine. Total Casualties Sick / Wounded 41 Div 29 / 69 Others 11 / 13 35 Division to relieve 41 Division tonight in the line. Bearer Divisions from 105 + 106 Field Ambulances arrived this ADS Capt W M Chesney RAMC reported for duty with this Field Amb.	Location RAPs 122 Bde. WRG

D. D. & L., London, E.C.
(1034.) Wt W3300/P713 750,000 3/15 E 2688 Forms/C2118/16

Instructions regarding War Diaries and Intelligence Summaries are contained in F. S. Regs., Part II. and the Staff Manual respectively. Title pages will be prepared in manuscript.

WAR DIARY
or
~~INTELLIGENCE SUMMARY.~~
(Erase heading not required.)

Army Form C. 2118.

VOLUME XXII Page 11.

Place	Date	Hour	Summary of Events and Information	Remarks and references to Appendices
SWEVEGHEM. ADS + HQ	27/10/18	–	Fine. Relief of Medical posts begun at dawn. Relief to be completed by 12.00 noon. Casualties treated up to noon. S. W. 41 Div 2 19 Others 2 11 4 30	WRG
		13.00	Personnel + transport of Field Ambulance moves off by route march to Rest area N.29 c 1.8 This Field Amb. responsible for collection of sick of 122 Inf Bde. 187 + 190 Bde RFA + two Field Co RE.	
BELLEGHEM N.29 c 1.8	28/10/18	–	Fine. Sick collected in accordance with instructions. Casualties received Wounded NIL Sick 24.	WRG
BELLEGHEM.	29/10/18	–	Fine. M.O. from this Field Ambulance attends at 187 Bde RFA HQ to see the sick of various Batteries at 11 am daily, whilst Field Ambulance is in present area. Casualties. Wounded NIL Sick 34.	WRG

D. D. & L., London, E.C.
(1034) Wt W5300/P713 750,000 3/15 E 2688 Forms/C2118/16

Instructions regarding War Diaries and Intelligence Summaries are contained in F. S. Regs., Part II. and the Staff Manual respectively. Title pages will be prepared in manuscript.

WAR DIARY
or
~~INTELLIGENCE SUMMARY.~~
(Erase heading not required.)

Army Form C. 2118.

VOLUME XXII Page 12

Place	Date	Hour	Summary of Events and Information	Remarks and references to Appendices
BELLEGHEM	30/10/18	-	Fine Casualties. Wounded NIL Sick 16.	WRG
BELLEGHEM	31/10/18	-	Dull - raining. O.O. No 68 received. 122 Inf Bde to relieve a portion of 35/Div night 31 Oct/1 Nov. This Field Amb to detail 2 Officers + 72 bearers to report to ADS 35 Div. 29/O 23 b.9.1. and in addition 6 Motor Amb Cars and 1 ADS limber. In connection with above 12 bearers and 2 wheeled stretchers posted to each Battalion of 122 Inf. Bde. Major J La F Lauder, RAMC, Capt W M Chesney, RAMC, remainder of bearers with ADS limber so reported in accordance with instructions. Capt C. G Moore, RAMC posted for temporary duty to DDMS. XIX Corps. Casualties. Wounded NIL Sick 25. Capt + QM J Starkie, RAMC reported back from leave.	WRG

W Rose Gardner
Lieut Colonel RAMC
O.C. 138th Field Ambulance

D. D. & L., London, E.C.
(1034-) Wt W3300/P713 750,000 3/15 E 2688 Forms/C2118/16

App 2

12 hours

From 8 pm 22/10/18 to 8 am 23/10/18

From 8 am to noon 23/10/18

41 Div.	S	W	S	W
12 E Surrey	1	10		1
15 Hants	1	3		
18 KRRC	1	-		1
11 Queens	-	-		
23 Mdx	-	7		3
10 Queens	1	6		
26 RF	1	3		
20 DLI	-	-		
41 MGC	1	-		
19 Mdx	-	-		
RFA 190 Bde	-	1		
RE 237 Fd			1	
101 MGC			3	
138 FA RAMC			1	
10 RWK		10		3
Totals	6	40	5	8
29 Div.				
2 SWB		1		
PofW		1		

8 pm to 8 am
23-24 Oct 1918

41 Div	S	W
11 Queens	12	9
10 RWK	3	25
23 Mdx	1	8
10 Queens	-	1
26 RF	-	8
20 DLI	-	1
RFA 190 Bde	-	1
~~[illegible]~~		
101 MG Bn	-	2
	16	55

9 Div	S	W
8 Black Watch	-	1
7 Seaforths	1	-
12 R Scots	1	-
	2	1

24/10/18.
8 am to 6 pm

41 Div	S	W
18 KRRC	3	
15 Hants	1	
41 MG Bn	7	
12 E Surrey	3	
11 Queens	1	3
10 RWK	1	11
23 Mdx	1	
10 Queens	1	2
26 R.F.	1	3
20 DLI	2	
190 Bde RFA	4	1
187 " RFA	4	
228 Field Co RE	1	
138 F. Amb	1	
139 F Amb.		1
101 MG Bn	6	
Total	37	21
29 Div		
1 Borders		1
Corps Troops		
RGA 4/Bde	1	

Oct 24 - 25th 1918
8. pm to 8. am.

	S.	W.
41 Div:		
26 R Fus.	1	5
10 Queens.	2	2
20 DLI.	9	8
11 Queens.	12	1
10 RWK.	-	4
23 Mdx.	1	-
41 MGBn.	2	1
41 Div Sig.	1	-
RAMC 140 Fa.	-	7
Total	28	28
34 Div.		
4 Cheshires	-	4
35 Div.		
18 HLI.	1	-
P of W.		
156 Inf Reg.	-	2

25/10/18. 08 00 hours to 16 00 hours

	SICK	WOUNDED
41 Div	27	189
9 "	1	7
34 "	1	16
35 "	5	2
Army Troops.	1	-
Corps "	1	-
P of W.	-	2
Totals	36	214

Included in the above 8 Officers 41 Div:

26 R. Fus.	Lt Legg K.B.	GSW Calf L.
— " —	2/Lt Waskett. L.	— " — Face
— " —	2/Lt Flockhart V.	— " — Scalp
20 DLI	2/Lt Donelly A	— " — Knee L
— " —	2/Lt Wood F	— " — Thigh L
23 Mdx	Capt Meester C.J.	— " — Arm R. Frac.
— " —	2/Lt Wallis F.V.	— " — Knee L
— " —	2/Lt Lewellen R.O	— " — Hip L.

From 20.00 hours 25/10/18 to 08.00 hours 26/10/18

	S	W
41 Div.		
26 R Fus.		13
20 DLI		14
10 Queens		1
10 RWK		1
11 Queens		4
23 Mdx.		1
12 E Surrey.		4
41 M G Bn.		3
190 Bde RFA		1
RE Sig	1	–
	1	47
34 Div.		
1/4 Cheshires		6
1/1 Herefords		3
9 Div. 5 Camerons		1
RAF 13 Kite Bn. Sect.	1	–
P of W.		1
Total	2	58

08.00 to 18 00 hours 26-10-18

41 Div:	S.	W
23 Mdx	2	8
18 KRRC	5	6
12 E Surreys	1	5
101 M G Bn.	1	-
233 F. Co RE	2	-
228 F Co RE	2	-
41 Bn M G C.	1	-
190 Bde RFA	4	-
41 DAC RFA	1	-
11 Queens	1	1
19 Mdx	1	-
10 Queens	1	-
20 DLI	3	1
15 Hants	1	1
10 RWK	1	-
139 F Amb RAMC	1	
	28	22

Officers
12 HLI 2/Lt Adam W. NYD Pyrexia
18 KRR. 2/Lt Walker A GSW Abdomen (Rem)
20 DLI Lt Heppell CA Dis[h]ex[?]

WD

35 Div	S.	W
35 MG Bn	1	-
7 R Scots	1	-
18 HLI	2	-
12 HLI	1	-
19 North Fus	1	-
	6	

Corps Troops	S.	W
17 H Batt AA	1	-
XIX Corps Cyclists	-	1

34 Div	S.	W
7 Cheshires	-	1
Army Troops		
119 Bde AFA	2	-
RAF		
39 Bn Sect	1	-

20.00 hours 26-10-18
to 08.00 – 27-10-18

	S	W
41 Div		
15 Hants	–	10
12 E Surreys	–	6
23 Mdx	1	1
26 R Fus	1	1
20 DLI	–	1
	2	19
35 Div		
18 HLI	1	1
17 R Scots	–	1
18 Lanc Fus	–	2
34 Div		
4 Cheshires	–	2
1/1 Hereford	1	1
9 Div		
5 Camerons	–	2
30 Div		
2/23 London	–	2
	4	30

Officers included in above.

4/Att 12/E Surrey	Lt Robinson W	GSW Arm (R)
12/E Surrey	2/Lt Summers W	GSW Thigh (L)
15 Hants.	2/Lt Langdon A	GSW Knee (R)
23 Mdx	2/Lt Bradshaw C	NYD Pyrexia

app. 1

MEDICAL SCHEME OF EVACUATION

138 Field Amb

1/ Initial Dispositions

A.D.S.	28/J.	21. b. 1.5.
Collecting Post (+ advanced Report centre)	K.	31. a. 5.9
Collecting Post.	K:	32. c. 3.9
Car Exchange	K	29. a. 6.4

2/ 1st Phase

(a) as above.

(b) Collecting Post + Ford. K 27 a. 9.3

Car Post. (at present RAP)

(c) Walking Wounded Post. Car Post + Main Medical Dump } K 31 a. 5.9

2nd Phase

Advanced C.P. or Car Post to be established in the vicinity of K. 34. a N. of GHELWE

3rd Phase

Advanced Collecting Post to be established on road running from Q 5 central K. 36 central L. 31 a and L 25 d 8. 0.

Medical Dumps

Blankets & Stretchers

K. 27. a 9. 3.
K 32. c. 3 9

12-10-18

22/10/18 20.00 hours

122 Inf Bde RAPs

12 E Surrey	O 16 c 0.9
15 Hants	O 16 c 3.8
18 KRRC	O 9 d 3.7
Relay Post, wheeled stretchers	O 15 a 3.8

123 Inf Bde RAPs

	N 24 b 3.7
23 Mdx	N 18 d 3.8
11 Queens	O 7 c 4.0
10 RW Kents	N 18 d 8.2
Car Post	

124 Inf Bde

	HQ	O 25 a 7.5
RAPs	26 RF	O 26 d 5.3
	20 DLI	U 3 d 0.7
	10 Queens	O 16 a 5.5

Evacuations from last mentioned RAP by wheeled stretchers to Car Post at O.14 b 6 7: thence direct to ADS Car Post at O 32 b 6 0 (DASI Cab.) [SWEVEGHEM] evacuate the 26 RF and 20 DLI RAPs

23/10/18 1200 hours

	120 Inf Bde. HQ.	29/	O 14 a 7 7
RAPs	18 KRRC		O 13 central
	15 Hants		O. 20 a.
	12 E. Surrey.		O 9 c 6 2
	123 Inf Bde. HQ.	29/	O 14 a 7 7
RAPs	23 Mdx		O 15 d 9 9
	11 Queens		O 16 b 9 8
	10 RW Kents		O 16 b 9 8
	124 Inf Bde. HQ.	29/	O 25 a 7 5
RAPs	26 RF		O 26 d 5 3
	20 DLI		U. 3 d 0 7
	10 Queens.		O 16 a 5 5

Car post O. 32. b. 6. 0.

Reference the evacuation of 123 Inf Bde a Canal carry party has been established at O. 16. c. 2. 8 This house is also the advanced RAP of 23 Mdx. Cases are carried from there across the foot bridge by RAMC bearers either to the main RAP of 23rd Mdx or to the Ford Car Post O 15 d. 6. 9 and from there to the Sunbeam Car Post at O 14 b. 8. 5. thence to ADS SWEVEGHEM

Number of cases evacuated from ADS attached.

ADMS. 35 Div:

09.15

Herewith medical Scheme of evacuation :-

SHEET 29

ADS.	O 1 c. 7. 5
Collecting Post	O 14 b. 6. 7
MDS.	H 33 a. 7. 9.
Right Bde (123) HQ.	O 14. a. 7. 7.
RAPs. 23 Mdx	O. 15 d. 9 9
11 Queens	O 16 b 9. 8
10 RWK	O. 16 b. 9. 8

A canal carrying party is established at O. 16. c. 2. 8. This house is also the advanced RAP of 23 Mdx, and cases are carried across the bridge by RAMC bearers either to the main RAP of 23 Mdx or to the Ford Car Post at O. 16. d. 6. 9.

Left Bde (124) HQ.	O 3 a 4. 8.
Car Collecting Post	O. 2 b. 8. 2
Ford Car Post	O. 9. b 8. 7.
RAPs. 20 DLI.	O 10 d. 1. 5
10 Queens	O 9 b 9. 9
26 RF.	O 3 d. 5. 1

Ambulances can run from RAPs direct to ADS via Lock 6. The bridge here has now been completed.

Field. Lt Col

24/10/18.

ADMS.
41/Div.

09.15.

SHEET 29

Locations herewith.

Collecting Post. O. 14. b. 6. 7.

Right Bde (123) HQ. O 14 a 7. 7.
RAPs. 23 Mdx. O 15. d. 9. 4.
11 Queens. O 16 b. 9. 8.
10 RWK. O. 16. b. 9. 8

Left Bde (124) HQ. O. 3. a. 4. 8.
Car Collecting Post. O 2 b. 8. 2
Ford Car Post. O. 9. b. 8. 7
RAPs. 20 D.L.I. O 10 d. 1. 5
10 Queens O. 9 b 9. 9
26. R.F. O 3. d. 5. 1

[signature] Lt Col

Field
24-10-18

ADMS
35/Div

at 16.00 hrs.

RAPs Left Bde

26 R Fus.	O 6 c 9 0
20 DLI	O 24 a 0 1
10 Queen	O 18 a 8 4
Car Park	O 11 a 9 1

Rt Bde

23 Mdx	O. 30 c. 1. 2
10 RWK	O. 29 b. 4 6 (approx
11 Queens	O. 24 a. 0 1

Field
25/10/18.

[signature]
Lt Col
138 Field Amb

ADMS.
41 Div.

16.40 hours.

Situation Report.

Left Bde
RAPs.

26 R Fus. 0.6.c.9.0

A fair number of stretcher cases are coming through here and a Car Post has been established at this RAP.

20 DLI 0.24 a.0.1
10 Queens. 0.18 a.8.4
Car Post 0.11.a.9.1.

The latter 2 posts are cleared via KNOKKE, but it is, necessary still to clear the Fusiliers RAP by the road running from 0.6 a to Lock 6. There is considerable shelling between the Fusiliers Aid Post and the Car Post making it unsafe to use that road as route of evacuation at present.

W Ross Gardner
Lt Col. RAMC
OC 138 Field Amb.

Field 25/10/18

ADMS
41st Div.
Location of RAPs. at Bde. at 16.00 hrs

23rd Middlesex D 30 c. 1. 2
10/ RW Kent D 29 b. 4. 6. (approx)
11/ Queens D 24 a 0 1

16.00 hours.

W Ross Gardner
A/Lt Col
OC 138th FA

25-10-18

Locations. 122 Brigade

HQ.		O	36	a	3	6
Left Bn	18/KRR.	P	26	c	1	7
Centre Bn	12/E Surrey	P	31	a	7	5
Right Bn	15/Hants	V	1	a	8	2
Car Post (temp)		P	25	a	5	5

Field
26-10-18

Appendix 3

SECRET

O.C. 106th Field Ambulance
Hd.Qrs 106th Infantry Bde.)
A.D.M.S. 41st Br. Division)for information
O.C. 138th Field Ambulance.)

---

1. The 106th Infantry Brigade has been placed at the tactical disposal of the G.O.C. 41st British Division, and will move today into the SWEVEGHEM Area.

2. O.C. 106th Field Ambulance will detail the necessary Bearer personnel and transport for duty in the event of the 106th Inf. Bde. going into action. Not more than 9 Stretcher Squads with Bearer Officer and N.C.Os., 1 Ford and 2 large Ambulance cars, are required at present.

3. The above detachment will report forthwith to O.C. 138th Field Ambulance at the Advanced Dressing Station, SWEVEGHEM.

4. O.C. 106th Field Ambulance will acknowledge and report completion of above arrangements.

H. A. Lowell. Major
for Colonel,
A.D.M.S. 35th Division.

24/10/18.

Nov. 1918

28

140/3524

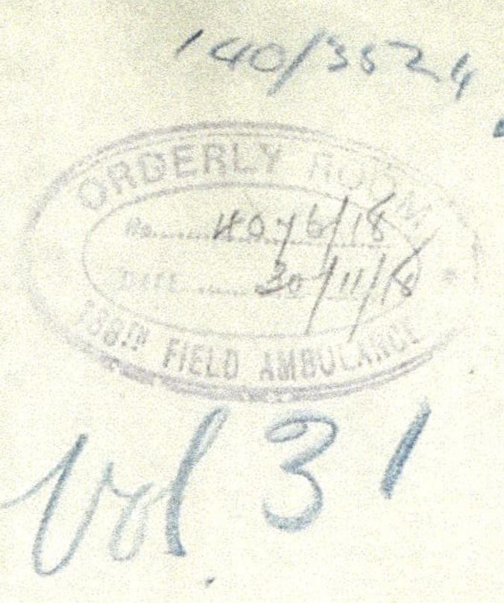

Vol 31

CONFIDENTIAL.

WAR DIARY

OF

138TH FIELD AMBULANCE

NOVEMBER 1ST TO 30TH - 1918.

(VOLUME XXIII)

(6392) Wt. W6192/P 75 1,500,000 4/18 McA & W Ltd (E 2815) Forms W3091/4. Army Form W.3091.

Cover for Documents.

Nature of Enclosures.

Notes, or Letters written.

Army Form C. 2118.

Instructions regarding War Diaries and Intelligence Summaries are contained in F. S. Regs., Part II. and the Staff Manual respectively. Title pages will be prepared in manuscript.

WAR DIARY
or
INTELLIGENCE SUMMARY.
(*Erase heading not required.*)

VOLUME XXIII. Page 1

Place	Date	Hour	Summary of Events and Information	Remarks and references to Appendices
BELLEGHEM Map References SHEET 29	1/11/18	-	Fine OO No 69 received 122 Inf. Bde will be relieved in the line midnight 1/2 Nov by Brigade of 30 Div:* 124 Brigade is relieving a Brigade of 35 Div. tonight as far south as P. 20 d. 0. 0 This Field Ambulance will be responsible for collection and evacuation of wounded in connection with above. Relief of 35 Div. Field Amb to be completed by 12.00 hours 2/11/18. An ADS will be established in vicinity of OOTEGHEM and HQ and wagon lines in vicinity of O.6. Evacuations from ADS will be via LOCK 6 - SWEVEGHEM to COURTRAI MDS. 140 Field Amb to detail 1 Officer, 1 bearer sub division, 4 runners and all available cars to report to this Field Amb. This Ambulance will be responsible for collection of sick and casualties of 123 Inf. Bde in Divisional Reserve in KNOKKE area.	* Locations of medical posts to be handed over to relieving Field Amb WRG
BELLEGHEM	2/11/18	- 7.00	Raining. Field Amb moved off by route march to OOTEGHEM. (vicinity) Relief of 106 Field Amb. completed by 10. am and upon posts taken over:- Car Post P. 17. d. 2. 9 Collecting Post P. 15. c. 1. 9. HQ + Transport lines } O. 6. a. 5. 2. ADS established at OOTEGHEM P. 8. a. 1. 4 Car post is being established in vicinity of OKKERWIJK as post at P. 17. d. 2. 9 is too far advanced for Sunbeam Cars. This post is therefore being made a relay post pending arrival of Fords. (Continued)	WRG

D. D. & L., London, E.C.
(1034.) Wt W5300/P713 750,000 5/15 E 2688 Forms/C2118/16

Instructions regarding War Diaries and Intelligence Summaries are contained in F. S. Regs., Part II. and the Staff Manual respectively. Title pages will be prepared in manuscript.

WAR DIARY
or
~~INTELLIGENCE~~ SUMMARY.
(*Erase heading not required.*)

Army Form C. 2118.

VOLUME XXIII Page 2

Place	Date	Hour	Summary of Events and Information	Remarks and references to Appendices
SHEET 29			Relief of posts in 122 Inf Bde area completed by 9 00 hours and O/c and bearers reported back to this HQ. Car post for evacuation of sick of 123 Inf Bde established at 123 Bde HQ. O 14 a 6.6 This Field Amb responsible for collection of sick of 122 Inf Bde in Divisional Reserve Area Evacuations from ADS wounded 3 Sick 23 1 civilian (XX)	RAPs 123 Inf Bde 10 RWK O 15 a 3.6 23 Mdx. O 7 d 2.8 11 Queens O 14 c 1 0 WRG
Sheet 29. HQ near OOTEGHEM O 6 a 5.2	3/11/18	–	Fine some rain during morning 2 Ford Cars sent to Collecting Post. One to be stationed in vicinity of relay post P17 d 1.8, the other at TIEGHEM Carpost. To evacuate to Sunbeam Car Post P10 d. 4 6. Lt Col W Ross Gardner OC this Field Amb acting ADMS during absence of ADMS. Lieut RC Manger RAMC from this Amb reported to 26 R Fus as temp. M.O.	RAPs 124 Inf Bde 10 Queens P.18 c 3.3 26 RF. O 18 b 4.3 20 DLI O 7 d 4 7 WRG
HQ. O.6 a 5 2	4/11/18	–	Fine. Bright sunshine: cold wind. O O No 70 received. Right Battalion of 124 Inf Bde will be relieved in the line tonight by a Battalion of 35th Div Left Battalion of 124 Inf Bde will be relieved in the line tonight by a Battalion of 123 Bde. Remainder of 123 Inf Bde will be disposed in the CASTER area. In connection with above operation. This Field Ambulance will hand over present medical posts to 106 Field Amb. and establish new ADS and HQ in the vicinity of INGOYGHEM. This ambulance will also be responsible for the collection of sick of 123 Bde in CASTER Area.	WRG

D. D. & L., London, E.C.
(1034) Wt W5300/P713 750,000 3/15 E 2688 Forms/C2118/16

Instructions regarding War Diaries and Intelligence Summaries are contained in F. S. Regs., Part II. and the Staff Manual respectively. Title pages will be prepared in manuscript.

WAR DIARY
or
~~INTELLIGENCE~~ SUMMARY.
(*Erase heading not required.*)

Army Form C. 2118.

VOLUME XXIII Page 3

Place (Sheet 29)	Date	Hour	Summary of Events and Information	Remarks and references to Appendices
HQ. O.6.a.8.2	5/11/18	-	Raining. ADS at OOTEGHEM and Collecting + Relay posts taken over by 106 Field Amb. This Field ambulance established ADS at WHITE HOUSE P.3.b.1.7. Evacuations from Divisional front will continue via TIEGHEM - OKKERWIJK - INGOYGHEM. Car post established in CASTER Area. HQ and transport moved off 11.00 hours and established new HQ and wagon lines on VICHTE - INGOYGHEM Road J.32.c.d.8 Relief completed by 12.00 hours. Locations at 13.00 hours. HQ rc J.32.c.9.8 ADS. P.3.b.1.7 * Sunbeam Car Post P.10.d.5.4. Collecting Post P.12.b.3.3. MDS established by 139 F. Amb at VICHTE. * This Car post will probably be vacated later as evacuation from forward RAP is taking place along the main TIEGHEM - OKKERWIJK - INGOYGHEM road to ADS. Considerable rain fell during the day and the roads in this area are in consequence in bad condition for transport. Ford Car broken down at P.9.a.3.6. and untowable.	Locations of RAPs at 13.00 hrs. 123 Bde HQ J.28.d.4.7 11 Queens O.7.d.5.8 23 Mdx J.34.c.4.8 10 RWK. K.31.b.6.6 WRL
HQ. J.32.c.9.8 Vicinity INGOYGHEM.	6/11/18	-	Still raining. 26 OR RAMC of 139 Field Amb. reported here to relieve personnel of this Unit attached as bearers to 123 Inf Bde. O.O. No. 71 received. MDS moved to DEERLYCK I.9.d.0.4. to open there 11.00 hours. 7/11/18 (140 F. Amb). Rain continued to fall throughout the day and night. About 6 hostile shells (? 4.2) during night vicinity HQ. No casualties. Evacuations from ADS Wounded 9. Sick 14 Civilians 12 Gassed. 2 sick.	WRL

D. D. & L., London, E.C.
(1034.) Wt W5300/P713 750,000 3/15 B 2688 Forms/C2118/16

Instructions regarding War Diaries and Intelligence Summaries are contained in F. S. Regs., Part II. and the Staff Manual respectively. Title pages will be prepared in manuscript.

WAR DIARY or ~~INTELLIGENCE SUMMARY.~~

(*Erase heading not required.*)

Army Form C. 2118.

VOLUME XXIII Page 4

Place SHEET 29	Date	Hour	Summary of Events and Information	Remarks and references to Appendices
HQ. J32.c.9.8.	7/11/18	-	Cloudy with some rain. Evacuations from ADS Wounded 32 Sick 20 Civilians Gassed 8 - 2 Civilian casualties brought in from village of TIEGHEM.	WRG
HQ — —	8/11/18	-	Raining. Evacuations from ADS. Wounded 3 Sick 34 Civilians - 1 - 1	WRG
HQ — —	9/11/18	-	Fine	
		11.00	Personnel of Field Amb. with cars and H Transport moved off by route march and arrived at Chateau Q 14 b 9.7 14.00 hours. A halt was made here while the marshy and heavy ground approaching river ESCAUT (SCHELDT) was examined and prepared for passage of transport.	See - Locations 123 and 124 Inf Bde.
		15.30	Holding party left at Chateau to await arrival of 140 Field Ambulance who open there as MDS at 12.00 hours 10/11/18. Remainder moved off and cars and transport successfully negotiated river approaches, with the exception of one GS Wagon*, and crossed the ESCAUT (SCHELDT) by pontoon bridge at Q 21 b 3.9 at 16.00 hours. HQ and ADS established on outskirts of BERCHEM Q 21 b 8.7 (GRIJKOORT) MAC cars crossed later for evacuation of cases to MDS VICHTE pending establishment of MDS at Chateau (KERKOVE) referred to above. ADS of this Field Amb at P 3 b 1.7 vacated, and personnel joined this HQ. 123 Inf Bde relieved in the line tonight by 122 + 124 Inf Bde.	WRG * Crossed next morning.

D. D. & L., London, E.C.
(1034.) Wt W5300/P713 750,000 3/13 E 2688 Forms/C2118/16

Instructions regarding War Diaries and Intelligence Summaries are contained in F. S. Regs., Part II. and the Staff Manual respectively. Title pages will be prepared in manuscript.

WAR DIARY
or
~~INTELLIGENCE SUMMARY.~~

(Erase heading not required.)

Army Form C. 2118.

VOLUME XXIII Page 5.

Place SHEET 29	Date	Hour	Summary of Events and Information	Remarks and references to Appendices
HQ + ADS GRIJKOURT Near BERCHEM Q.21 b.8.7	10/11/18	–	Fine. Bright + sunny. Operation Order No 72 received from ADMS. MDS at VICHTE. Subsidiary Dressing Station Chateau, KERKOVE. 138 + 140 Field Ambulances to mutually arrange for carriage of casualties across SCHELDT. Horse Ambulances to be used.	
		14.00	This Field Ambulance moved off by route march with transport, leaving a small party with one Horse Ambulance for evacuation of casualties across the River until relieved by 140 Field Amb. Owing to numerous mine craters along the route of march to new site, the progress of transport was slow and difficult. Personnel arrived at NUKERKE R.21 b.38 about 18.00 hours, but the transport was unable to negotiate the steep ascent to this village until the following morning.	WRG See Locations 122 Inf Bde.
		18.00	HQ and ADS established	
HQ + ADS. NUKERKE R.21 b.38	11/11/18	–	Dull + misty. Rain. Holding party from late ADS Q.21 b.8.7 rejoined HQ Operation Order No 73 received. This Amb to move forward and establish HQ + ADS at NEDERBRAKEL 30/N 17 central leaving small Collecting Post at NUKERKE until relieved on 12/11/18. 139 Field Amb. move from VICHTE and establish themselves at KERKOVE & BERCHEM to evacuate casualties across SCHELDT. ~~[illegible] to NEDERBRAKEL~~ The 123 and 124 Inf. Bdes resume advance at 9.00 hours. Objective River DENDRE. This Field Amb to keep in touch with these forward Brigades.	WRG.
		10.00	Wire received from ADMS reference cessation of hostilities at 11.00 hours. (Continued)	

D. D. & L., London, E.C.
(10340) Wt W5300/P713 750,000 5/18 E 2188 Forms/C2118/16

Army Form C. 2118.

WAR DIARY
or
INTELLIGENCE SUMMARY.
(*Erase heading not required.*)

Instructions regarding War Diaries and Intelligence Summaries are contained in F. S. Regs., Part II. and the Staff Manual respectively. Title pages will be prepared in manuscript.

VOLUME XXIII. Page 6

Place	Date	Hour	Summary of Events and Information	Remarks and references to Appendices
NUKERKE	11/11/18	–	(Continued) In accordance with instructions Officer + advance party proceeded to establish Collecting Post conveniently situated to 123 + 124 Brigades. A.D.S. established 13.00 hours at NEDERBRAKEL. (30/N 17 central) Holding party left at NUKERKE. Main body with transport + cars moved off by route march 14.00 hours. HQ established Sheet 30/N 17 central NEDERBRAKEL Evacuations to 139 Field Amb. BERCHEM.	WRG
SHEET 30				
HQ & ADS NEDERBRAKEL N 17. central	12/11/18	–	Fine. Bright + sunny. 124 Inf Bde moved forward to occupy positions as shewn on location table. MDS + DRS established by 140 Field Amb at NUKERKE. Holding party rejoined this HQ. All bearers attached to 123 Inf Bde with wheeled stretchers rejoined this HQ. Runners left with Battalions and suitable car posts established. (see margin) Casualties through ADS 27 sick. Evacuations to BERCHEM.	See Location table Car post for 124 Bde O. 17. d. 8. 8. WRG
HQ + ADS NEDERBRAKEL	13/11/18	–	Fine. Bright sunny weather continues. Brigade Operation Order received. 123 Inf. Bde take over outpost line P.27 c.0.0 to V7.c.0.0 from 31st + 35th Divisions. Casualties attended to at ADS. included released British Prisoners of War from HAL. 12 evacuated. 6 others treated. Several civilians treated and a few evacuated Ordinary evacuations 1 Officer 5 OR sick. Evacuations to BERCHEM. Brigade Operation Order (123 Bde) received. Details relating to position + duties of outposts. Bridges at Q 20 a 8 6 and P.36 c 36 open for lorry traffic from 13.00 hours today.	Car post 123 Bde. M.18 d. 3. 3. WRG

D. D. & L., London, E.C.
(10341) Wt W3300/P713 750,000 3/18 E 2088 Forms/C2118/16

Instructions regarding War Diaries and Intelligence Summaries are contained in F. S. Regs., Part II. and the Staff Manual respectively. Title pages will be prepared in manuscript.

WAR DIARY
or
INTELLIGENCE SUMMARY.
(Erase heading not required.)

Army Form C. 2118.

VOLUME XXIII Page 7.

Place SHEET 30	Date	Hour	Summary of Events and Information	Remarks and references to Appendices
HQ & ADS NEDERBRAKEL	14/11/18	–	Bright sunny weather continues. RAMC operation Order No 74 received. 140 Field Amb. move this morning from NUKERKE to LIERDE ST MARTIN 30/O.16 (124 Inf Bde area) 139 Field Amb move tomorrow from BERCHEM & KERKOVE to NEDERBRAKEL 5 wards each accommodating 16 patients now open at this ADS. No cases evacuated today. Waiting arrival MAC Cars. RAMC Operation Order No 75. received. This Field Amb to act as DRS until Division moves forward, and to be responsible for collection of sick of 122 Inf Bde. 139 Field Amb move 16th inst to GRAMMONT (123 Inf Bde Area)	WRG
HQ + DRS. NEDERBRAKEL	15/11/18	–	Fine bright weather. Personnel of this Amb assisting with arrangements for relieving evacuated civilians returning through NEDERBRAKEL. Party of 50 British P of W. collected from NINOVE by MAC cars and evacuated to 36 CCS. SWEVEGHEM. Other evacuations 33 sick – to 36 CCS.	WRG
HQ & DRS. NEDERBRAKEL	16/11/18	–	Bright sunny weather. Cold. 122 Inf Bde relieve 124 Inf Bde in outpost line west of GRAMMONT - VRIJHEID road. On relief sick of 124 Inf Bde to be evacuated by this Unit.	WRG

(Continued)

D. D. & L., London, E.C.
(1034 :) Wt W3300/P713 750,000 3/18 E 2188 Forms/C2118/16

Instructions regarding War Diaries and Intelligence Summaries are contained in F. S. Regs., Part II. and the Staff Manual respectively. Title pages will be prepared in manuscript.

WAR DIARY
or
INTELLIGENCE SUMMARY.
(Erase heading not required.)

Army Form C. 2118.

VOLUME XXIII. Page 8.

Place	Date	Hour	Summary of Events and Information	Remarks and references to Appendices
SHEET 30			(Continued) Evacuations to 17 CCS DEERLYCK. Sick 40. Capt L. W Bain proceeded on leave to UK. ADMS Administrative Instructions dated 16/11/18 relative to march of 41 Div to Germany, received. Div: Order No 284 ref: advance 2/Army received.	WRG
HQ + DRS NEDERBRAKEL	17/11/18	–	Weather fine. Cold. Conference ADMS Office. 10.45 am. 96 sick cases evacuated to 17 + 36 CCS.	See Copy Medical Arrangements from 18/11/18 onwards. WRG
HQ + DRS NEDERBRAKEL	18/11/18	–	Cold. Snow fell during morning. Rain in the evening. Bde Operation Order 252 received. Field Ambulance moved off with transport 7.30 hours and proceeded by route march through (SHEET 30) N 33. 24. O 25 26 32 U 3 10 17. 24. 29 to DEUX ACREN Sheet 38 C.6.a 4.2 and established HQ at Chateau. Capt Cheney & small party RAMC OR remained behind with cars at DRS to complete evacuations (see Appendix) Brigade Sick collected with Ford Cars.	Positions of lines to be taken up by 41 Div. during advance
SHEET 38			Capt. Cheney's party after completion of evacuations at DRS NEDERBRAKEL reported with cars to this HQ.	WRG
HQ. Chateau DEUX ACREN C.6.a 4.2	19/11/18	–	Fine in the morning with rain later in day. ADMS Instructions M117 received ref evacuation of sick on line of march. 138 Field Amb collects sick of 122 Bde + HQ group 139 + 140 Field Amb collect sick of 123 + 124 Bdes and evacuate to 138 Field Amb. 138 Field Amb evacuate to AUDENARDE Group of CCS. (Continued)	WRG

D. D. & L., London, E.C.
(10341) Wt W5300/P713 750,000 3/15 E 2188 Forms/C2118/16

Instructions regarding War Diaries and Intelligence Summaries are contained in F. S. Regs., Part II. and the Staff Manual respectively. Title pages will be prepared in manuscript.

WAR DIARY
or
~~INTELLIGENCE SUMMARY.~~

(*Erase heading not required.*)

Army Form C. 2118.

VOLUME XXIII Page 9.

Place	Date	Hour	Summary of Events and Information	Remarks and references to Appendices
			(Continued) 138 Field Amb leave behind small party if necessary when Unit moves forward, to complete evacuation. ADMS 41 Div visited HQ this Ambulance.	
HQ. DEUX ACREN	20/11/18	-	Weather dull and misty. Brigade Operation Order No 283 received. 41 Div to be replaced by another Division in the line today. In connection with above this Field Ambulance moved off in rear of Brigade at 10.45 hours and proceeded to SARLARDINGE by march route: established HQ at Sheet 30/V 10 a. 6. 4. (Schoolhouse). Hospital in Convent. DRO 988 dated 19/11/18. Lt Col W. Ross Gardner DSO. RAMC OC this Field Amb. awarded bar to DSO. Major J. La F Lauder. DSO. MC. RAMC. of this Field Amb. awarded bar to M.C.	WRG
HQ. SARLARDINGE 30/V 10 a 6 4	21/11/18	-	Weather cold, dull, misty. Ambulance cars evacuating to CCS had to turn back with patients owing to road being congested with French lorries - some detached. Sick cases dealt with for past week average 25 daily. Reference 41 Div G 217 - Active Service Army Schools, Capt W. M. Chesney RAMC selected as Education Officer of this Unit.	WRG
HQ. SARLARDINGE	22/11/18	-	Weather bright, frosty. All cases evacuated from Hospital to CCS 6.00 hours.	WRG

D. D. & L., London, E.C.
(1034) Wt W3300/P713 750,000 3/15 E 2688 Forms/C2118/16

Instructions regarding War Diaries and Intelligence Summaries are contained in F. S. Regs., Part II. and the Staff Manual respectively. Title pages will be prepared in manuscript.

WAR DIARY
or
INTELLIGENCE SUMMARY.
(*Erase heading not required.*)

Army Form C. 2118.

VOLUME XXIII Page 10

Place	Date	Hour	Summary of Events and Information	Remarks and references to Appendices
HQ. SARLARDINGE	23/11/18	-	Fine, bright frosty weather. Divisional Commander visited HQ & Hospital.	WRG
— do —	24/11/18	-	Bright frosty weather. All M.A.C cars returned to No 2 MAC (ADMS instructions)	WRG
— do —	25/11/18	-	Bright frosty weather. Thaw later in day. Presentation of Medals & awards by G.O.C Division at EVERBECQ 10.00 hours. Recipients of this Field Amb. Lt Col W Ross Gardner. Bar to DSO. Major J Le F Lauder. " " MC. 66309 Pte W. J. Terry RAMC. Military Medal 71952 " G.E. Shea —"— —"— 74099 " L.G. Coles —"— —"— Evacuations to 17 CCS. HAL.	WRG
— do —	26/11/18	-	Fine. Evacuations to AUDENARDE (3 Aus. C.C.S) Bde Warning Order No R259 received:- 41 Div: will move commencing on or after 1st Dec 1918 to an area just EAST of NAMUR. This move from the present area will probably be divided into six days march.	WRG
— do —	27/11/18	-	Rain. Two civilians admitted to Hospital from EVERBECQ suffering from wounds from hand grenade left behind by Germans. One died in Hospital: the other evacuated to CCS.	WRG

D. D. & L., London, E.C.
(1034) Wt W5300/P713 750,000 3/1? E 2688 Forms/C2118/16

Instructions regarding War Diaries and Intelligence Summaries are contained in F. S. Regs., Part II. and the Staff Manual respectively. Title pages will be prepared in manuscript.

WAR DIARY
or
~~INTELLIGENCE SUMMARY.~~

(Erase heading not required.)

Army Form C. 2118.

VOLUME XXIII Page 11

Place	Date	Hour	Summary of Events and Information	Remarks and references to Appendices
SARLARDINGE HQ.	28/11/18	-	Raining	WRG
do	29/11/18	-	Raining	WRG
do	30/11/18	-	Dull. Admissions of sick to Hospital remain normal - averaging about 25 daily. Personnel of Unit evacuated sick during Month:- RAMC 16. ASC 12. Reinforcements received RAMC 12 ASC 6.	WRG

W. Ross Gardner
Lieut Colonel RAMC
O.C. 138th Field Ambulance.

D. D. & L., London, E.C.
(1031) Wt W5300/P713 750,000 3/15 B 2688 Forms/C2118/16

A.D.M.S.
41 Div.

Locations of 122 Inf Bde and Medical Posts 18.00 hours 1/11/18

Brigade HQ	O 36	a	3. 2
C.P.	P 25	c	5. 6
ADS	O 23	b	9. 2

(MAC cars are evacuating from this ADS)

RAPs

15 Hants	P 31	c	0. 8
18 K.R.R.	P 33	b	8 8
Relay posts	P 26	a	8. 0
12 E Surrey	O 24	b	4 8

These posts are being handed over to relieving Field Ambulance 30 Div. commencing tonight 12 midnight

It is also notified for your information that a bridge over

the canal at KNOKKE capable of carrying 10 to 20 tons is now being erected

W. Ross Gardner
Lt. Col.

Field
1/11/18

The positions of the various lines to be taken up by 41 Div during advance are as under:-

A LINE. ENGHIEN - SOIGNIES - LOUVIERE
B " HAL - BRAMLOIGNTE - MANIGGE JUNC
C " S.E. BRUSSELS - TILLET - FLEURES - - TENNIES
D " GEMBLOUX - NAMUR
E " ARDENNES - JAUCHE
F " LINE N & S through HUY
G " " " " AMAY
H " " " " FLAMMIEL - COMBLAIN
I " S of LIEGE through DOLEMBREUX to CHEBRON
J " MAGMEL E of LIEGE to TROIS POINTS
K " On the RHINE at COLOGNE

[signature] Lt Col
R.A.M.C.
O.C. 138th Field Ambulance.

MEDICAL ARRANGEMENTS

From 18th onwards all cases will be evacuated to group of CCS at AUDENARDE.

On 18th these will be evacuated by Div. Cars and not by M.A.C.

During the advance all roads will be one way roads only – one East & one West. Drivers of M.T. Cars must be instructed under no circumstances will they be allowed to proceed against the traffic.

The 122nd Infantry Brigade Group will include:–

228 Field Coy. R.E.
No 2 Coy Div Train
11 Army Bde R.F.A.

One M.O. will visit the Train Coy and Field Coy. R.E. daily as required

W. Mc Gardner
Lt Col R.A.M.C.
O.C. 138th Field Ambulance.

Field
17/11/18

LOCATIONS -- A.D.S. C.Ps. R.A.Ps. ETC. –

Date →	Nov 5		6		7		8		9		10		11	
	Location	Time hours	Location	Time	Location	Time	Location	Time	Location	Time	Location	Time	Location	Time
H.Q. 138 F. Amb	J32, c9.8	13.00							Q21 b8.7	18.00	R21, b3.8	20.00	R21	
A.D.S.	P3, b1.7	13.00							do		R21 a7.8		M27, a6.9 Marquette	9.00
Coll^g Post	P12, b3.3	13.00							—					
Car Post	P10, d5.4	13.00							—					
M.D.S. (140 FA)			I9. a0.4	9.00					[illegible]	[illegible]				
Div. H.Q. (advanced)									Q21 a5.2	[illegible]				
H.Q. 122 Inf. Bde													Nukerke	9.00
18 K.R.R.	H12, b2.8	18.00	H12 a05.75	9.00							R16, b4.3	22.00	R16 b4.3	
12 E. Surreys			H12, b3.7	9.00							R17, d4.2	22.00	R17 d4.2	
15 Hants.	H12 b2.8	18.00	H12, b3.7	9.00							R21, b90.45	22.00	R21, b90.45	
H.Q. 123 Inf. Bde	J28, d4.7	13.00	J27, d9.1	9.00					Q24 d.2.4	20.00			M22 b8.8	9.00
11 R.W. Surreys	Q7, d5.8	13.00							R25 b (SW 8906) ~~R19 b.c.d.~~	18.00				
10 R.W. Kents.	K31, b6.6	13.00							R19 b5.2	20.00				
23 Middlesex	J34, c4.8	13.00							Q12 d5.3	20.00				
H.Q. 124 Inf. Bde									Q29 central	18.00			M22 b8.8	9.00
20 D.L. Inf									Q10, d8.0	19.00			M11 c4.3	
10 R.W. Surreys									TIEGHEM	18.00			M16 b7.3	
26 R. Fus.			I30, a3.5						Caster	18.00			M21 d3.7	

LOCATIONS.

	Nov. 12 (time)	Nov 13 (time)	Nov 14	Nov. 15	Nov. 16	Nov. 17	Monday. Nov 18.	Nov. 19.
H.Q.) 138 F.A. ADS}	N.17 central						Sh. 38 C 6, a 4.2 13.00	
Car post 124 Bde	O.17.d.8.8 16.00							
Car post 123 -		U 11 a 7.5 17.00 M 18 d.5.3. 10.00						
A.D.M.S. Div (H.Q)	Schoorisse 16.00							Sh. 30 Q 15 b 3.1 9.00
122 I. Bde				O 16 a 7.2 12.00			VIANE	
18 KRR				O 14 b 7.7 d 2.7 12.00			Bn. HQ. VIANE	
15 Hants				O 16, c 5.8 12.00			Bn HQ BIEVENE	
12 E Surreys.				U 8, b 9.6 12.00			Bn HQ. BIEVENE	
Car Post				O 16, c 5.8 12.00				
123 I. Bde.		U 10, b 3.3 17.00 M. 16. d. 4.5 10.00						Sammerages 9.00
23 Mdx. RAP		U 6 c 9.4 17.00 M. 12. c. 1.3 "						Shullenbeek "
10 R.W. Kents "		U 10, b 2.4 17.00 N. 13. d. 8.3 "						Tollezeel "
11 Queens "		U 5, d 5.7 17.00 M. 18. d. 3.7 "						Herennes "
139 Fd Amb								Sh. 30 N 15 c 8.7 9.00
124 I. Bde	P. 21.b Schendelbeke} 16.00							Sh. 30 R 19 b 4.8 "
20 D.L.I. RAP	O.17.b.d, O.18 a c O.17. d. 5.8. 16.00							Sh. 30 R 5 d 4.3
10 R.W.S. RAP	Gemeldorp. P. 19. c. 5.5. 16.00							Sh. 30 Q 33 b 2.2
26 R.F. RAP	O.12 d+ P. 7. a c O. 12. d. 4.3. 16.00							Sh. 30 R 19 b 7.7
140 Fd Amb				N 13 d 5.5 16.00				Sh. 30 Q. 17 c 3.7 9.00
141 D.A.C.								
19 Middlesex								Q 19, d 7.5

LOCATIONS

	Nov 20	time	Nov 21	time	Nov 22	Nov 23	Nov 24	Nov 25
41 Div. HQ	Santbergen		Grammont					
No 2 Co Div Train	–		Everbecq					
ADMS	–		Grammont					
122 Inf Bde	Everbecq		Everbecq					
138 Field Amb	30/V10. a 6.4 (Sarlardinge)		SARLARDINGE					
12 E Surrey	–		Everbecq					
15 Hants	–		Geofferdinge					
18 KRR	–		Sarlardinge					
123 Inf Bde								
139 Field Amb	Ghoy		Ghoy					
124 Inf Bde								
140 Field Amb	Bosch Straat N of Bievene		Bosch Straat				Gammerages	
19 Mdx	Ideghem		Ideghem					
41 DAC	30/P 22. a 2.8		30/P 22. a 2.8					
11 A.F. Art.			Overboulaere					
228 Field Co RE			Plankm					

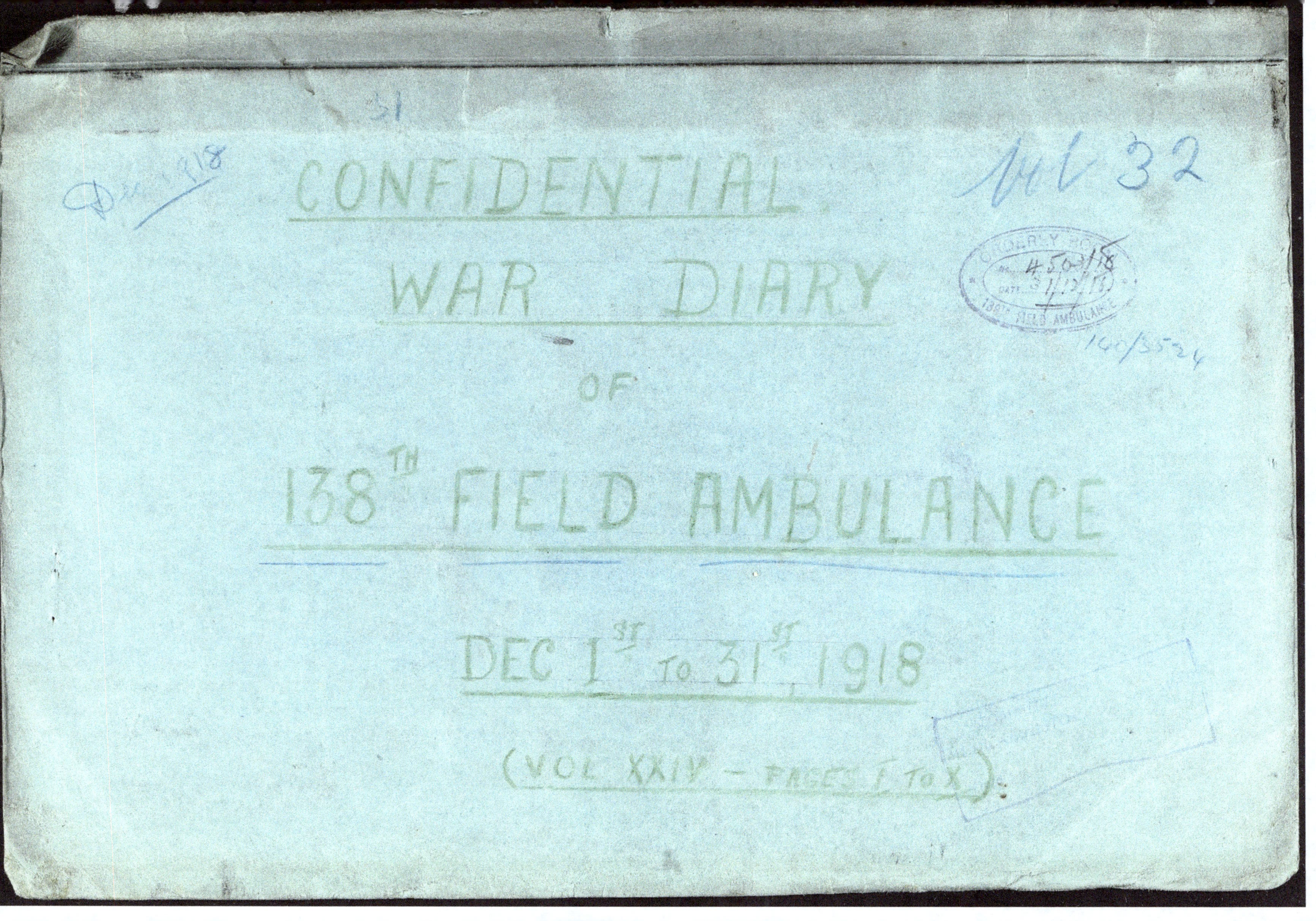
31
Dec 1918
Vol 32
CONFIDENTIAL
WAR DIARY
OF
138TH FIELD AMBULANCE
DEC 1ST TO 31ST 1918
(VOL XXIV - PAGES I TO X)
ORDERLY ROOM
No. 450/18
DATE 1/12/18
138TH FIELD AMBULANCE
140/3524

Instructions regarding War Diaries and Intelligence Summaries are contained in F. S. Regs., Part II. and the Staff Manual respectively. Title pages will be prepared in manuscript.

WAR DIARY
or
INTELLIGENCE SUMMARY.
(*Erase heading not required.*)

Army Form C. 2118.

VOLUME XXIV Page 1

Place	Date	Hour	Summary of Events and Information	Remarks and references to Appendices
HQ - DRS SARLARDINGE Sheet 30 U 10 a 6.4	1/12/18	-	Fine Cold & bright ADMS 41 Div M 194 - This Division is transferred from Second to Fourth Army at 23.59 hours 28/11/18 (X Corps) ADMS 41 Div M 199. Arrangements to be made to keep cases amenable to treatment for a few days in this DRS with a view to curtailing evacuations to CCS. 3 wards now open for treatment of sick cases includes one ward for Scabies Total Admissions this date Sick 27. Evacuations NIL.	WMB
HQ & DRS SARLARDINGE	2/12/18	-	Fine bright weather Evacuations to be restricted to not more than 25 daily. 3 Aus CCS at Audenarde closed. Evacuations from today to 17 CCS HAL. Total Admissions 16 Evacuations 25 Capt Sherry & 1 NCO RAMC proceeded to Reception Camp COURTRAI for temporary duty	WMB
do	3/12/18	-	Raining ADMS M 216 received. O.C 140 Field Amb will not transfer cases in future to 138 Field Amb. but will evacuate direct to CCS HAL 138 Field Amb to transfer 1 large car to 140 Field Amb. On arrival of car with evacuations at 17 CCS it was found that this CCS had moved. Cases were taken to 1 Canadian CCS near CHARLEROI Admissions 18.	WMB

D. D. & L., London, E.C.
(1034) Wt W5300/P713 750,000 3/15 E 2688 Forms/C2118/16

Instructions regarding War Diaries and Intelligence Summaries are contained in F. S. Regs., Part II. and the Staff Manual respectively. Title pages will be prepared in manuscript.

WAR DIARY
or
~~INTELLIGENCE~~ SUMMARY.
(Erase heading not required.)

Army Form C. 2118.

VOLUME XXIV Page 2.

Place	Date	Hour	Summary of Events and Information	Remarks and references to Appendices
			122 Inf Bde BM 753 received. Units who will shortly be marching into new area will carry out route marches on alternate days. Lorries may not be available so men should march in full equipment. Marches not to exceed 8 miles and foot inspections to be made	MMB.
HQ + DRS. GARLARDINGE	4/12/18	-	Raining 4 Wards now open. No evacuations are taking place pending instructions. Admissions 57 Cases were received from details of Reception Camp who were moving forward from COURTRAI. to new Area.	MMB.
— do —	5/12/18	-	Fine. Capt Chesney + NCO reported back to HQ. ADMS 41 Dn. M 236 received Evacuations until further orders to CCSs at CHARLEROI & NAMUR. 140 Field Amb to evacuate direct. 139 Field Amb to evacuate to 138 Field Amb on 6th + 7th afterwards direct to CCS. This Field Amb will commence clearing DRS on 6/12/18 2 Ambulance Cars and one lorry reporting to this Field Amb to assist in evacuations Admissions	MMB.

D. D. & L., London, E.C.
(10341) Wt W5300/P713 750,000 3/15 E 2688 Forms/C2118/16

Army Form C. 2118.

Instructions regarding War Diaries and Intelligence Summaries are contained in F. S. Regs., Part II. and the Staff Manual respectively. Title pages will be prepared in manuscript.

WAR DIARY
or
~~INTELLIGENCE SUMMARY.~~

(Erase heading not required.)

VOLUME XXIV. Page 3

Place	Date	Hour	Summary of Events and Information	Remarks and references to Appendices
HQ + DRS SARLARDINGE	6/12/18	-	Fine. Evacuation of DRS commenced in accordance with ADMS Instruction. Conference ADMS Office 3.0 pm today. points to be discussed:- Medical arrangements for march and new area Training and recreation in new area. Leave for Officers and men. Evacuations 56 6 cars and 1 lorry Admissions 15.	WMB
— do —	7/12/18	-	Fine. Cars and lorry returned from CHARLEROI after evacuating to 20 CCS + 55 CCS. Admissions 25. Evacuations NIL	WMB
— do —	8/12/18	-	Fine. 49 Cases evacuated this morning to CHARLEROI 8.30 hours. 122 Inf Bde Administrative Instructions and Brigade Operation Order No 257 received reference move of 41 Div from present area into NAMUR - HUY Area. This Field Ambulance to provide Horse Ambulance to bring in men who cannot march. Route taken by cars to to CHARLEROI :- GRAMMONT - ENGHIEN - HAL - NIVELLES - CHARLEROI. Cars returned 22.00 hours. Admissions 30. 2 MAC cars reported for duty.	WMB

D. D. & L., London, E.C.
(1034.) Wt W3300/P713 750,000 3/15 E 2688 Forms/C2118/16

Instructions regarding War Diaries and Intelligence Summaries are contained in F. S. Regs., Part II. and the Staff Manual respectively. Title pages will be prepared in manuscript.

WAR DIARY
or
~~INTELLIGENCE SUMMARY.~~
(Erase heading not required.)

Army Form C. 2118.

VOLUME XXIV Page 4

Place	Date	Hour	Summary of Events and Information	Remarks and references to Appendices
HQ & DRS SARLARDINGE	9/12/18	-	Raining in morning. Later fine. 17 Cases evacuated to CHARLEROI Admissions 14.	WMB
— do —	10/12/18	-	Fine Rain later in day. Evacuations 32 Received from Inf Bde. Memo No 5.C.H.47 All men considered unfit to undertake march to be sent to this Field Amb. tonight by 20.00 hours. These men will be disposed of by this Field Amb early tomorrow morning. 1. MAC. car returned to X Corps. Admissions 22. Medical Arrangements No 2 received from ADMS. Arrangements on March and on arrival at final destination.	WMB
do	11/12/18	.	Dull, with rain Evacuations 37 Presentation of French Croix de Guerre by G.O.C. Div at Grammont 11.00 hours Detachment of RAMC from this Amb. 2 Officers 38 Other Ranks Recipients of this Field Amb. Croix de Guerre à la Division. Lt Col W. Ross Gardner DSO RAMC Croix de Guerre à la Brigade. Sgt Major E Ratcliffe. DCM RAMC. Admissions 6	WMB
"A" Day of March program				

D. D. & L., London, E.C.
(1031) Wt W5300/P713 750,000 3/1? E 2188 Forms/C2118/16

Instructions regarding War Diaries and Intelligence Summaries are contained in F. S. Regs., Part II. and the Staff Manual respectively. Title pages will be prepared in manuscript.

WAR DIARY
or
~~INTELLIGENCE SUMMARY.~~
(Erase heading not required.)

Army Form C. 2118.

VOLUME XXIV Page 5

Place	Date	Hour	Summary of Events and Information	Remarks and references to Appendices
			Extract Medical Arrangements (ADMS) No 2 dated 10/12/18.- Field Ambulances to make necessary arrangements with their Brigade Groups to bring in men who fall out on the march. Evacuations on line of march will be to CCS Group at CHARLEROI and NAMUR whichever is nearest.	WMB.
SARLARDINGE Brussels 6 Map	12/12/18 B Day	- 9.00	Rain. This Field Ambulance moved off by route march via Grammont, Moerbeke, Viane, Herinnes to TERLINDEN and billeted there for the night. Hospital established. Rain fell throughout the march. Admissions 7. Evacuations 4.	WMB.
TERLINDEN	13/12/18 C Day	- 11.00	Dull. cloudy. Field Ambulance proceeded by route march to BIERGHES. Hospital established in Convent. Admissions 32 (This number included NYD Pyrexia 8 Sore feet 9) Evacuations NIL.	WMB.
BIERGHES	14/12/18 D Day	- 8.00	Fine. Evacuations to CHARLEROI 42. Field Ambulance proceeded by route march via Tubize, Clabecq, Braine le Chateau to WAUTHIER BRAINE, and billeted in Cotton Factory. Hospital established. Admissions 20. Capt C. C. Moore RAMC posted to 10 Queens for temporary duty.	WMB.

D. D. & L., London, E.C.
(1034) Wt W3300/P713 750,000 3/15 S 2188 Forms/C2118/16

Instructions regarding War Diaries and Intelligence Summaries are contained in F. S. Regs., Part II. and the Staff Manual respectively. Title pages will be prepared in manuscript.

WAR DIARY
or
~~INTELLIGENCE~~ SUMMARY.

(*Erase heading not required.*)

Army Form C. 2118.

VOLUME XXIV Page 6.

Place Brussels 6 Map	Date	Hour	Summary of Events and Information	Remarks and references to Appendices
NAUTHIER BRAINE	15/12/18 E Day	–	Fine Admissions 24. Evacuations 29 to Charleroi Major J. La T. Lander RAMC proceeded on leave.	WMB
— do —	16/12/18 F Day	– 11.00	Raining Roads in bad condition. Field Ambulance moved off and proceeded by route march via Braine l'Alleud to PLANCENOIT Hospital established there Admissions 11. Evacuations 10 to Charleroi.	WMB
PLANCENOIT	17/12/18 G Day	– 8.30	Raining. Roads in bad condition Field Ambulance moved off & proceeded by march route via Genappes and Quatrebras to TILLY Hospital established in School Admissions 5 Evacuations 6 to 20 CCS Charleroi. Capt L W Bain reported back from leave – posted to 10 Queens for temporary duty in relief of Capt C G Moore.	WMB

D. D. & L., London, E.C.
(1034 A) Wt W3300/P713 750,000 3/18 E 2688 Forms/C2118/16

Instructions regarding War Diaries and Intelligence Summaries are contained in F. S. Regs., Part II. and the Staff Manual respectively. Title pages will be prepared in manuscript.

WAR DIARY
or
~~INTELLIGENCE SUMMARY.~~
(Erase heading not required.)

Army Form C. 2118.

VOLUME XXIV. Page 10

Place	Date	Hour	Summary of Events and Information	Remarks and references to Appendices
MOHA	28/12/18	-	Rain. Admissions 8 Evacuations. 6	WMB
— do —	29/12/18	-	Rain. Admissions 7. Evacuations. 7 Warning Order G 15. received. This Division (41) will be transferred to Second Army to form part of Corps to relieve Canadian Corps in COLOGNE Bridgehead. Transfer to be completed as early as possible in January.	WMB
— do —	30/12/18	-	Rain - morning. later Fine. Admissions 9 Evacuations. 8	WMB
— do —	31/12/18	-	Fine Admissions 8 Evacuations 8	WMB

W M B Heaney Capt R.A.M.C.
O.C. 138th Field Ambulance.

D. D. & L., London, E.C.
(1034.) Wt W5300/P713 750,000 3/1: E 2688 Forms/C2118/16

Instructions regarding War Diaries and Intelligence Summaries are contained in F. S. Regs., Part II. and the Staff Manual respectively. Title pages will be prepared in manuscript.

WAR DIARY
or
~~INTELLIGENCE SUMMARY.~~
(Erase heading not required.)

Army Form C. 2118.

VOLUME XXIV Page 7

Place	Date	Hour	Summary of Events and Information	Remarks and references to Appendices
Brussels 6 Map				
TILLY	18/12/18	–	Rain. Cold + windy.	
	H day	12.30	Field Ambulance moved off and proceeded by route march to SOMBREFFE. Hospital established in School.	
			Capt C.G. Moore Rame reported to DMS V Army for posting as OC No 4 MAC.	
			Admissions 14	
			Evacuations 10 to 55 CCS Charleroi	MMB.
SOMBREFFE	19/12/18	–	Rain.	
		9.00	Field Ambulance moved off and proceeded by route march to ST SERVAIS, outskirts of Namur. Hospital established.	MMB
	I day		Admissions 4	
			Evacuations 17 to 48 CCS Namur.	
			Capt Bain reported back to this Field Amb. for duty.	
Namur 8 Map				
ST SERVAIS.	20/12/18	–	Rain.	
	J day	8.45	Field Ambulance moved off and proceeded by route march to LAVOIR, from where they were brought on by lorry and cars to final destination MOHA.	
			Hospital established.	MMB
			Admissions 5	
			Evacuations 1 to 48 CCS Namur	

D. D. & L., London, E.C.
(10341) Wt W3300/P713 750,000 3/15 E 2688 Forms/C2118/16

Instructions regarding War Diaries and Intelligence Summaries are contained in F. S. Regs., Part II. and the Staff Manual respectively. Title pages will be prepared in manuscript.

WAR DIARY
or
~~INTELLIGENCE SUMMARY.~~
(Erase heading not required.)

Army Form C. 2118.

VOLUME XXIV Page 8.

Place (Liege No 7 Map)	Date	Hour	Summary of Events and Information	Remarks and references to Appendices
MOHA	21/12/18 K day	–	Fine Extract Medical Arrangements No 2. 140 Field Amb. will open DRS at HUY and collect sick from 124 Inf. Bde. 139 Field Amb will open DRS in Chateau near WARNANT and collect sick from 123 Inf Bde and 122 Inf. Bde. 138 Field Amb. will remain closed. They will collect from Artillery Group in OTEPPE-BORDINNE Area and HQ Group in WANZE-VILAMONT Area and evacuate to 140 Field Amb. A CCS will be established at HUY for evacuation from Division. Field Ambulances will change monthly. 1st change 140 Field Amb and 138 Field Amb. 2nd change 139 Field Amb and 140 Field Amb. Admissions 9. Evacuations 18. Lt Col W. Ross Gardner, OC this Field Amb. proceeded on leave.	WMB
MOHA	22/12/18	–	Rain. Admissions 4. Evacuations 5.	WMB
MOHA	23/12/18	–	Fine Admissions 3 Evacuations 2. 7 Other ranks proceeded to United Kingdom for demobilization (6 miners 1 pivotal)	WMB

D. D. & L., London, E.C.
(10341) Wt W3300/P713 750,000 3/18 E 2688 Forms/C2118/16

Instructions regarding War Diaries and Intelligence Summaries are contained in F. S. Regs., Part II. and the Staff Manual respectively. Title pages will be prepared in manuscript.

WAR DIARY
or
~~INTELLIGENCE~~ SUMMARY.
(*Erase heading not required.*)

Army Form C. 2118.

VOLUME XXIV. Page 9.

Place	Date	Hour	Summary of Events and Information	Remarks and references to Appendices
MOHA	24/12/18	–	Fine morning. Rain later in day. Medical arrangements No. 3 received from ADMS. This Field Ambulance will collect sick from R.A. Group, the 3 Field Co RE at MOHA, 41 MGC at COUTHOIN and 19 Mdx at BAS OHA and any other troops located in the area. Evacuations from division to 48 CCS Namur. CCS at HUY not yet established. This Field Amb continue to evacuate to 140 Field Amb. at HUY. Admissions 4 Evacuations 5	wmb.
— do —	25/12/18	–	Fine. Admissions. 3. Evacuations. nil	wmb.
— do —	26/12/18	–	Fine Admissions 2 Evacuations 4 Lt. R.C. Mauger MORC posted to this Field Amb. for duty.	wmb.
— do —	27/12/18	–	Rain. Admissions 9 Evacuations 10	wmb.

D. D. & L., London, E.C.
(1032 1) Wt W3300/P713 750,000 3/18 E 2688 Forms/C2118/16

CONFIDENTIAL

MAY. 1919

41st DIV

Box 2444

May 1919

WAR. DIARY.

Jan 19 to May 19

138 FIELD AMB.

1 Confidential

Vol 33.

Jan. 1919

140/3534

War Diary

of

138 Field Ambulance RAMC

Went to Germany. 8/1/19.

From 1-1-1919 To 31-1-1919

Volume XXV

Instructions regarding War Diaries and Intelligence Summaries are contained in F. S. Regs., Part II. and the Staff Manual respectively. Title pages will be prepared in manuscript.

WAR DIARY
or
~~INTELLIGENCE SUMMARY.~~
(Erase heading not required.)

Army Form C. 2[illegible]

VOLUME XXV. Page 1.

Place Map 7 Rege	Date	Hour	Summary of Events and Information	Remarks and references to Appendices
MOHA.	1/1/19	-	Fine Rain later in day. Admissions 5. Evacuations 5	WRS
— do —	2/1/19	-	Fine Admissions 4. Evacuations 4.	WRS
— do —	3/1/19	-	Fine Intermittent rain. Admissions 8 Evacuations. 8 1 RAMC personnel died. 64356 Sgt A. Lindsay.	WRS
— do —	4/1/19	-	Fine. Rain later in day. Admissions 7. Evacuations. 7. RAMC Warning Order No 76 received. 41 Div. will relieve 1/Canadian Div. at the Cologne Bridgehead. Moves will commence on 6/1/19. Orders for moves of Field Ambulances will be issued later. All Field Ambulances will hold an advance party in readiness to move at sudden notice.	WRS

D. D. & L., London, E.C.
(10341) Wt W5300/P713 750,000 3/15 E 2488 Forms/C2118/16

Army Form C. 2118

Instructions regarding War Diaries and Intelligence Summaries are contained in F. S. Regs., Part II. and the Staff Manual respectively. Title pages will be prepared in manuscript.

WAR DIARY
or
~~INTELLIGENCE SUMMARY.~~
(Erase heading not required.)

VOLUME XXV. Page 2

Place	Date	Hour	Summary of Events and Information	Remarks and references to Appendices
MOHA.	5/1/19	-	Fine - rain during afternoon. Admissions 6 Evacuations 6	WRC
		15.00	Funeral of Sgt Lindsay RAMC. Moha Cemetery. 41 Div. Order No 287 dated 4/1/19 reference move of 41 Div to COLOGNE to relieve 1st Canadian Division, received. 41 Div Medical Administrative Instructions No 3 dated 5/1/19 received. 138 Field Amb will entrain 8/1/19. They will move from MOHA on the morning of 7/1/19 and take over buildings etc at HUY occupied by 140 Field Amb. and function that place until relieved by a Canadian Field Amb. O.C. 138 Field Amb will arrange to send an advance party of maximum of 10 men leaving 7/1/19 to take over their location at URBACH. Reference Warning Order No 76. Advance party will leave early 6/1/19.	
MOHA	6/1/19	-	Fine 1 NCO and 9 men proceeded to report to DMS 2/army COLOGNE for duty in connection with sick British Prisoners of War. Advance party of 1 NCO + 9 men proceeded to URBACH to take over location. Admissions 6 Discharges 6	WRC

D. D. & L., London, E.C.
(1034 ?) Wt W5300/P713 750,000 3/18 E 2188 Forms/C2118/16

Instructions regarding War Diaries and Intelligence Summaries are contained in F. S. Regs., Part II. and the Staff Manual respectively. Title pages will be prepared in manuscript.

WAR DIARY
or
~~INTELLIGENCE~~ SUMMARY.
(*Erase heading not required.*)

Army Form C. 2[illegible]

VOLUME XXV Page 3.

Place	Date	Hour	Summary of Events and Information	Remarks and references to Appendices
MÖHA	7/1/19	–	Fine.	
		9.00	Field Ambulance moved off by route march and proceeded to occupy buildings etc vacated by 140 Field Amb at HUY.	
			Admissions 6.	
			Discharges 6 to 50 CCS. Huy	WRG
HUY.	8/1/19	–	Fine. Admissions 13. Discharges 13 to 50 CCS.	
		11.00	Transport proceeded to Station for entrainment.	
		12.00	Ambulance Cars left and proceeded by road to URBACH	
		15.00	Field Ambulance moved off to Station.	
		16.30	No 9 Train moved off with Field Amb + Transport.	WRG
No 9 Train	9/1/19	8.30	Fine Arrived COLOGNE	
		10.30	Arrived HOFFNUNGSTHAL. Detrained	
		12.00	Transport all detrained	
		13.00	Field Ambulance proceeded by route march to URBACH.	
		16.00	Arrived URBACH.	WRG

D. D. & L., London, E.C.
(10312) Wt W5300/P713 750,000 3/15 B 2688 Forms/C2118/16

Instructions regarding War Diaries and Intelligence Summaries are contained in F. S. Regs., Part II. and the Staff Manual respectively. Title pages will be prepared in manuscript.

Army Form C. 21[illegible]

WAR DIARY
or
~~INTELLIGENCE SUMMARY.~~
(Erase heading not required.)

VOLUME XXV. Page 4.

Place	Date	Hour	Summary of Events and Information	Remarks and references to Appendices
URBACH 7 miles SE of COLOGNE	10/1/19	-	Fine. Admissions } NIL. Discharges } Major J Le F Lauder RAMC returned from leave.	WRG
URBACH	11/1/19	-	Fine Admissions 1 Discharges 1 to 1 Can CCS BONN. OC Field Amb. Lt Col. W Ross Gardner. RAMC returned from leave.	WRG
— do —	12/1/19	-	Fine Admissions 6 Discharges 6 to 2 Can CCS BONN	WRG
— do —	13/1/19	-	Rain. Admissions 3 Discharges 3 to 44 CCS COLOGNE Extract Medical Arrangements for 41 Bn MGC. 138 Field Amb will be responsible for the medical care and sanitation of C Coy at PORZ.	WRG

D. D. & L., London, E.C.
(10343) Wt W5300/P713 750,000 3/15 E 2488 Forms/C2118/16

Instructions regarding War Diaries and Intelligence Summaries are contained in F. S. Regs., Part II. and the Staff Manual respectively. Title pages will be prepared in manuscript.

WAR DIARY
or
~~INTELLIGENCE SUMMARY.~~
(*Erase heading not required.*)

Army Form C. 2118.

VOLUME XXV Page 5

Place	Date	Hour	Summary of Events and Information	Remarks and references to Appendices
			ADMS Instructions M 107/21/5 dated 12/1/19 :- 139 Field Amb will open D.R.S at WAHN on 15/1/19. 138 + 140 Field Amb will transfer all cases to 139 Field Amb on + after 15/1/19. 139 Field Amb will send back overnight to affiliated Field Ambulances all RTDs for distribution to Units. OCs 138 + 140 Field Amb will each detail 1 Medical Officer for duty at DRS to report 14/1/19.	WRG
URBACH.	14/1/19	-	Fine. Major L S C Roche, RAMC proceeded to duty at D.R.S. WAHN. Capt W M Chesney, RAMC proceeded to 15 Hants for duty as M.O. Admissions 3 Discharges 1 to CCS Cologne.	WRG
— do —	15/1/19	-	Rain. Admissions 10 Discharges 8 to 44 CCS Cologne 4 to 41 D.R.S. WAHN.	WRG

D. D. & L., London, E.C.
(1934.) Wt W3300/P713 750,000 3/15 E 2688 Forms/C2118/16

Instructions regarding War Diaries and Intelligence Summaries are contained in F. S. Regs., Part II. and the Staff Manual respectively. Title pages will be prepared in manuscript.

WAR DIARY
or
~~INTELLIGENCE SUMMARY.~~
(Erase heading not required.)

Army Form C. 2118.

VOLUME XXV. Page 6.

Place	Date	Hour	Summary of Events and Information	Remarks and references to Appendices
URBACH	16/1/19	-	Fine Admissions 11 Discharges 9 Extract Medical Arrangements ADMS, M 163/2/13 15/1/19. 138 Field Ambulance will be responsible for medical care and sanitary supervision of :- No 2 Co Divisional Train situated at ROSRATH by arrangement with MO i/c 18 KRRC, ROSRATH. 41 Div M.T. Co situated at PORZ.	WRG
— do —	17/1/19	-	Rain Admissions 5. Discharges 7	WRG
— do —	18/1/19	-	Rain Admissions 13. Discharges. 13.	WRG
— do —	19/1/19	-	Fine Admissions 4 Discharges 4	WRG

D. D. & L., London, E.C.
(10341) Wt W5300/P713 750,000 3/15 E 2688 Forms/C2118/16

Instructions regarding War Diaries and Intelligence Summaries are contained in F. S. Regs., Part II. and the Staff Manual respectively. Title pages will be prepared in manuscript.

WAR DIARY
or
~~INTELLIGENCE SUMMARY~~.
(Erase heading not required.)

Army Form C. 2[illegible]

VOLUME XXV Page 7

Place	Date	Hour	Summary of Events and Information	Remarks and references to Appendices
URBACH	20/1/19	-	Dull - cloudy. Admissions 11 Discharges 7	WRS
- do -	21/1/19	-	Fine. Cold bright weather. Admissions 8 Discharges 8	WRS
- do -	22/1/19	-	Fine Cold & bright. Admissions 9 Discharges 9	WRS
- do -	23/1/19	-	Fine Admissions 10 Discharges 9	WRS
- do -	24/1/19	-	Fine Admissions 10 Discharges 10.	WRS

D. D. & L., London, E.C.
(10341) Wt W5300/P713 750,000 3/15 E 2688 Forms/C2118/16

Instructions regarding War Diaries and Intelligence Summaries are contained in F. S. Regs., Part II. and the Staff Manual respectively. Title pages will be prepared in manuscript.

WAR DIARY
or
INTELLIGENCE SUMMARY.
(Erase heading not required.)

Army Form C. 21

VOLUME XXV Page 8

Place	Date	Hour	Summary of Events and Information	Remarks and references to Appendices
URBACH	25/1/19		Fine but Cold. Admissions 6 Discharges 6	WRG
— do —	26/1/19.		Fine & Cold Admissions 4. Discharges 4.	WRG
— do —	27/1/19		Cold with Snow Admissions 5. Discharges 4	WRG
— do —	28/1/19		Cold with Snow Admissions 9 Discharges 9 Capt W.J.S. Selkirk RAMC arrived for duty with this unit & is taken on the strength.	WRG
	29/1/19.		Cold & Frosty Admissions 8 Discharges 6	WRG
	30/1/19		Cold & Frosty Admissions 5 Discharges 9	WRG
	31/1/19		Cold & Frosty. Admissions 8 Discharges 7 1 Motor cycle returned from [illegible] Workshops.	WRG

31/1/19.

W Ross Gardner
Lieut Colonel RAMC
Commanding 135th Field Ambulance

D. D. & L., London, E.C. (A6945) Wt W5300/P1. 750,000 3/16 E 2688 Forms/C2118/16

WAR DIARY. 138 Field Amb.

MARCH 1919. VOL XXVII

APPENDICES. MARCH 1919

I DEFENCE SCHEME.

I A. First amendment to MEDICAL DEFENCE SCHEME

II Div: Admin: Instruction No 7.

III MARCH TABLES.

IV BRIGADE OPERATION ORDER No 263.

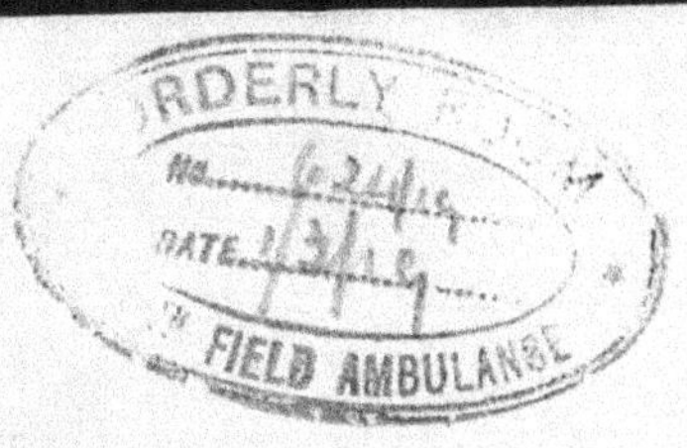

Appendix 1

Copy No. 8

[illegible].

DEFENCE SCHEME.

Right Sub-Sector, Left Division. X Corps.

Reference maps:- Sheet 2910 - 1/25,000 - OVERATH,
" 2911 - " - ENGELSKIRCHEN.

CONTENTS.

1. Brigade Sector,
2. Boundaries.
3. Description of the country,
4. Defensive system,
5. Policy of occupation,
6. Disposition of troops and action in case of attack,
7. Vickers Guns.
8. Points of Observation,
9. Defensive Organisation of Artillery.

APPENDICES.

"A" Table of Permanent Guards and Picquets,

MAPS.

"A" Boundaries, Defensive Line, Machine Gun Positions,

-0-0-0-0-0-0-0-0-0-0-0-0-0-

DISTRIBUTION:-

1. File,
2. War Diary.
3. 12th E. Surrey Regt.
4. 15th Hampshire Regt.
5. 1/7th Middlesex Regt.
6. 12[illegible]th Army Bde, R.F.A.
7. 228th Field Coy, R.E.
8. 138th Field Ambulance.
9. "B" Coy, 41st Bn. M.G.C.
10. No.2 Co, 41 Div. Train.
11. 41st Division "G".
12. 41st Division "Q".
13. C.R.A., 41st Division.
14. C.R.E., 41st Division.
15. A.D.M.S. 41st Division.
16. D.A.P.M. 41st Division.
17. 123rd Infantry Brigade.
18. 124th Infantry Brigade.
19. 103rd Infantry Brigade.
20. Staff Captain Civil Duties.
21. [illegible].P.M. ROSRATH.
22. G.O.C. Brigade.
23. Brigade Major.
24. Staff Captain.
25. Bde. Signal Officer.
26. Spare.
27. "
28. "
29. "
30. "

1. Brigade Sector.

The 122nd Infantry Brigade, 41st British Division, holds the Right Sub-Sector of the front of the Left Division, X Corps, (Cologne Bridgehead).

The 103rd Infantry Brigade, 34th British Division, is on the Right, junction at T 9,3 - 6,6.

The 124th Infantry Brigade, 41st British Division, is on the Left, junction at S 8,8 - 4,9,

2. Boundaries.

The Military Northern and Southern Boundaries are shewn on Map "1".

The Boundaries for Civil Administration do not necessarily coincide with the Military Boundaries: the Civil Boundaries are drawn to coincide as far as possible with the present German Boundaries of each respective Burgermeistorei.

The Perimeter of the Bridgehead is twenty miles, but the Eastern boundary has been adjusted to conform with the Communal Civil Boundaries and runs:-

From junction with Southern Division at the bend of the NAAF, three-quarters of a mile N.E. of HOLL - along the NAFF B to ABELSNAAF - HECK - along road to DRABENDERHOHE (exclusive) - N. along road through BRUCHEN, thence along stream to HALTENBACH (exclusive) to HARDT (inclusive)

3. Description of the Country.

From the valley of the Rhine Eastwards, the ground gradually rises in gentle slopes as far as the River SULZ: East of the River SULZ the country becomes very hilly and broken, being inter-sected with deep valleys, and ravines with steep convex slopes. The ravines are wooded, affording good cover, and there are numerous copses on the hillsides.

From the River RHINE to a general line drawn North to South about one mile East of the Main HEUMAR - AHN Road, the country is open, and, being thickly populated, is covered with innumerable small houses and factories.

Further East, as far as the R. SULZ, the area is entirely forest, called KONIGSFORST, through which are cut numerous straight "Rides" and tracks.

The area topographically divides itself into three zones, these divisions being made by the AGGER and SULZ Rivers, both running approx. North and South across the area. These are both fordable, except after heavy rains.

The roads along the valleys of the river AGGER and SULZ, together with the MARIALINDEN - MUCH Road, form the main arteries of traffic.

There are three lines of railways:-

1. Running from Cologne to SIEGBURG, then up the valley of the AGGER through OVERATH to ENGELSKIRCHEN, and thence on th the neutral zone.
2. Running from COLOGNE via ROSRATH to LINDLAR up the valley of the SULZ. A lateral connects the line from HOFFNUNGSTHAL to OVERATH.
3. Running from COLOGNE via BERG GLADBACH to ROSRATH where it joins No.2.

The main tactical features within the area forward of the river AGGER are:-

(a) Hill 229. BUSCHOVEN.
(b) Hill 248. East of [illegible]RATH.
(c) MARIALINDEN.
(d) Hill 324. East of MUCH.
(e) Hill 309. South of HUNDELAUSEN.
(f) Hill 302. S.E. of DRABENDERHOHE.

4/-

4. Defensive System. Map "..".

At present no trenches, wire or defences exist.

The primary object of the Bridgehead Position is to secure the passages of the RHINE so as to enable a force being concentrated East of the RHINE without interference by the enemy.

With this object in view, work on defences will be commenced in the following order:-

(a) Wire.
(b) Spitlocking of trenches.
(c) Digging, draining and revetting.

The construction of the concrete pill-boxes will be carried out simultaneously with the other work.

The Brigade Area is organised on the following lines :-

(a) i. The outpost line, which consists of a series of nine posts along the outer perimeter, commanding all roads, approaches, and exits to and from the neutral zone.

ii. The Line of Resistance of the Outpost Line, consisting of a series of Strong Points and Defended Localities.

(b) The Main Line of Resistance, which is the front line of the Battle Zone, consisting of a series of Defended Localities and Strong Points along the main tactical features described in para. 3. Each Locality will be strongly wired and be capable of all round defence.

The Main Line of Resistance is divided into three sub-sections. Right, Centre and Left, Sub-sections, respectively.

(c) The Support Line of the Main Line of Resistance, also composed of mutually supporting localities; which will be placed in a state of defence.

The Infantry will be supported by Field Artillery and Machine Guns as follows:-

(a) By Field Guns, so sited to support the Defence of the Main Line of Resistance, and by the Field Guns of forward batteries supporting the outposts. The guns will not be actually placed in position, but positions and O.P's will be selected and marked.

(b) By Machine Guns placed in Defended Localities, and in position to cover the ground between Strong Points. The Machine Guns will not actually be placed in position, but positions will be sited and prepared.

5. Policy of Occupation.

The tactical organisation of the area is drawn up with a view to offensive rather than defensive action; and preparations are made to permit of the rapid concentration of the Division prior to a further advance Eastward.

Principle of Defence.

When completed the sector will be held in depth, the Outpost Line as lightly as possible.

In each company there will always be one platoon, and in each Battalion one company, available for counter-attacks.

There will be no withdrawal from the Main Line of Resistance.

In the event of a general attack along the line, the troops occupying the Front System, that is, the ground forward of the Main Line of Resistance defined in para. 4, will not be reinforced from or behind the above mentioned line.

The role of the troops in advance of the Main Line of Resistance is to give warning of an enemy attack, to repulse it if possible, or failing that, to delay the enemy advance for sufficient length of time to enable the Support Battalion to move up and occupy the Main Line of Resistance.

If ultimately forced by superior numbers to evacuate the Outpost Zone, they will withdraw fighting behind the Main Line of Resistance and reform behind [illegible]ARTH. (S.W. of [illegible]RIALIN[illegible]).

In addition/-

para.5 contd.

In addition, the two Reserve Companies of the Outpost Battalion will be prepared, on receipt of orders, to move forward and occupy the high ground immediately East of MUCH (Exclusive) - DRABENDERHOHE, (i.e., Hills 324 - 309 - 302) to co-operate with troops of the Division on the Right, occupying with advance troops, the General line HULSCHEID - MUCH (inclusive).

6. Disposition of troops & Action in case of attack.

1. "A" battalion in the Outpost System, disposed as follows:-
Six Platoons holding nine posts in the Outpost Line.
Two platoons in support of posts numbers 1 and [illegible]
X -- Four Platoons in Battalion Reserve accommodated in MARIALINDEN.
[illegible] 8 to 9 accommodated in MARIALINDEN.
Battalion Headquarters are at MARIALINDEN.

In the event of a hostile attempt to penetrate the Outpost Line, the forward posts will offer the greatest resistance and delay the enemy as long as possible; when forced to retire, will do so fighting and will concentrate in MARTH. The six platoons in support will move to and occupy the "Line of Resistance of the Outpost Line" from which there will be no withdrawal without orders from Brigade Headquarters.

The company in reserve will concentrate at LANDWEHR.

Battalion Battle Headquarters will be established at LANDWEHR,

2. "B" Battalion in support is accommodated in OVERATH (3 companies) and BOMBACH (1 Company).
Battalion Headquarters are in OVERATH.

On receipt of orders from Brigade Headquarters, the Battalion in support will move to and occupy the Main Line of Resistance, with three companies in the Line.

One company will remain in Battalion Reserve at BURG.

The Battalion Battle Headquarters will be in BURG.

The Battalion in Support will not be used for counter-attacks in front of the Main Line of Resistance, except to re-establish the front system in case of penetration in a purely local attack.

3. "C" Battalion in Brigade Reserve is accommodated in VOLBERG and HOFFNUNGSTHAL.
Battalion Headquarters are in HOFFNUNGSTHAL.

On receipt of orders from Brigade Headquarters the Battalion in Brigade Reserve will move to the area East of the River AGGER between CIRIAX and WASSER, and be prepared to reinforce the Main Line of Resistance between the Brigade Boundaries or carry out counter-attacks upon:-

BUSCHOVEN.
Hill 248, East of MARTH.
MARIALINDEN,

or form a defensive flank, and protect the road Bridge over the River AGGER on the OVERATH - MARIALINDEN Road. (W 8,9 - 0,8.)

On arrival in area CIRIAX - WASSER, "C" Battalion will take over all permanent guards and picquets found by "B" Battalion as shewn on Appendix "A" of defence scheme,, under heading "Battalion in Line of Resistance".

The following orders will be sent from Brigade Headquarters:-
(1) "Move to positions of readiness".
(2) "Man Battle Positions".
(3) "Occupy MUCH- DRABENDERHOHE.Line".

<u>In the event of (1)</u>:-

"A" Battalion will stand by ready to resume the advance,. or move to Battle positions.

"B" Battalion -do-

"C" Battalion will move at once to area E, of River AGGER as described above.

Battaries/-

para.5 contd.

In addition, the two Reserve Companies of the Outpost Battalion will be prepared, on receipt of orders, to move forward and occupy the high ground immediately East of MUCH (exclusive) - DRABENDERHOHE, (i.e., Hills 324 - 309 - 302) to co-operate with troops of the Division on the Right, occupying with advance troops, the General line HULSCHEID - MUCH (inclusive).

6. Disposition of troops & Action in case of attack.

1. "A" battalion in the Outpost System, disposed as follows:-
Six Platoons holding nine posts in the Outpost Line.
Two platoons in support of posts numbers 1 and 2, accommodated at WARTH, 1½ miles South-West of MARIALINDEN.
X - Four platoons in Support of posts Nos. 3 to 9 accommodated in MARIALINDEN.
Battalion Headquarters are at MARIALINDEN.

In the event of a hostile attempt to penetrate the Outpost Line, the forward posts will offer the greatest resistance and delay the enemy as long as possible; when forced to retire, will do so fighting and will concentrate in WARTH. The six platoons in support will move to and occupy the "Line of Resistance of the Outpost Line" from which there will be no withdrawal without orders from Brigade Headquarters.

The company in reserve will concentrate at LANDWEHR.

Battalion Battle Headquarters will be established at LANDWEHR,

2. "B" Battalion in support is accommodated in OVERATH (3 companies) and BOMBACH (1 Company).
Battalion Headquarters are in OVERATH.

On receipt of orders from Brigade Headquarters, the Battalion in support will move to and occupy the Main Line of Resistance, with three companies in the Line.

One company will remain in Battalion Reserve at BURG.

The Battalion Battle Headquarters will be in BURG.

The Battalion in Support will not be used for counter-attacks in front of the Main Line of Resistance, except to re-establish the front system in case of penetration in a purely local attack.

3. "C" Battalion in Brigade Reserve is accommodated in VOLBERG and HOFFNUNGSTHAL.
Battalion Headquarters are in HOFFNUNGSTHAL.

On receipt of orders from Brigade Headquarters the Battalion in Brigade Reserve will move to the area East of the River AGGER between CIRIAX and WASSER, and be prepared to reinforce the Main Line of Resistance between the Brigade Boundaries or carry out counter-attacks upon:-

BUSCHOVEN.
Hill 248, East of WARTH.
MARIALINDEN,

or form a defensive flank, and protect the road Bridge over the River AGGER on the OVERATH - MARIALINDEN Road. (W 8,9 - 0,8.)

On arrival in area CIRIAX - WASSER, "C" Battalion will take over all permanent guards and picquets found by "B" Battalion as shewn on Appendix "A" of defence scheme,, under heading "Battalion in Line of Resistance".

The following orders will be sent from Brigade Headquarters:-
(1) "Move to positions of readiness".
(2) "Man Battle Positions".
(3) "Occupy MUCH- DRABENDERHOHE.Line".

In the event of (1):-
"A" Battalion will stand by ready to resume the advance,. or move to Battle positions.
"B" Battalion -do-
"C" Battalion will move at once to area E, of River AGGER as described above.

Battaries/-

para.6 contd.

Batteries located in the forward area will occupy positions in support of the Outpost Battalions, and remaining batteries of affiliated Artillery Brigade will move forward, by previously reconnoitred routes, to previously selected assembly areas.

228th Field Coy. R.E. will stand by at HOHRATH.

"B" Coy. 41st Bn. Machine Gun Corps will move to OVERATH.

The Reserve Brigade will be moved forward, under Divisional Orders, to an assembly area about ESCHBACH ½ IMMEKEPPEL.

In the event of (2):-

"A" Battalion will occupy Battle positions.

"B" Battalion will move to and occupy the Main Line of Resistance between the Brigade Boundaries. The Northern Boundary for this operation will be a line drawn through points:- X 0,3 - 9,7. to S 2,9 - 0,7 (SIEFEN exclusive)

The Southern Boundary remains unchanged.

"C" Battalion will stand fast, keeping in touch with "B" Battalion by patrols.

Affiliated Batteries of Divisional Artillery and "B" Coy. 41st Bn. Machine Gun Corps will move to and occupy positions already prepared to cover the Main Line of Resistance.

228th Field Coy. R.E. will stand by.

122nd Inf. Bde. Headquarters will move to OVERATH.

The Reserve Brigade will move, under Divisional Orders, to the Main Line of Resistance N. of the Brigade Boundary as described above.

In the event of (3):-

"A" Battalion will send two companies to occupy the high ground - Hills 324 - 309 and 302 described in para. 5; routes forward will be via MARIALINDEN - FEDERATH - HECK B (No. 6 post) - road bifurcation S 7,8 - 0,9: thence one Company via DRABENDERHOHE, and one company via OBR ½ OBERBUSCH - HUNDHAUSEN: and the remaining two Companies will concentrate (S.W. of SCHEID &) S.W. of HELLERSCHEID respectively.

"B" Battalion will move to FEDERATH.

"C" Battalion will concentrate in MARIALINDEN.

Batteries located in the forward area will take up positions to cover the MUCH - DRABENDERHOHE Line, and remaining batteries of Affiliated Artillery Brigades will move forward to MARIALINDEN.

228th Field Coy. R.E. will concentrate at MARIALINDEN.

"B" Coy. 41st Bn. Machine Gun Corps will send six guns to take up positions in the MUCH - DRABENDERHOHE Line, the remaining 10 guns concentrating in FEDERATH.

122nd Inf. Bde. Headquarters will move to MARIALINDEN.

para 7/-

7. Vickers Machine Guns.

One Company, 16 guns, covers the Brigade Sector and are sited in pairs and are disposed as follows:-

6 guns covering the Line Of Resistance of the Outpost Line.
10 guns covering the Main Line of Resistance.

Company Headquarters will be at BURG.
Positions are shown on Map "A".

8. Points of Observation.

Points from which observation may be obtained are:-
(a) Hill 248 East of Warth.
(b) MARIALINDEN.

9. Defensive Organisation of Artillery.

The Sector is covered by the 126th Army Brigade R.F.A.? which is accommodated as follows:-

1 Forward Battery at OVERATH.
3 Batteries in vicinity of PORZ.
Brigade Headquarters are at PORZ.

The role of the forward Battery is to maintain touch with, and be in immediate support of, the Outpost Battalion by engaging routes of approach etc.

On receipt of Orders from Divisional/Artillery Headquarters, Brigade H.Q. and the remaining three Batteries will move forward, concentrating in the first place in ROSRATH, and from there moving forward and occupying positions in support of the Main Line of Resistance, in accordance with the situation.

126th Army Briggde R.F.A. Headquarters will be established at OVERATH.

Acknowledge

S R Hogg

Captain,
Brigade Major,
122nd Infantry Brigade.

28thFebruary 1919.

APPENDIX "A".

TABLE OF PERMANENT GUARDS AND PICQUETS FOUND.

Found by	Party.	Detail.	Remarks.
1. Battalion in Outpost Line	1 Officer 1 Platoon,	Posts in Outpost Line along perimeter of Cologne Bridgehead.	
2. "	1 " 1 "		
3. "	1 section.		
4. "	1 " 3 "		
5. "	1 " 2 "		
6. "	2 "		
7. "	1 " 1 platoon.		
8. "	1 " 2 sections.		
9. "	2 "		
1. Battalion in Line of Resistance.	2 N.C.O's 12 men.	Bridge, junction of road and river 1500 yds,(approx) NNE of "F" AUFLERE.	
2. "	2 " 12 "	Small railway bridge over stream due N. of "H" in HONSBACH.	
3. "	2 " 6 "	Small railway bridge over stream due N. of "S" in SCHOENAUE.	
4. "	2 " 12 "	Railway Bridge at first "8" in mark 88.5 S. of H in BALBACH.	
5. "	1 " 6 "	Railway Bridge 400 yds (approx) N.E. of "H" in COMBACH.	
6. "	1 " 6 "	Railway Bridge 800 yds.(approx) S.S.E. of "G" in GIRLAX.	
7. "	1 " 6 "	River bridge at 88.6 mark N.W..of "G" in GIRLAX.	
8. "	1 " 6 "	Railway Bridge 800 yds. (approx) N. of Bridge at 88.6 mark	
9. "	1 man	Sentry on OVERATH Station	From Batt. H.Q. Guard.
10. "	1 " 6 men.	River Bridge where River AGGER crossed BURG Road.	
1. Battalion in Reserve.	2 " 13 men	Battalion H.Q. Guard and Guard over Main Road Bridge in VOLBERG, over River SULZ.	
2. "	1 " 4 "	HOFFNUNGSTHAL Station.	
3. "	2 " 6 "	UREACH Town Guard.	

ORDERLY ROOM 8/3/19 138th FIELD AMBULANCE

Appendix II

41st Division Administrative Instruction No. 7

1. The following moves will take place under Brigade arrangements on March 9th 1919 :-

23rd Bn.Middlesex Regt from HACKENBURGER SCHOOLS,KALK to Barracks BENSBERG.

53rd Bn.Middlesex Regt from OVERATH to Barracks BENSBERG. (To be absorbed by 23rd Middlesex on arrival.)

2/4 R.W.Surrey Regt from WIPPERFURTHER Strasse and KANT Strasse Schools to HACKENBURGER Schools,KALK.

2.TRANSPORT.

Lorries will report to Units Headquarters to assist in move of Stores as under :-

23rd Middlesex Regt.	2 lorries	08.00 hours	March 9th.
53rd Middlesex Regt.	4 "	10.00 "	" 9th.
2/4 R.W.Surrey Regt	1 "	08.00 "	" 9th.

3.ADVANCE PARTIES.

Advance parties will be sent forward on March 8th to take over accommodation.

Parties will proceed by civilian train where necessary. Information as to accommodation at BENSBERG Barracks can be obtained from 86th Infantry Brigade HQ at BENSBERG.

4.SUPPLIES.

O.C.Divisional Train will arrange for rations for 23rd and 53rd Middlesex for consumption 11th instant to be delivered to BENSBERG Barracks on the 9th, after which,rations for 53rd Middlesex will be included in 23rd Middlesex indents.

ACKNOWLEDGE.

March 7th.1919.

Major,
for/A.A.&.Q.M.G.
41st Division.

Distribution:-

122nd Infantry Brigade.
41st Divl. Train.
"G.S."
Xth Corps "Q"
D.A.D.V.S.
D.A.P.M.
123rd Infantry Brigade.
S.S.O.
29th Division "Q"
D.A.D.O.S.
A.D.M.S.
41st Divl.M.T.Company.

138 F.A

ORDERLY ROOM
No. 575/19
DATE 8/3/19
138TH FIELD AMBULANCE

Appendix 1a

S E C R E T

Copy No. 8

1st AMENDMENT TO 41st DIVISIONAL MEDICAL DEFENCE SCHEME dated 24-2-19

Delete para. 2 and substitute the following :-

Evacuation from M.D.S. and D.R.S. to C.C.Ss. will be by M.A.C. cars for lying cases and lorries for walking cases.

W Rose Gardner

41st Divisional Headquarters
March 6th 1919
B.

Lt-Col. R.A.M.C.
A/A.D.M.S. 41st Division.

Issued to all Recipents of Medical Defence scheme.

Appendix III

ORDERLY ROOM
No. 701/19
DATE 11/3/19
138th FIELD AMBULANCE

8.

SECRET.

Headquarters,
41st. Division "G".

B.M.538.

In reply to 41st. Division G.630/38/1, dated 5th. March 1919:-

(1) Herdwith March tables "A", "B" & "C", shewing routes to be followed by each Unit, and times taken from the time of "passing the starting point in each case."

(2) The tables have been worked out on the following basis:-
(a) That a previous warning had been received and Units were standing to, ready to move at half an hours notice. 30 minutes must therefore be added to each time to include time taken to "turn out."
(b) That the average rate of marching would not exceed more than two miles per hour, in view of the steep and long hills and also the heavy surface of certain of the roads and tracks which will necessarily have to be followed.
(c) That in all marches exceeding four hours, an hour's halt will be necessary. The extra hour has been allowed for in the table.

(3) The march of the affiliated Field Ambulance is not included as it is not yet known which ambulance will be allotted to the Brigade.

Ack.

S R. [illegible] Capt
for. Brigadier General,
Commanding 122nd. Infantry Brigade.

March 10th. 1919.

Copies to all recipients of 122nd. Infantry Brigade Defence Scheme dated 28th. February 1919.

March Table "A", "Move to Positions of Readiness."

Serial No.	Unit.	From.	To.	Starting Point. Position.	Time.	Route.	In final position by.	Remarks.
1.	'A'. Battn.	-	-	-	-	-	-	Will not move
2.	'B'. Battn.	-	-	-	-	-	-	- do -
3.	'B', Coy. M.G.C.	Durbusch.	Overath.	Cross Roads W. 4.8 - 3.0	Z.	Via Heiligenhaus.	Z + 1 Hr. 28 mins.	
4.	'B', Batt. 126th. Bde. A.F.A.	Overath.	Marialinden.	Overath Church.	Z.	Via Bridge over Agger at W 8.[illegible] -9.8	Z + 1 Hour.	
5.	'C'. Battn.	Hoffnungsthal.	Overath.	Bridge over Sulze at Volberg.	Z.	Level Crossing W 3.2 - 7.5. Klein - Linden - Honrath Station.	Z + 3 Hrs. 28 mins.	
6.	'A'. 'C' & 'D'. Batt. 126th. A.F.A.	Porz.	Overath area.	Under orders of O/C 126th. Bde. A.F.A.	Z.	Via Bensberg.	Z + 4 Hrs.	
7.	228th. F.C.R.E.	-	-	-		-	-	Will not move
8.	122nd. Inf. Bde. H.Q.	-	-	-		-	-	- do -

March Table "B" "Move to Battle Positions."

Serial No.	Unit.	From.	To.	Starting Point. Position.	Time.	Route.	In Final position by.	Remarks.
1.	'A'.Battn. Supporting Co.only.	Marialinden.	Line of Resist. of Outpost Line.	-	-	Direct.	Z + 36 Mins.	
2.	'B'.Battn.2 Coys.	Overath.	Main Line of Resistance.	Battn.H.Q.S Overath.	12min.	Via Marialinden.	Z + 1 Hr.37mins.	To be clear of Bridge at W8.8-9.8 by Z + 20mins.
	1 Coy.	Hs.Auel.	-do-	Road at W 6,8 - 5,5	Z	Via Bridge over Agger W 7,1-5,9 Kern.	Z + 1 Hr.25mins.	
	1 Coy.	Overath.	Burg.	Battn.H.Q. Overath.	Z 16mins.	Via Bridge over Agger at W 8,8-9,8	Z + 36mins.	
3.	'B'.Co.M.G.Battn. 1½ Sections.	Durbusch.	Line of Resist. of Outpost Line.	Cross Roads W4,8-8,0	Z.	Via Heiligenhaus-Overath-Marialinden.	Z + 3Hrs.37min.	To be clear of Bridge at W8,8-9,8 by Z + 1 Hr.47 mins.
	2½ Sections.	-do-	Main Line of Resistance.	-do-	Z.	-do-	Z + 3Hrs.5mins.	
4.	'F'.Batty.126 A.F.A.	Overath.	Marialinden area.	Overath Church.	Z.	Via Bridge over Agger W8,8-9,8.	Z.+ 1Hr.	
5.	'C'.Battn.	Hoffnungsthal.	Overath area.	Bridge over Sulze at Volberg.	Z.	Level Crossing at W3,2-7,5.Klein-Linden-Honrath Station.	Z + 3Hrs.35mins.	
6.	'A'&'D'.Batty.126 A.F.A.	Porz.	Overath area.	Under orders of O/C 126 A.F.A.	Z.	Via Bensberg.	Z + 4Hrs.	
7.	228th.F.S.B.	-	-	-	-	-	-	Will not move.
8.	122nd.Inf.Bde.H.Q.	Rosrath.	Overath.	Rosrath Church.	Z.	Same as Serial 5.	Z + 3Hrs.45mins.	

March Table "C", "Occupy Much - Drabenderhohe Line."

Serial No.	Unit.	From.	To.	Starting Point Position.	Time.	Route.	At final position by.	Remarks.
1.	'A'.Battn. 2 Cos.only.	Marialinden	Much-Drabenderhohe Line.	Marialinden Church.	Z.	Via Federath-Rd Bifurcation.at W7,8 - 0,9.	Z + 4Hrs.30min.	1 Hr.long halt not included.
2.	'F'.Battn.	Overath.	Federath.	Battn.H.Q. Overath.	Z 12min.	Via Marialinden.	Z + 1Hr.47min.	To be clear of Bridge at W8,8-9,8 by Z + 20mins.
3.	'B'.Co.M.G.C. 1½ Sections.	Durbusch.	Much-Drabenderhohe line.	Cross Roads W 4,8-8,0	Z.	Via Heiligenhaus, Overath, and then as per Serial 1.	Z + 8Hrs.14mins.	To be clear of Bridge at W8,8-9,5 by Z + 1Hr.47mins.
4.	2½ Sections	-do-	Federath.	-do-	Z	-do-	Z + 3Hrs.37mins.	
4.	'B'.Batty.126 A.F.A.	Marialinden	Wellerscheid area.	Overath Church.	Z	Via Marialinden Gerlinghausen.	Z + 3Hrs.30mins.	
5.	'C'.Battn.	Hoffnungsthal.	Marialinden.	Bridge over Sulze at Volberg.	Z	Via Level Crossing at W 3,2 - 7,5 Klein-Li[..]den-Honrath -Overath.	Z + 5Hrs.25mins.	
6.	'A'.C'.& 'D' Batty. 126 A.F.A.	Porz.	Marialinden.	Under orders of O/C 126 A.F.A.	Z	Via Bensberg-Overath.	Z + 6Hrs.	
7.	228th.F.C.R.E.	Honrath.	Marialinden.	Bridge over Agger at W 7,1-5,9	Z	Via Kern-Warth.	Z + 2Hrs.12mins.	
	122nd.Inf.Bde.H.Q.	Rosrath.	Federath,	Rosrath Church.	Z	Same as Serial 5.	Z + 6Hrs.20 mins.	To be clear of Bridge over R.Agger at Z + 3Hrs. 20mins.

Appendix IV

SECRET.

Copy No. 11

122nd.INFANTRY BRIGADE OPERATION ORDER No.263.

-o-o-o-o-o-o-o-o-o-o-o-o-o-o-o-o-o-o-o-o-o-o-o-o-

Reference maps - Sheets 2910 and 2911-1/25,000.

1. The 9th.East Surrey Regt. will relieve the 15th.Hampshire Regt. in the Outpost Line on March 22nd.1919.

2. The 15th.Hampshire Regt. will on relief move to VOLBERG area, into Brigade reserve, taking over Headquarters at present occupied by 122nd.Infantry Brigade Headquarters.

3. All arrangements for relief to be made by Battalion Commanders concerned.

4. Command of the Outpost Line will pass to Lieut.Colonel E.A.CAMERON, C.M.G., D.S.O., on completion of relief.

5. Completion of relief to be reported to this office.

6. 122nd.Infantry Brigade Headquarters will close at present location at noon 22nd.instant, and re-open at ROSRATH - W 1,5-6,5- at the same hour.

7. Ten lorries will report to Headquarters 9th.East Surrey Regt. at 07.30 hours on March 22nd; six for conveying the six platoons due to relieve the picquets on the perimeter of the Bridgehead, and four for packs, blankets etc. The same lorries will be available for the 15th.Hampshire Regt. on the return journey.

8. The company attached to the 123rd.Inf.Bde. and the company at OVERATH at present working on the range, both of the 9th.East Surrey Regt., will rejoin the Battalion on the 22nd.March at MARIALINDEN.

9. The 15th.Hampshire Regt. will be relieved on the 24th.March by the 17th.Royal Fusiliers, who are detraining at HOFFNUNGSTHAL.

10. The 15th.Hampshire Regt, complete with Transport and horses, will entrain at HOFFNUNGSTHAL by the train bringing the 17th.R.F.'s on the 24th.instant, en route for OPLADEN.

11. Acknowledge. (Units of Brigade group only)

S. R. Hogg

Captain,
Brigade Major,
122nd.Infantry Brigade.

Issued at 22.00 hours
20th.March, 1919.

-o-o-o-o-o-o-o-o-

1. File.
2. War Diary.
3. London Division.
4. -do-
5. 9th.East Surrey Regt.
6. 15th.Hampshire Regt.
7. 7th.Middlesex Regt.
8. C.R.A.London Division.
9. A.D.M.S. -do-
10. D.A.P.M -do-
11. 138th.Field Ambulance.
12. 228th.Field Coy.R.E.
13. "B"Coy.41st.Bn.M.G.C.
14. 2/B.Batt.126th.A.F.A.
15. 126th.A.F.A.
16. 123rd.Infantry Brigade.
17. 124th. -do-
18. No.2,Div.Train.
19. Brigade Major,
20. Staff Captain.
21. Brigade Signal Officer.

-o-o-o-o-o-o-o-o-o-

Appendix 1.

SECRET.

Copy No.....11.....

122ND INFANTRY BRIGADE OPERATION ORDER NO.264.

Reference maps - Sheets 2910 and 2911 - 1/25,000.

1. 23rd Middlesex Regt. will relieve the 9th East Surrey Regt. in the Outpost Line on Saturday 12th instant.

2. The 9th East Surrey Regt. will, on relief, move to VOLBERG Area, into Brigade Reserve.

3. All arrangements for relief to be made by Battalion Commanders concerned.

4. Command of the Outpost Line will pass to Lt.Col.HEATH, C.M.G., D.S.O., on completion of relief.

5. Completion of relief to be reported to this office.

6. 20 Lorries will report to H.Q. 23rd. Middlesex Regt., HOFFNUNGSTHAL, at 07.30 hours on April 12th., 14 for conveying the 8 Platoons due to relieve the picquets on the perimeter of the Bridgehead, and 6 for packs, blankets etc.

The same lorries will be available for the 9th East Surrey Regt. on the return journey.

7. Demonstration Platoon detailed for the Brigade School will now be found by the 9th East Surrey Regt., and will be accommodated with the Battalion in HOFFNUNGSTHAL.

8. Units of Brigade Group to Acknowledge.

S. R. Hogg

Captain,
Brigade Major,
122nd. Infantry Brigade.

Issued at 22.00 hours
6.4.19.

-0-0-0-0-0-0-0-0-

1. File.
2. War Diary.
3. London Division.
4. -do-
5. 9th East Surrey Regt.
6. 7th Middlesex Regt.
7. 23rd Middlesex Regt.
8. C.R.A., London Division.
9. A.D.M.S. -do-
10. D.A.P.M. -do-
11. 138th Field Ambulance.
12. 228th Field Company, R.E.
13. B. Company, M.G.Corps.
14. B. Battery, 190th Bde. R.F.A.
15. 190 Brigade, R.F.A.
16. 123rd Infantry Brigade.
17. 124th Infantry Brigade.
18. 103rd -do-
19. No.2. Company, Div. Train.
20. Brigade Major.
21. Staff Captain.
22. Brigade Signal Officer.

-0-0-0-0-0-

Instructions regarding War Diaries and Intelligence Summaries are contained in F. S. Regs., Part II. and the Staff Manual respectively. Title pages will be prepared in manuscript.

WAR DIARY
or
~~INTELLIGENCE SUMMARY.~~
(Erase heading not required.)

Army Form C. 2118.

VOLUME XXVIII Page 1.

Place	Date	Hour	Summary of Events and Information	Remarks and references to Appendices
URBACH. 7 miles SE of Cologne	1/4/19	-	Fine	
			Admissions 8. Discharges 8	
			London Div: Order No 292.	
			On April 1st + 2nd 126 Bde RFA will be transferred from VI Corps (London Div:) to II Corps (Lowland Div.)	WMB.
			On April 1st - 3rd 93 Bde RFA will be transferred from II Corps to VI Corps and accommodated in PORZ-EIL + KALK Area.	
			138 Field Amb. will collect the sick in PORZ-EIL Area.	
			140 " " " " " " " KALK Area.	
			Capt P. McGowan RAMC returned from leave.	
	2/4/19	-	Fine. cold bright weather.	WMB.
			Admissions 7 Discharges 7	
	3/4/19	-	Fine	WMB.
			Admissions 7. Discharges 7	

(A9175) Wt W2355/P360 600,000 12/17 D. D. & L. Sch. 52a. Forms/C2118/15.

Instructions regarding War Diaries and Intelligence Summaries are contained in F. S. Regs., Part II. and the Staff Manual respectively. Title pages will be prepared in manuscript.

WAR DIARY
or
~~INTELLIGENCE SUMMARY.~~
(Erase heading not required.)

Army Form C. 2118.

VOLUME XXVIII Page 2.

Place	Date	Hour	Summary of Events and Information	Remarks and references to Appendices
URBACH	4/4/19	-	Fine	
			Admissions 2 Discharges 2	MMB
			Capt. P.D. McGowan RAMC reported to 10th Queens as M.O.	
	5/4/19	-	Fine	
			Admissions 8 Discharges 8	MMB
	6/4/19	-	Fine	
			Admissions 4 Discharges 4	MMB
			Conference ADMS Office on Sanitation.	
	7/4/19	-	Fine	
			Admissions 15 Discharges 15	
			Posted as under and struck off strength of this Unit.	MMB
			Capt L W Bain RAMC to 23 Mdx.	
			Capt P D McGowan RAMC to 10 R W Surrey.	
			Capt T.S. Evers RAMC taken on strength of this Unit.	

Instructions regarding War Diaries and Intelligence Summaries are contained in F. S. Regs., Part II. and the Staff Manual respectively. Title pages will be prepared in manuscript.

WAR DIARY
or
~~INTELLIGENCE SUMMARY.~~
(Erase heading not required.)

Army Form C. 2118.

VOLUME XXVIII Page 3.

Place	Date	Hour	Summary of Events and Information	Remarks and references to Appendices
URBACH	8/4/19	-	Fine	
			Admissions 6. Discharges 6.	
			122 Inf Bde Operation Order No 264 received.	Appendix 1. Bde OO 264
			Relief of 9. E Surrey in Outpost line by 23 Mdx.	
			Instructions from ADMS. O.C. Field Ambulances to visit their Brigade Forward Area for next week or so in the capacity of SMO Brigade for the purpose of organising + facilitating the Sanitation.	WMB
	9/4/19	-	Fine	
			Admissions 18. Discharges 18.	WMB
	10/4/19	-	Fine	
			Admissions 6. Discharges 6.	WMB
			Capt W M Chesney reported for duty to 1/7 Mdx.	
	11/4/19	-	Fine	
			Admissions 8 Discharges 8	WMB.

(A9175) Wt W2358/P560 600,000 12/17 D. D. & L. Sch. 52a. Forms/C2118/15.

Army Form C. 2118.

Instructions regarding War Diaries and Intelligence Summaries are contained in F. S. Regs., Part II. and the Staff Manual respectively. Title pages will be prepared in manuscript.

WAR DIARY
or
~~INTELLIGENCE SUMMARY.~~
(Erase heading not required.)

VOLUME XXVIII Page 4.

Place	Date	Hour	Summary of Events and Information	Remarks and references to Appendices
URBACH	11/4/19	(Continued)	Lt. Col W. Ross Gardner DSO RAMC proceeded to United Kingdom on leave	
			Capt W. J B Selkirk. RAMC. proceeded United Kingdom for demobilization	MMB.
			Copy. VI Corps Defence Scheme received.	
	12/4/19	.	Fine Rain later in day.	
			Admissions 16. Discharges 16.	
			ADMS London Division paid farewell visit to Field Ambulance.	
			Medical arrangements forward area.	MMB.
			23 Mdx relieve 9 E Surrey in outpost line.	
			Capt L.W. Bain to take over medical charge 1/7 Mdx OVERATH 23 Mdx MARIALINDEN	
			Capt W M Cheesney " " " " 9 E Surrey VOLBERG 19 Mdx ESBACH UNTER and Units in IMMERKEPPEL.	
	13/4/19	.	Rain	
			Admissions 8. Discharges 8.	MMB.
		.	Capt. A E Schokman. RAMC reported for duty	
			New ADMS London Div. Col. C.H Lindsay. CMG. DSO assumed duties 12/4/19 vice Col. L. N. Lloyd CMG. DSO to Home Estab.	

(A9475) Wt W2358/P360 600,000 12/17 D. D. & L. Sch. 52a. Forms/C2118/15.

Instructions regarding War Diaries and Intelligence Summaries are contained in F. S. Regs., Part II, and the Staff Manual respectively. Title pages will be prepared in manuscript.

WAR DIARY
or
~~INTELLIGENCE SUMMARY.~~
(Erase heading not required.)

Army Form C. 2118.

VOLUME XXVIII Page 5.

Place	Date	Hour	Summary of Events and Information	Remarks and references to Appendices
URBACH	14/4/19	-	Rain very windy.	
			Admissions 5 Discharges 5	[initials]
			122 Inf. Bde renamed 1st London Inf Bde. (9th E. Surrey. 1/7 Mdx 23 Mdx)	
	15/4/19	-	Weather variable.	
			Admissions 10 Discharges 10	[initials]
			Capt W. McChesney returned to his HQ. Permanent M.O resumed medical charge 9 E Surreys. 19 Mdx and Units in IMMERKEPPEL Area.	
	16/4/19	-	Fine.	
			Admissions 18 Discharges 18	[initials]
	17/4/19	-	Fine	
			Admissions 9 Discharges 9.	
			Major J La F Lauder, RAMC Acting OC this Unit proceeded to United Kingdom for Course of Instruction in Venereal Laboratory Work at Rochester Row Military Hospital.	[initials]

(A9175) Wt W2355/P360 600,000 12/17 D. D. & L. Sch. 52a. Forms/C2118/15.

Instructions regarding War Diaries and Intelligence Summaries are contained in F. S. Regs., Part II. and the Staff Manual respectively. Title pages will be prepared in manuscript.

WAR DIARY
or
~~INTELLIGENCE SUMMARY.~~
(Erase heading not required.)

Army Form C. 2118.

VOLUME XXVIII. Page 6.

Place	Date	Hour	Summary of Events and Information	Remarks and references to Appendices
URBACH	18/4/19	-	Good Friday.	
			Fine.	[initials]
			Admissions 6. Discharges 6.	
	19/4/19	-	Fine.	
			Admissions 10 Discharges 10.	[initials]
			Capt T.F. Wilson RAMC joined for duty	
	20/4/19	-	Fine.	
	Easter Sunday.		Admissions 2 Discharges 2	[initials]
			ADMS London Division visited Ambulance	
	21/4/19	-	Fine	
			Admissions 3 Discharges 3	[initials]
			Elementary Education class started daily 11 am.	

(A9175) W1 W2353/P360 600,000 12/17 D. D. & L. Sch. 52a. Forms/C2118/15.

Instructions regarding War Diaries and Intelligence Summaries are contained in F. S. Regs., Part II. and the Staff Manual respectively. Title pages will be prepared in manuscript.

WAR DIARY
or
~~INTELLIGENCE SUMMARY.~~
(Erase heading not required.)

Army Form C. 2118.

VOLUME XXVIII Page 7

Place	Date	Hour	Summary of Events and Information	Remarks and references to Appendices
URBACH	22/4/19	-	Fine	
			Admissions 9 Discharges 9.	
			Capt A.E. Schokman RAMC took over medical charge 1/7 Mdx.	WMB
			Acting O.C. Capt W.M. Chesney visited 64 CCS to meet Major Gen. Sir W. Babtie.	
			Our Disinfestor at OVERATH now in operation	
	23/4/19	-	Fine	
			Admissions 8 Discharges 8	WMB
			O.C. 142 Fd Amb. inspected Unit Demobilization Register	
	24/4/19	-	Change in weather. Cold rain	
			Admissions 11 Discharges 11.	WMB.
	25/4/19	.	Morning. Cold with sleet. Afternoon fine.	
			Admissions 19. Discharges 19.	WMB

(A9475) Wt W2353/P360 600,000 12/17 D. D. & L. Sch. 52a. Forms/C2118/15.

Instructions regarding War Diaries and Intelligence Summaries are contained in F. S. Regs., Part II. and the Staff Manual respectively. Title pages will be prepared in manuscript.

WAR DIARY

or

~~INTELLIGENCE SUMMARY.~~

(Erase heading not required.)

Army Form C. 2118.

VOLUME XXVIII Page 8.

Place	Date	Hour	Summary of Events and Information	Remarks and references to Appendices
URBACH	26/4/19	-	Weather variable.	
			Admissions 6 Discharges 6	mmb.
	27/4/19	-	Variable. Cold. sleet.	
			Admissions 8 Discharges 8	mmb.
	28/4/19	-	Fine, cold.	
			Admissions 8 Discharges 8	mmb.
	29/4/19	-	Fine. warmer.	
			Admissions 7 Discharges 7	mmb.
	30/4/19	-	Fine	
			Admissions 5 Discharges 5	mmb.

mmbhown Capt R.A.M.C.
for O.C. 188th Field Ambulance.

(A9475) Wt W2358/P360 600,000 12/17 D. D. & L. Sch. 52a. Forms/C2118/15.

Instructions regarding War Diaries and Intelligence Summaries are contained in F. S. Regs., Part II. and the Staff Manual respectively. Title pages will be prepared in manuscript.

WAR DIARY
or
~~INTELLIGENCE SUMMARY.~~
(Erase heading not required.)

Army Form C. 2118.

VOLUME XXIX Page 1.

Place	Date	Hour	Summary of Events and Information	Remarks and references to Appendices
URBACH	1/5/19	-	Rain	
			Admissions 9 Discharges 9.	
			London Division Warning Order G 760 received	WMB.
	2/5/19	-	Rain	
			Admissions 11 Discharges 11.	WMB.
			ADMS M.1920 received. Precautions for personal safety of Officers.	
	3/5/19	-	Rain	
			Admissions 8 Discharges 8	WMB.
			Capt T.F. Wilson. RAMC proceeded to 17th R. Fus for temporary duty.	
	4/5/19	-	Fine	
			Admissions 8 Discharges 8.	WMB.
	5/5/19	-	Fine Admissions 10 Discharges 10	WMB.
			Classes commenced for Regimental Stretcher bearers (Appendix 1)	Appendix 1

Instructions regarding War Diaries and Intelligence Summaries are contained in F. S. Regs., Part II. and the Staff Manual respectively. Title pages will be prepared in manuscript.

WAR DIARY
or
~~INTELLIGENCE SUMMARY.~~
(Erase heading not required.)

Army Form C. 2118.

VOLUME XXIX Page 2.

Place	Date	Hour	Summary of Events and Information	Remarks and references to Appendices
URBACH	6/5/19	-	Fine	
			Admissions 13 Discharges 13	WMb.
			Commanding Officer, Lt Col. W. Ross Gardner, DSO. RAMC returned from leave.	
			First party of Infantry attachments (prospective transfers to RAMC) arrived	
	7/5/19	-	Fine	
			Admissions 9 Discharges 9	WMb.
	8/5/19	-	Fine	
			Admissions 10 Discharges 10	WMb
	9/5/19	-	Fine	
			Admissions 10 Discharges 10	WMb
	10/5/19	-	Fine Further reinforcements for attachment to RAMC + RASC arrived	
			Admissions 7 Discharges 7.	WMb.
			Received 1st London + 3rd London Brigade Operation Orders relative to moves of these Brigades.	

(A9175) Wt W2358/P360 600,000 12/17 D. D. & L. Sch. 52a. Forms/C2118/15.

Instructions regarding War Diaries and Intelligence Summaries are contained in F. S. Regs., Part II. and the Staff Manual respectively. Title pages will be prepared in manuscript.

WAR DIARY
or
~~INTELLIGENCE~~ SUMMARY.
(*Erase heading not required.*)

Army Form C. 2118.

VOLUME XXIX Page 3

Place	Date	Hour	Summary of Events and Information	Remarks and references to Appendices
URBACH	10/5/19		(Continued)	
			RAMC Administrative Instruction No 31 received.	
			3rd London Inf Bde is relieving 1st London Inf. Bde Rt sub. sector Div. Front on May 12th 13th & 14th 138 Field Amb will collect sick from Units of 3rd London Inf. Bde.	WMb
			Conference at 64 CCS. DMS. Rhine Army. OC's Medical Units.	
	11/5/19	-	Fine.	
			Admissions 10 Discharges 10	WMb.
	12/5/19	-	Fine	
			Admissions 9 Discharges 9.	WMb.
	13/5/19	-	Fine	
			Admissions 11 Discharges 11.	WMb.

(A9475) Wt W2358/P360 600,000 12/17 D. D. & L. Sch. 52a. Forms/C2118/15.

Instructions regarding War Diaries and Intelligence Summaries are contained in F. S. Regs., Part II. and the Staff Manual respectively. Title pages will be prepared in manuscript.

WAR DIARY
or
~~INTELLIGENCE~~ SUMMARY.
(Erase heading not required.)

Army Form C. 2118.

VOLUME ~~XXIX~~ Page 4

Place	Date	Hour	Summary of Events and Information	Remarks and references to Appendices
URBACH	14/5/19	-	Fine.	
			Admissions 7 Discharges 7	WMb
			O.C. Lt Col Gardner delivered farewell address to NCOs + men.	
	15/5/19	-	Fine	
			Admissions 9. Discharges 9.	
			Lt. Col. W. Ross Gardner proceeded to report to War Office, London.	WMb
			Command of Field Ambulance taken over by Capt W. M. Chesney. M.C RAMC	
	16/5/19	-	Fine	
			Admissions 4 Discharges 4	WMb.
	17/5/19	.	Fine	
			Admissions 2 Discharges 2.	WMb.
			Instructions received from ADMS. All demobilizable personnel down to 50% War Estab to be sent to Dispersal Centres.	

Instructions regarding War Diaries and Intelligence Summaries are contained in F. S. Regs., Part II. and the Staff Manual respectively. Title pages will be prepared in manuscript.

WAR DIARY
or
~~INTELLIGENCE SUMMARY.~~
(*Erase heading not required.*)

Army Form C. 2118.

VOLUME XXIX Page 5.

Place	Date	Hour	Summary of Events and Information	Remarks and references to Appendices
URBACH	18/5/19	-	Fine Admissions 10 Discharges 10	WMB
	19/5/19	-	Fine Admissions 9 Discharges 9. Capt T.F. Wilson. RAMC rejoined Unit.	WMB
	20/5/19	-	Fine Admissions 6 Discharges 6	WMB
	21/5/19	-	Fine Admissions 6 Discharges 6.	WMB
	22/5/19	-	Fine Admissions 6. Discharges 6. 26 Horses transferred to Animal Reception Camp in accordance with instructions.	WMB

(A9475) Wt W2352/P360 600,000 12/17 D. D. & L. Sch. 52a. Forms/C2118/15.

Instructions regarding War Diaries and Intelligence Summaries are contained in F. S. Regs., Part II. and the Staff Manual respectively. Title pages will be prepared in manuscript.

WAR DIARY
or
~~INTELLIGENCE SUMMARY.~~
(Erase heading not required.)

Army Form C. 2118.

VOLUME ~~XXX~~ Page 6.

Place	Date	Hour	Summary of Events and Information	Remarks and references to Appendices
URBACH	23/5/19	-	Fine Admissions. 5 Discharges. 5	[signature]
	24/5/19	-	Fine Admissions 7 Discharges 7	[signature]
	25/5/19	-	Fine Admissions 3. Discharges 3 Instructions received to transfer all Cars with exception of 1 Ford + 1 Cycle to 139 + 140 Field Ambulances.	[signature]
	26/5/19	.	Fine Admissions 5 Discharges 5 RAMC Administrative Instructions No. 34 received: 139 Field Amb. will establish D.R.S. at VOLBERG	[signature]

Instructions regarding War Diaries and Intelligence Summaries are contained in F. S. Regs., Part II. and the Staff Manual respectively. Title pages will be prepared in manuscript.

WAR DIARY
or
~~INTELLIGENCE SUMMARY.~~
(Erase heading not required.)

Army Form C. 2118.

VOLUME XXIX Page 7.

Place	Date	Hour	Summary of Events and Information	Remarks and references to Appendices
URBACH	27/5/19	-	Fine.	
			Admissions 5. Discharges 5.	
			Cars, cycles & drivers transferred to 139 & 140 Field Ambulances with M.T. personnel.	[initials]
	28/5/19	-	Fine	
			Admissions nil Discharges nil	[initials]
	29/5/19	-	Fine	
			Admissions 2 Discharges 2	[initials]
	30/5/19	-	Fine	
			Admissions nil Discharges nil	[initials]
	31/5/19	-	Fine	
			Admissions 2 Discharges 2	[initials]

[signature] Capt.

Appendix 1

Syllabus of Training for Regimental Stretcher Bearers

Times	Monday	Tuesday	Wednesday	Thursday	Friday
9 a.m. to 10.30 am	Stretcher Drill with 6 & 5 Bearers per Squad.	Stretcher Drill with 4 & 3 Bearers per Squad.	Preparing & Loading Stretchers with 6, 5, 4, 3, & 2 Bearers per Squad.	Improvised Carriage of Wounded in the Field.	Treatment & Collection of Wounded in the Field.
11 am. to 12 noon	The Skeleton. Bones, Joints & Muscles	Circulation. Haemorrhage & Pressure Points. Application of Tourniquet.	Bandaging Roller & Triangular	Sprains, Dislocations & Fractures. Application of Splints.	First Field Dressing. Shell Dressing. Surgical Haversack & Medical Companion.

ADMS
London Div.

Herewith WAR DIARY for month of May 1919

W. M. Brown [signature] Capt.

Urbach
1/6/19

www.ingramcontent.com/pod-product-compliance
Lightning Source LLC
Chambersburg PA
CBHW080900230426
43663CB00013B/2589
9781474520171